A NIGHT TO REMEMBER

Passenger Charles Hayes was also awakened by the jolt. He might have wondered, then, what had urged him, just a few hours earlier, to raise his glass and proclaim "that the time has come for the greatest and most appalling of all disasters at sea." But, no—it couldn't be *that* bad.

Within three hours he would be dead.

"Mystery and majesty...
Provocative...Spectacular...
The most thorough account yet of
the whole *Titanic* story"
Kirkus Reviews

"Impressionistic.
Surrealistic, like walking through
a Stanley Kubrick film.
But it is impossible to pull off
this sort of thing
without knowing the facts,
and Charlie Pellegrino knows his
Titanic inside and out."
Walter Lord

HER NAME, TITANIC

THE UNTOLD STORY OF THE SINKING AND FINDING OF THE UNSINKABLE SHIP

CHARLES PELLEGRINO

AVON BOOKS  NEW YORK

AVON BOOKS
A division of
The Hearst Corporation
1350 Avenue of the Americas
New York, New York 10019

Copyright © 1988 by Charles Pellegrino
Cover art courtesy of The Bettmann Archive
Published by arrangement with McGraw-Hill Publishing Company, a division of McGraw-Hill Inc.
Visit our website at **http://AvonBooks.com**
Library of Congress Catalog Card Number: 88-13212
ISBN: 0-380-70892-2

First Avon Books Printing: June 1990

AVON TRADEMARK REG. U.S. PAT. OFF. AND IN OTHER COUNTRIES, MARCA REGISTRADA, HECHO EN U.S.A.

Printed in the U.S.A.

OPM   20   19   18   17   16   15   14

HER NAME, TITANIC

To my parents and my friends,
who stood with me on a cold April night

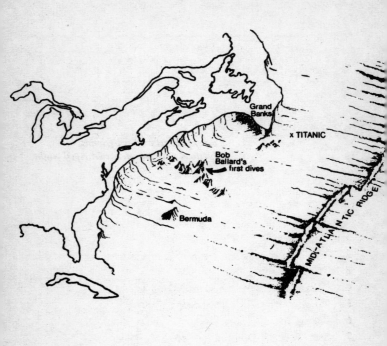

CONTENTS

Not even the geologist-astronaut Harrison Schmitt, poking among rocks on the surface of the moon for the first time, could have been happier than I was when I first saw a hot spring surrounded by a field of giant clams nearly two miles down on the bed of the Pacific. Exploring that unknown world was, all by itself, a fantastic adventure. Still...it was only the beginning. I was sailing with Robert Ballard, who had just led the expedition that discovered the wreck of the *Titanic*. He was hiding then. And I was in hiding with him, though I cannot understand to this day exactly why he was hiding, or why he brought me along, or how I came to be the one he opened up to and told what the *Titanic* had done to him.

His eyes filled with tears as he told me. And suddenly my eyes were stinging, too. At that time, I was not planning to write a book about the *Titanic*. My main interests were space exploration and robots—not marine archaeology. To me, the *Titanic* began as just another interesting thing that was happening on the way to Jupiter and its moons. I was perfectly content to be probing the edge of creation with the robot *Argo*, two miles below us on the East Pacific Rise. But Bob seemed to be warning me that the space program I cherished so much would soon be facing a modern-day

Titanic. "I think there's a parallel with NASA and the people who built the *Titanic*," he said. "And I think you can see it. When we conquer a new field of technology, we become overconfident... sooner or later it's bound to happen."

"What? A *Titanic* in space?" I asked.

"Exactly," was the reply.

That was December 20, 1985, aboard the research vessel *Melville*. As if prodding me toward this book, he approached me on the fantail the next morning and handed me two pieces of metal. They were from *Argo,* the robot that had found the *Titanic*. "Sooner or later," he'd warned. I agreed with him, though I had no idea that it could happen so soon, and to the ship that made me feel both humble and proud the night she was launched, to the ship I'd hoped to fly in. Only a month later, the *Challenger* was killed by ice—ice where it did not belong... ice warnings that were ignored in order to meet a schedule. That's when the *Titanic* came roaring out of the past and into my life: the day the *Challenger* was ripped open and blown apart and strewn about. There are very few people in the world who can tell you that their lives have been touched and disrupted by the *Titanic*. Yet, by a chain of seemingly unrelated and unlikely events, I happen to be one of them.

I guess you could say it began about ten years ago. I was a marine biology student then, with an ever-present interest in astronomy. Insects were also among my favorite things, and when it came time to write a master's thesis in marine science, I turned naturally to crabs. (After all, what are crabs and lobsters but giant seagoing cockroaches?) At about the same time, a professor introduced me to Big Brook Creek, a fossil site in New Jersey dating from the days of the last dinosaurs. My digs there raised many questions about ancient climate and mass extinctions, and ultimately sent me flying to New Zealand in search of answers. As it turned out, one of my New Zealand digs was not only punctuated by evidence of climatic upheavals, mass extinctions, and whole new varieties of fossil crabs; an asteroid impact, too, seemed to have been thrown into the bargain.

At that time, I was looking forward to spending the rest of my life in New Zealand, where glaciers and tropical evergreens grew side by side. The place was like a new planet: startlingly beautiful, strange, and rippling with unanswered questions. I'd found a treasure, and nothing in the world could have seemed farther from the *Titanic* and Bob Ballard. But trouble was brewing. It was brewing fast.

Evolutionary biologist Jesse Stoff had given me stony meteorites whose contents suggested that life's origins, as well as its crises, might be written in the sky. What Jesse and I eventually ended up with were the original models suggesting that underground streams once existed inside asteroids, and that new oceans would inevitably turn up in the outer solar system, beneath the ice cover of certain Jovian and Saturnian moons. And then Ballard's Rise project group found strange oases thriving around volcanic vents on the bottom of the Pacific. The oases began to look like windows on other worlds—which, perhaps, they were.

Speculating about what might be on (or rather in) those new worlds was not enough. I wanted some reasonable assurance that I could see answers in my lifetime. By 1982 I was designing robot helicopters to probe Titan. Colleagues at NASA/JPL suggested that blimps would be better. Meanwhile, my supervisors at Victoria University, in New Zealand, began wondering why a paleobiologist was getting so much mail from NASA, and why I was suddenly talking about such madness as launching helicopters into space. Increasingly, their feelings about me were shifting from curiosity to utter confusion and mild annoyance—and at the worst possible time. The fall of 1982 was a period of growing animosity and suspicion toward Americans. Before long all my notebooks and specimens were confiscated (the vice chancellor and the minister of education denied that it was confiscation: I was simply told that my belongings had been removed from my laboratory and I was not allowed to have them back), my work was censored (they denied that it was censorship: I was simply told that reasonable restrictions were being placed on what I was allowed to publish), and I was asked to leave (actually, I was told to "get the [fill in appropriate noun] out!").

censorship: I was simply told that reasonable restrictions were being placed on what I was allowed to publish), and I was asked to leave (actually, I was told to "get the [fill in appropriate noun] out!"). For an encore, a similar request was made of the United States Navy.

I took the hint, and returned to America (with, I might add, a much overdue appreciation for our civil liberties).

During the three years that followed, I turned more and more to advanced preliminary design of spacecraft—antimatter rockets and that sort of thing. It was a path that was eventually to lead me back into the oceans (albeit through the back door). In 1985, our brainstorming sessions at Brookhaven National Laboratory turned toward robot submarines, with which we one day hoped to explore a new ocean that almost certainly exists under the ice of Jupiter's moon Europa. There are other oceans in the solar system, but Europa seems to be the most accessible. And the pressures at its bottom are about what you will find on the floor of the Pacific.

It was time to familiarize myself with deep-sea robots, to learn what conditions they must work under, to know the state of the art, and to extrapolate from there to what might be the state of the art in twenty years. "And, who knows?" I said. "One might even make an interesting book out of deep-sea exploration." As it turned out, that was the understatement of the decade.

This book is, in part, a you-are-there biography of explorer Robert Ballard, who launched the most amazing adventure since the landings on the moon. *Her Name, Titanic* and Ballard's *Discovery of the Titanic,* the only two books covering the Ballard expeditions, were coordinated to avoid overlap. In fact, there are deliberate gaps and crossovers in both books. If you want to know about Bob's adversary, Jack Grimm, you must read Ballard's *Discovery of the Titanic.* If you want to understand what makes Bob Ballard tick, how a child who was afraid of the water came to spend his life on the high seas, and deep under them, you must read *Her Name, Titanic.* The reader will note that even the illustrations and photographs are unique to each book. Both projects were conceived and executed as companion pieces to each other, not as competitors. The color photographs in Ballard's book are nothing short of astonishing, and one of these will undoubtedly be included among the top 100 photographs of the century when we look back from New Year's Eve, A.D. 2000. It was through an analysis of such photographs that I came up with the downblast scenario during Expedition *Argo*-Rise. The *Titanic* looks as if it were caught in the aftermath of a stupendous explosion. The damage appears to be the result of a phenomenon never seen before, and it all occurred in the space of a hiccup on that cold April morning in 1912. The downblast theory is now viewed by Bob Ballard and historian Walter Lord as the most significant new insight to emerge from the expeditions. Ballard and I agreed that this would be covered much more extensively in my book, to which he refers the reader in his book. There are other interesting crossovers. At one point in Ballard's book, Bob wonders what submarine pilot Ralph Hollis must be thinking as they sit on the *Titanic*'s bridge eating peanut butter sandwiches. Bob regrets momentarily that he will probably never know, because he and Ralph are not on speaking terms. In this book, we learn what Ralph Hollis is thinking as he watches Bob and wonders what could possibly be going through *his* mind.

This book also recaptures the essence of a strange and frightening thing—rarely spoken about—that occurred during and shortly after the discovery of the *Titanic*'s grave. I was not on that first expedition, but weeks later, when I disappeared with the Ballard team and began examining those first fuzzy images, I felt it too. Time seemed to have come unstuck. Even today, crystal-clear photographs taken by oceanauts on the actual decks of the *Titanic* do not have the same emotional impact as those first *Argo* transmissions. They do not send chills through me. They cannot move me to tears. They do not have the power to cause what Robert Ballard and others who saw them when they were new refer to as "a minor nervous breakdown." In *Her Name, Titanic*, we are from the start unstuck in time, shifting abruptly from the sinking liner to the expeditions and back again. And the material on the sinking is a gold mine of new information—derived in part from such things as wireless operator Harold Bride's report to the Marconi Company, passengers' unpublished diaries (provided by Walter Lord), analysis of the wreckage, and conversations with survivors (who were especially helpful with respect to unexpected opinions about the Ballard expeditions). Indeed, this will probably be the last book written while *Titanic* survivors are still alive and can contribute details.

And so, I ended up sailing with Robert Ballard some three months after one of his robots found the *Titanic*.

And then, on January 28, 1986, the *Titanic* and *Challenger* became one.

And then, unexpectedly, a more personal tragedy joined the *Titanic* and *Challenger* to form an ugly trinity. Beneath the surface, this book is about watching someone I loved very much descending irretrievably into cocaine addiction—which explains, perhaps, why the ship itself takes on a personality. *"A man can hate a ship worse than he can a human being, although he sails on her. Likewise a ship can hate her men, then she frequently becomes known as a killer."*[1] *Thomas Andrews knew that the ship meant to kill him...She did seem determined to drag him down with her—yes. Oh, yes. She'd get Andrews. The poor fool, he loved her—*[2] Watching the *Titanic* die was, to me, like the peculiar horror of watching someone very young and beautiful and full of power and life turning destructively against herself and everyone around her. Yet even at her most obscene there were faint glimmers of beauty and strength. *Up the Grand Stairway began a small procession of elegantly dressed men and women, orderly, quiet and regal....She watched the procession and she knew what it must become, knew that the night was shifting from familiar faces and familiar settings into something else; shifting like wax...into a fancy-dress ball in Dante's Hell.*[3] And finally, through Bob Ballard's 1986 dives to the wreck, we visit a grave. *They peered into the shimmering pool of light, while all around them the* Titanic *lay in state in her orange shroud.*[4]

And last night I dreamed of her again. And when I dream of

---

[1] From Charles Lightoller, *Memoirs*. See Chapter 8.
[2] See Chapter 20.
[3] See Chapter 4.
[4] See Chapter 27.

her, I dream also of *Titanic* and *Challenger;* and no one gets out alive. Like the *Titanic* and the *Challenger,* those who knew her best believed her to be unsinkable—so much so that two of her closest friends had always avoided confiding their problems in her, because they thought it embarrassing to let someone who so clearly had the world under control, who had everything to live for, know that their own lives were less than perfect. She seemed so strong, so full of promise; but like Richard Cory and the *Titanic,* she only seemed so.

This book was an exorcism, of sorts. A final release. And I do not wish ever to repeat the experience.

CHARLES PELLEGRINO, PH.D.
Rockville Centre, New York
2:20 A.M., April 15, 1987

Watching that great ship fly up, and up, and up against the night was an awakening, a vivid flash of—something like God, something more powerful than nature itself. And it is us.

And we know. We who have seen.

Charles Pellegrino at the launch of Challenger, *August 30, 1983*

Not even God himself could sink this ship.

A White Star employee at the launch of Titanic, *May 31, 1911*

SYNOPSIS

They built a ship.
It struck an iceberg and sank.
Almost everyone died.
Many years later some people found the ship.
The End.

No, that is not all.
This is a book about men who loved and sometimes worshiped their machines.
And God help me.
I'm one of them.

—Charles Pellegrino
April 15, 1987

1

To Dare God

The cradle lay in starlight. A cradle for giants: thick webs of iron scaffolding broad enough to enclose a half dozen cathedrals; cranes at the top, perched higher than most of the world's tallest buildings; below them, a skeleton in the shape of a ship—her name, *Titanic;* and below her, the Belfast shipyards of Harland and Wolff, where Thomas Andrews stood with his bride. The two were virtually invisible against the cyclopean scale of everything: propellers as wide as windmills; a rudder six stories high. To Helen Andrews the towering rows of vertical supports looked like the Industrial Age imitating the Acropolis. Here was unearthly beauty, made more unearthly and more beautiful by the apparition in the sky.

Once again Phaeton borrowed the Chariot of the Sun, driving it dangerously close to Earth....

On this chilly spring morning in the otherwise uneventful year 1910, the thin veils of Halley's Comet glowed across half the sky. Far off to one side was a flying mountain of dirt and ice larger than the city of London, yet invisible, at an immeasurable distance, through even the most powerful telescopes. It boiled up there. A head of vapor and dust streamed out from the nucleus in every direction, appearing as wide as a cricket ball held out at arm's length. It was almost bright enough to read by.

"It's beautiful," Helen said.

"The comet."

"Yes, that too. But the ship. Your ship."

Planting a kiss on the back of her neck, he nudged her gently; and, taking the signal, she leaned back against him. He clasped both hands around her abdomen—swollen, now, with the promise of a child. His breathing quickened. As much as he loved designing and building ships—as much as he truly loved his work—here, bundled in his arms, was the actual center of his life.

At that moment, the center of his life was mildly worried about keeping him up too late. Surely he needed *some* sleep. By 6:00 A.M. her husband would be weaving his way through that modern-day Acropolis, a paint-smeared hat on his crown, grease on his boots, the pockets of his blue jacket stuffed with plans. She imagined him shouting directions over the persistent uproar of riveting tools, calling attention to the smallest details of his ship. And now, looking at the thing and knowing it to be the greatest of technology's achievements, her admiration for him went up a notch. All the more reason to see to it that he slept.

"Shouldn't we be leaving soon?" Helen said.

"Soon...soon..."

Directly overhead, a green star winked on and darted out of view behind the scaffolding. Then another. And another. Meteoritic ice lanced down from heaven—a backdrop for *Titanic*.

"Three million rivets," said Thomas Andrews. "Three million rivets will go into her hull alone—twelve hundred tons of them."

"A fantastic adventure."

"Yes. We're putting four passenger elevators into her. Eight electric cargo cranes, a fifty-telephone switchboard, and the world's most modern kitchens—equipped with electric freezers, ovens, and slicing, peeling, and mincing machines."

"And you say she'll be unsinkable?"

"Safer than a lifeboat. Yes, each ship its own lifeboat."

Something shuddered in the sky. The normally white cometary veils, swept back on a wind of reflected sunlight, were laced now with shimmering greens and blues. Helen craned her neck to kiss

Thomas on the lips. She could see his face in the glow of the comet, pale, without detail.

More ice streaked down, more and more ice, scratching fire over Belfast.

Earth was deep in the tail of Halley.

2

The 70,000-Ton Sky

EXCERPT FROM THE LOG OF CHARLES PELLEGRINO
Research Vessel: *Melville*
Expedition: *Argo*-Rise
Date: Wednesday, December 18, 1985
Time: 4:00 A.M.
Place: Somewhere on the East Pacific Rise
Depth: 1.7 miles

At first glance, it might have been built by intelligent beings. But if you moved closer you could see immediately that the stone pillars were merely nature mimicking the Acropolis. The pillars, some of them standing three stories tall, were cast from solid obsidian when trapped seawater leapt up from the bottom of a lava lake, chilling columns of rock from floor to ceiling. As the lake receded, only the pillars remained to support a frozen skin transformed suddenly into a roof. Most of the roof has fallen in, replaying the story of the real Acropolis long before the coming of Greece, or geometry, or architecture. The floor of this lava ruin is littered with glittering slabs of glass. And over there, in the middle, a tangle of organ pipes and chimneys has sprouted on top of the wreckage. A sulfide-spouting fountain of life once grew there. But it weakened and died centuries ago, as testified to by dozens of empty, mineral-encrusted clam shells strewn at its feet. And there, in the corner, a natural bridge spans the tops of two pillars—a piece of the roof intact. And up there, on the roof...sea lilies...*life*.

The sea lilies resemble their cousins, the starfishes, except that they are turned on their backs and have feathers for legs and are attached to stalks. They are famous as fossils, but have declined from several thousand species to only a few dozen. They live today in the cold and the dark, where food is scarce, but where the deep range belongs almost entirely to them. It is as if they are unable to compete in more crowded, daylit waters, as if they manage to keep a foothold on Earth only by being able to survive in environments so difficult that no other creatures can move in and thrive and become competitors. One key to their survival is happy circumstance. The intense cold of the deep does not kill them, it merely slows their metabolism some twenty-seven times. This has two results. First, they don't have to eat very often—which has its advantages in the ocean's deserts. Secondly, a sea lily takes about eighty years to reach adulthood, meaning that the inhabitants of the undersea Acropolis must be fully one hundred years old.

One hundred years of peace and quiet. And then, a great calamity came out of the sky. There was a brightness out there. It spread from the south, growing brighter and brighter each passing second. The thing skimmed low and fast—approaching purposefully, as if on a collision course....

The steel compartment was a commotion of activities, each orderly in itself, and the whole surprisingly orderly for such cramped quarters. Tapes were being plugged into consoles, maps were made, numbers called out and data logged. The array of screens showed pillars sweeping up ahead. At the flyer's station, Earl Young pulled back on the winch. At precisely that moment, the little finned robot nearly two miles below us climbed up on its tether. The altimeter clicked up five meters...six meters... seven meters…and still that column was in front of us, higher and higher…"It's absolutely huge"…ten meters…It covers half the screen…coming straight at us…and what were those on top? …Crinoids!…That's what we call sea lilies—crinoids….And here we go!…The robot scraped the top of the column….A down-looking camera glimpsed chips of lava spiraling down…and crinoid arms floating.

The screens flickered, and for a moment they appeared to be on the verge of winking out—but the picture and the data read-outs flashed back to normal. Our robot was still alive down there on the bottom. Flying into a dead lava pool was a dangerous ma-neuver, but *Argo* was proving to be a very forgiving machine.

"Crinoside!" someone shouted. "One hundred years sitting on top of a lava pillar, with nothing at all happening down there, and then this UFO—this thing with lights comes out of the sky and smashes into their home. And here we are, up here, taking pictures of it happening."

Elsewhere in the room, an aspiring Rich Little put on his best Bogart: "Of all the pillars in all the oceans in all the world, *Argo* blunders into mine."

"Oh, you better not pout," someone sang. "You better not *cri*noid."

And, as the laughter died away, a loud rumble played out from the hydrophone. We were listening to the voice of the Earth's crust as it groaned and snapped across the glassy landscape more than a mile beneath our feet.

At the data logging station, I leaned forward in my chair, look-ing into TV screens displaying shapes that seemed to have been, quite literally, squirted up through uncountable tubes of tooth-paste—and I tried to separate the creaking of *Argo*'s tether from the imagined murmur of a lava pool out there in the dark, tried to project myself into that fierce, alien world from which I was sheltered, way up here in the research vessel *Melville*. Someday, I knew, I must go down into that world and see with my own eyes the pillars and the organ pipes—see them real and alive, standing against a sky so black as to be brilliant.

I knew also that the dark wilderness was far more hostile than the moon or Mars. The same spacecraft that took Neil Armstrong and Buzz Aldrin down to the Sea of Tranquility would implode long before it reached *Argo* on the East Pacific Rise. In places, *Eagle*'s hull was as thin as two sheets of newspaper. It would crack at a depth of one hundred feet. By comparison, the manned submersible *Alvin*, the deep-ocean equivalent of the Apollo lunar module, has as its crew compartment a seven-foot-diameter hollow sphere whose skin is titanium two inches thick. On a typical dive, the immense pressure exerted by more than two miles of overlying water actually shrinks the sphere—so that the portholes close like mighty fists around the Plexiglas windows, trying to squeeze them out into the sea like watermelon seeds pressed between thumb and forefinger. The only thing holding the windows in place is a precisely cut angle in the metal that balances the force trying to squirt them out against the pressure trying to push them in. Fortunately for ascending explorers, titanium has a "memory" and springs back into its original dimensions as the craft returns to lower pressures (otherwise the windows *would* squirt out).

At *Alvin*'s maximum depth of two and a half miles, the total pressure on the crew compartment is seventy thousand tons. No diving suit or airlock has yet been conceived that can allow an oceanaut to step out onto the East Pacific Rise or to touch the decks of the *Titanic*. The difference between space exploration and deep-sea exploration is that you are always confined to your capsule in the deep sea. On the moon, if you want to see what is behind you, you simply turn around and look. On the ocean floor you have to turn the entire bulk of *Alvin* around—very carefully. It's a little easier if you happen to be looking at the deep through the eyes of a robot. Then you need only punch a button and switch to a new camera angle.

The knowledge that we will probably ride antimatter rockets to Alpha Centauri before we are able to walk on the ocean bottom and place a gloved hand on a lava pillar is one reason that Robert Ballard, leader of the *Argo*-Rise expedition and the very same man who fought for a decade to transform *Alvin* into a viable scientific tool, has now begun to develop *Argo,* the world's most sophisticated and deepest-diving undersea robot.

He reasons that if an oceanaut cannot walk there and directly sense her surroundings, then why not let a machine do most of the exploration for us? So, for all of us aboard *Melville,* the robot *Argo* has become a giant mental transporter. It is quite different from an *Alvin* mission. *Alvin* can carry only three people down to the bottom, and nobody learns what they have seen until they pop up to the surface seven hours later. The whole scientific party can descend with *Argo*—all thirty of us—not just three lucky passengers. And we can see and hear the bottom in real time. In a manner of speaking, we are leaving our kidneys and gallbladders at the surface and, through *Argo*'s eyes and ears, sending our spirits into the new world. Still…armchair exploration is just…not enough. It is like an expensive dinner with something missing. One actually wants to go there.

But *Argo* does have the distinct advantage of not having to come up for air. It can stay, and stay, and stay. And we, too, through this emerging science of "telepresence," can glide along the bottom until our little hearts are content.

To me, this is all a dress rehearsal for deep space. Even in the *Argo* control room, my mind often wanders up from the bottom of the ocean to the stars—to that part of the sky now occupied by *Voyager 2.* The spacefaring robot is two billion miles away, and in only a few weeks it will hurtle past Uranus and Miranda at twenty miles per second—which makes our one-mile-per-hour traverse of the rise seem ludicrous by comparison. (But, oh! To be able to study Miranda in such detail!) Ballard and the others know me well enough to guess when my mind wanders, and where to. My habit of thinking about space while, at the same time, looking at the bottom of the ocean is not as strange as it seems at first glance. Indeed, Ballard is largely responsible for it.

Years ago, Jesse Stoff and I came up with models suggesting that underground streams once existed inside asteroids, and that actual oceans might now exist inside certain icy moons of Jupiter,

Saturn, Uranus, and Neptune—even inside Pluto and Charon. It was, of course, fun to speculate about the possibility of life in those oceans, especially after *Voyagers 1* and *2* swept past Europa and Ganymede and found evidence that the oceans might actually exist; but I remember asking Jesse, early in 1979, what our hypothetical beasties could be eating. On what do you base a food chain *inside* a world, where there is no sunlight, where chlorophyll, the molecule that sustains life on this planet, cannot possibly function? Jesse was ready for me. He had stacks of papers from Ballard, whose team had just made one of the biological discoveries of the century. Protruding from the bottom like organ pipes, hot springs on the East Pacific Rise were spouting continuous jets of sulfide-laden water. Bacteria living near the springs were slowly burning, or oxidizing, hydrogen sulfide and using it as a source of energy, much the same way that chlorophyll in green plants uses energy provided by the sun. Around the springs the ocean floor had become an oasis, supporting dense communities of clams, mussels, limpets, and crabs, with the bacteria forming the base of the food chain. One species of worm grew twelve feet long and lived in clusters of thousands. They were white, with scarlet, petal-shaped gills around their heads, and their colonies looked to Ballard like rose gardens grown out of control. And strangest of all to learn that the worms did not feed on the carbohydrate-producing bacteria, but were themselves carbohydrate-producing organisms, the only animals on Earth known to synthesize their own food, like plants. They had no stomachs, no digestive system at all. Not even a mouth.

Ballard had found creatures who drew life from sulfides instead of sunlight. Having seen them, Jesse and I thought immediately of the stony, claylike meteorites we had been studying. They were chock-full of sulfides. And Io, the moon next door to Europa, was spewing mountains of the stuff—so it was reasonable to expect life-sustaining sulfides in Europa, and in still other ice worlds waiting to be seen through *Voyager's* eyes.

My preoccupation with space is a favorite subject of friendly ribbing from Ballard.

"What is the most you can hope to find out there, when *Voyager* flies past Uranus next month?"

"Oceans."

"And what is the most you can hope to see in those oceans, assuming they exist, and assuming you can break through miles of ice, and assuming anyone is ever willing to give you a budget to explore them?"

"Sulfide oases. Life. Fishlike things, maybe."

"Then look down here. We already have what you're looking for. And more. What's so important about life in Miranda or Titan?"

"Because it's somewhere else!"

—somewhere else...There really is no bigger answer. Even if the world revealed by *Voyager*'s seagoing cousin *Argo* is to me a mere window through which I can see, at a distance, a piece of the universe, that of course does not diminish my sense of wonder about the Rise. If anything, it adds another layer of spice to the landscape. Spreading before us on the Pacific range are frozen streams of polished black glass. Here and there we have encountered hollow bulbs of obsidian. They look like eggshells cracked open. As *Argo* moves farther from the center of the ridge, the glass grows older and we witness an ever-deepening accumulation of sediment. The range is swept by a never-ending snowfall of silt from muddy rivers, pollen from the continents, the smoke of dead meteors, and the skeletons of surface-dwelling microbes. I am told that twenty-five miles from the ridge, the "snow" is 700,000 years old. It completely covers the lava formations.

"It gets much deeper toward the continents," explains Jean Francheteau, one of the French members of the *Argo*-Rise team. "The 'snow' is miles deep out there, and everywhere you go in the ocean, if you drill down far enough through the mud, you will strike lava formations just like the ones we observe on the Rise. At the very bottom, all the oceans in all the world are lava."

The oceans are also a vault of the ages, filling now with the substance of archaeology. We have seen a soda can lying on the Rise. It may still be there thousands of years from now. In the deep, objects tend to become flash-frozen in time. I have been told by Ed Bland of the day, way back in 1968, when he was forced to abandon *Alvin* during a launch that went awry. He watched his ship fill with water and disappear, taking with it his lunch. A year later, when *Alvin* was hauled up from its resting place one mile under the Atlantic, the steak in his sandwiches was found to be salty but still edible. Near-freezing temperatures had forestalled all decay, and this led to speculation that carpeting, wooden furnishings, and even meat sealed in refrigerators might still be preserved aboard the *Titanic*. The wine might still be drinkable, the decks still intact, and, in deep interior sections unreachable by fish, bodies might still be identifiable through use of the *Titanic* Historical Society's records.

Three months before we set sail for the East Pacific Rise, *Argo* had photographed the *Titanic* and shown her to be in such a remarkable state of preservation as to be downright scary. Somehow, that seemed to be in character with everything else about the *Titanic*'s history.

Tom Dettweiler, one of *Argo*'s builders, was in the control room when the TV screens filled with pictures of huge brass bollards showing barely any signs of tarnish. A passenger's suitcase was on the bottom. It could have been dropped there days ago. Early robot reconnaissance suggests that all the damage was done on that cold April night in 1912. The ship pounded down almost horizontal under the Grand Banks, having lost her stern during the two-and-a-half-mile fall. Once she stopped descending, the funnel of water that trailed behind her punched through the roof of the first-class entrance hall and shattered the grand stairway. The crow's nest, from which crewman Fred Fleet had sighted the iceberg, looked as if it had been blown apart by the downblast....Behind it, two cargo cranes had been slammed down and the cargo hold doors kicked in. He could not see into the hold, but Tom knew that it was strewn with bales of rubber...a cask of china for Tiffany's...William Carter's Renault Town Car. And then the lifeboat davits showed up in *Argo*'s cameras—empty. Tom noticed that Sharon Callahan, the security officer, was standing in the back of the room. Tears were streaming down her face.

"What's wrong?" he asked.

"I don't know," she said.

"She was already feeling this strange, unexpected outburst of emotion that was eventually to hit us all," recalls Tom. "It hit her first. And then all of a sudden Bob Ballard looked up at the clock and said, 'Fellas, do you realize what time it is?' Of course we all did, because we had been reading the books about the *Titanic,* and we realized that we were very close to the time that it had actually gone under. And Bob said, with tears beginning to appear in his eyes, 'I don't know about you people, but I want to get together on the fantail and have just a moment of silence for the 1,500 souls that died very close to this moment.' And we stood there, over the spot where hundreds of people had stood in the dark waiting for the deck to go under, and no more lifeboats. And that was quite a thing to be thinking about, as we quietly raised the flag of the *Titanic*'s builders. That's when it hit me. I began to cry.

"When I got home, of course, everybody wanted to ask me about it and there were some things I just couldn't talk about without getting all emotional, so I'd just skip the issue. And the night I got home Bob gave this news conference and I remember watching him on TV and I just got sort of emotionally overwhelmed because he was experiencing the same difficulty. I could see that he was choking up. He just couldn't talk about the ship. And that got to me.

"It's so odd, and unexpected, the way it affected us. I've explored the wreck of the *Empress of Ireland.* That was the biggest loss of passengers in maritime history. It put the *Titanic* to shame. Yet nobody seems to remember it. Even to me, even after I'd read all the books on it and interviewed a survivor, the *Empress of Ireland* was simply an exploration, an adventure—just like looking at these strange lava formations on the Rise. It had none of the *Titanic*'s impact on me. It did not overpower me with sadness."

"Why?" asked Ballard as we sat over cups of Coke (Classic) in the *Melville*'s library. "Why has the word *Titanic* become part of our vocabulary? Why does a four-year-old or a six-year-old know about it? Everyone knows that word. It's part of our culture. Why is that?"

"I don't know," I answered. "Perhaps this whole mystique about the *Titanic* is little more than fascination for something that was spectacular and yet very sad. I think that combination touches something in the heart. Also, people like narrow focus. By focusing on just one part of a picture, it becomes easier to understand the whole picture. For any number of reasons, including all the ironies surrounding the *Titanic* disaster, that ship has been chosen to speak for all disasters. It's the same thing with Jack the Ripper. History has seen murderers worse than him. But he's the one who sticks in our minds. There have been many great scientists, yet one, Albert Einstein, has become almost a symbol for scientific brilliance."

"That could be it, or part of it," Ballard said. "But do you know what one of the strangest things about the *Titanic* expedition is? The real justification for that expedition was not to go look for the *Titanic*. The real justification was to conduct the final sea trials of *Argo*. They were a prerequisite for *Argo*-Rise—for this expedition. Ironically, you won't see people writing about *this* expedition in the history books. No. Not a single word."

3

The Argossey

EXCERPT FROM THE LOG OF CHARLES PELLEGRINO
Research Vessel: *Melville*
Expedition: *Argo-Rise*
Date: Thursday, December 19, 1985
Time: 4:00 P.M.
Place: Somewhere over the East Pacific Rise, with 1.5 miles of water below

Most people think that the oceans, like sinks, end at the bottom. Not so. They reach beneath the East Pacific Rise and the Challenger Deep, into the Earth itself. According to Francheteau, a volume of water equivalent to the entire contents of the oceans has, over the last eight million years, seeped down into the crust and returned through hydrothermal vents.

Ballard bemoans the fact that we will soon know more about a distant moon of Uranus than about the East Pacific Rise. "Of the deep sea we have only fragmented knowledge," he says. "What we do know is that the deep sea is as complicated as any land is, or any damned Uranian satellite. The mid-ocean ridge is a 40,000-mile-long seam running around the planet. The East Pacific Rise is only a tiny piece of it. Fully twenty-three percent of the Earth's total surface is wrapped up in this mountain range. Very few people know that. People should be aware of the biggest geologic feature on Earth, but they aren't. If you walked up to the average guy on the street and asked, 'What's the largest single geologic feature on Earth?' he might say, 'Oh, it must be the Rocky Mountains.' Not bad! A pretty good guess, but it isn't. The whole Rocky Mountain chain could fit in a small corner of the ocean ridge system. Do you know that there are more volcanoes under water than on the land surface? Do you know that? Most people don't. That speaks a lot about our ability to transmit information."

Poor *Argo* is transmitting no new information this morning. Sooner or later, a collision was bound to happen. To imagine what towing a robot across a field of submarine volcanoes is like, picture yourself trying to photograph hot-dog stands at Coney Island using a camera suspended from a helicopter at the end of a mile-long string. It's just bound to happen. *Bound to*. And so, inevitably, *Argo* ran up against a vertical cliff last night and started a major landslide. Volcanic glass punched down through her carapace, severing lines and killing the robot.

Francheteau was troubled enough without this latest setback. Yesterday afternoon a cartoon appeared on the *Argo* bulletin board depicting his plight:

Right! It looked so easy, four days ago, when *Argo* was sent to the bottom and many of us saw, for the first time, a live hydrothermal vent. We found it in the middle of a frozen lava lake so new that glass sparkled everywhere in a million points of reflected torchlight. Hot, sulfide-laden water emerged from obsidian tubes cracked open, and around them grew an oasis of worms, unidentified fish known only as "polywags" because they resemble tadpoles, blind crabs as white as ivory, and brittle stars. The *Argo* room was filled with *Oohs!* and *Ahhs!* and *Oh, shits!* Francheteau and Ballard were impressed with the reaction they saw in us; but it was to them an overreaction to what they knew from previous encounters to be a rather boring vent. Ballard decided, then, to turn the ship toward the big vents to show us a *real* roaring piece of machinery—"just to blow our brains away."

Three days ago *Argo* was sent down into what should have been "vent city." The trouble is that we have found no vents. Lava there is—tubes and bulbs and frozen rivers of it everywhere—sometimes evil and wondrous in appearance, as alien as another planet. We know, each of us, that we are the very first people ever to see them; yet, after viewing lava formations every day, all day long, for nearly a week, they begin to be a bore. That in itself is fascinating: how fast the human mind adapts. The fantastic has become commonplace. The mood is underscored by a sign over the TV monitors that warns in bold black crayon letters:

YOU ARE HAVING FUN

Indeed we are. This is a day of rest for most of the scientific party, while *Argo* is under repair. So we sit in the plywood "swimming pool" Ballard has constructed on the fantail, discussing column formation in lava pools nearly two miles below. And we watch the sharks. And a flying fish lands on deck. And we pass around the *Argo* sample: a piece of rubble from last night's avalanche. It was lying there, Bible black and opal bright, amidst severed lines when we hauled the robot up. Glass on the sea floor tends to lose its polish after only a few decades. Yet the *Argo* sample still has a fresh sheen to it—*very* fresh; it could have formed yesterday.

Close. We were close. We might have been there with our cameras just in time to catch an eruption. That's the point: one of these days we're going to get one.

In a day *Argo* will be repaired and on the bottom again photographing lava fields and mapping places where the Earth is forming new crust and pushing it west and east as fast as seven inches per year.

In three years *Argo* will fly as high as one hundred feet above the ocean floor, taking the high view with her down-looking cameras and side-scanning sonar while, at the same time, dispatching a smaller robot named *Jason* for close-up views. The two machines will operate as a team—reminiscent of the *Viking* orbiter and lander exploration of Mars. Together, *Argo* and *Jason* (named affectionately after Jason and the Argonauts) will beam sonar maps, 3-D images, and the sounds of the deep to the surface—allowing us to see and hear other worlds without actually having to go there—a goal Ballard refers to as "telepresence." He says it may take him ten years to fully develop his vision of it. *Jason* will have hands and stereo color eyes. *Argo* will be *Jason's* garage; but the garage will have the ability to see from above, with her own high-resolution color TV cameras. Imagine a control room with TV screens arranged side by side to give a 180° robot's-eye view. It will be bigger and better than the *Star Trek* bridge screen.

"At the level of technology we see on this ship today," explains Ballard, "telepresence is still back in the days of a guy yelling into a tin can on a string, compared to where it can go. I mean, we're still using black-and-white TV cameras, for crying out loud. Ultimately we can go toward that personal experience of being there, in other words the *Wow!* In ten years you'll be making simulated dives, and when I put you in *Alvin* you'll be disappointed because you're not going to have the freedom of vision that *Argo/Jason* can give you. You'll be looking out a little porthole. Compared to the robot's-eye view, an *Alvin* dive will be somewhat like crawling around on the bottom of a cave with a flashlight...and blinders around your eyes. And remember: *Alvin* can only accommodate three. We can't transport everyone down to a hydrothermal vent in a minisub. But we can put their minds there. Telepresence is the ability to share. What is an experience if it's not shared? You know, it's one thing to be wowed and zapped, but it's another to turn to a person and say, 'Wasn't that great?' It's as important as being wowed. If you're just wowed and you can't tell anybody about it, then it's—did you really have the experience?

"*Sharing.* That's the concept of an epic journey. I think the epic journey is part of our lives. It's a part of human development in literature and exploration and everyday life. The journey's goal is to attain a truth, a new knowledge. But unless it's brought back and shared, the journey isn't complete.

"I will be going on journeys till I die, and I want to bring more and more people into that experience—like what's happening now on this ship. I think that the perfect way of sharing is to participate in the journey. Telepresence technology makes it possible for people to tune in. One day our expeditions will be broadcast live on cable television, in 3-D, from the bottom of the Pacific."

But that technological dream is years away. There is a possibility that it may never be funded at all. Ballard explains that even in the short term he needs dynamic-positioning equipment for the ship, so that he can hold *Jason*'s garage still, and fiber-optic cable. Those two items, or rather the lack of them, are cause for despair. Building the robots is easy. It's the bureaucratic machinery that slows everything down.

Not to worry, though. Ballard has a way...of having his way. He told me of the day he visited MIT and met a graduate student with a footing in artificial intelligence. He decided in an hour that he wanted that man on his team—and he was going to get him. He went after him like a barracuda. "I wooed him," Ballard recalls. "I lied to him. I did everything possible and I infected him with my disease. And he's hooked in. He's the long-term expert. He's *Jason*."

It begins to look, from time to time, as if we are witness to a peculiar parasitism, wherein Ballard serves the robot's interests, instead of the other way around. And strangest of all to think that, to a greater or lesser degree, he has infected us all with this disease. We have learned to look with affection upon a machine named *Argo*. Sometimes we even lose sleep over her.

The next big step in *Argo/Jason*'s evolution, the next epic journey, will take place sometime next summer, when a prototype for *Jason,* a two-foot-wide robot called *Jason Jr.,* will be dispatched from *Alvin* into the *Titanic.*

Now that *Argo,* assisted by its predecessor *Angus,* has mapped guy wires, fallen masts and other traps in waiting, *Alvin* can descend to three predetermined safe spots. Seated on the *Titanic*'s decks, Ballard will send *Jason Jr.* where he and *Alvin* cannot go: into the cargo holds...through the collapsed crystal dome of the first-class Grand Stairway, to point fingers of light up and down hallways...onto the bridge where Captain Smith had stood, thinking perhaps of the five ice warnings he'd ignored, as he listened to the sea gurgling across the A Deck and spilling down the ventilators.

If shipbuilder Thomas Andrews were alive today, he would be fascinated—utterly fascinated—to learn of the computerized instruments that would see into his *Titanic* and uncover its secrets. We can only guess what he might think of the other marvels of our age. As he watched the *Titanic* growing, steel plate by steel plate, in the Belfast shipyard, men had barely learned to fly in flimsy, kitelike airplanes. Could he have imagined that three-quarters of a century later we'd be sailing an interplanetary sea? Could he have guessed, in his wildest fantasy, that Halley's Comet, which is making its first appearance since 1910, would be greeted this time by a flotilla of spacefaring robots? What would he think of *Voyager*? or *Challenger*?

We have come to love our machines. We who know them. We who have touched them. And Thomas Andrews would have understood us. Andrews' affection for his creation could not have been very different, seventy-four years ago.

4

A Fancy-Dress Ball in Dante's Hell

It is difficult to understand why the owners and builders named this ship *Titanic*. The Titans were a mythological race who came to believe they'd conquered nature, who thought they'd achieved power and learning greater than Zeus himself, to their ultimate ruin. He smote the strong and daring Titans with thunderbolts; and their final abiding place was in some limbo beneath the lowest depths of the Tartarus, a sunless abyss below Hades.

—*From an editorial in the* Belfast Morning News, *June 1, 1911*

A man standing in a crow's nest. That is how it began: with a man perched halfway up the foremast peering out into the cold and the dark at 11:40 P.M. on Sunday, the 14th of April, 1912.

Lookout Frederick Fleet found the sea unusually calm. The air screamed thinly through rigging as the *Titanic* steamed through it at twenty-two knots. And the cold stars burned. And his warm breath hissed out into the moonless night.

The contrast between the ocean and the sky was a vivid dark line. Below that line was only the black Atlantic. Above it, rising from the horizon in every direction, the sky was a dome of stars.

Fleet noticed a strange commotion directly ahead, right on the dividing line. First one at a time, then by twos and threes, the stars appeared to be winking out. He squinted into the night. A silhouette was moving against the starlight. Every second it loomed larger and closer—spreading and sharp-edged.

Oh, God. Can that be? . . . a mountain? . . . *coming down our throats?*

Instinctively, he banged the crow's nest bell three times, warning of danger ahead.

Up on the bridge, First Officer Will Murdoch picked up the phone.

"What did you see?"

"Iceberg dead ahead!"

At that moment the *Titanic* was bearing down on a wall of pale blue ice that dropped vertically below the waterline. The next day, a scar of red paint at the iceberg's base would reveal the cruelest *Titanic* irony: Fleet's warning to Murdoch was the last domino in a chain of events that had been set in motion more than two years before, by the kind of blind confidence that ruled no more than twenty lifeboats need be installed because sixteen watertight compartments running from stem to stern made the ship unsinkable. Indeed, the ship would have floated if Fleet had never seen the iceberg. Had Murdoch driven head-on into that vertical wall, he would only have squashed the bow and flooded the first two forward compartments. The *Titanic* could even have floated with the first four compartments gone. But, as Murdoch was quickly learning, blind confidence—even in the most lofty of technology's achievements—was potentially more unstable than nitroglycerin, and stability diminished proportionally with every bump in the road.

In response to Fleet's warning, Murdoch pulled the engine-room telegraph handle all the way to STOP and ordered quartermaster Hitchens to turn the wheel hard to starboard.* He followed, twenty seconds later, with an order for "Full speed astern," but the iceberg was too close. The starboard side grazed the wall, bringing a small avalanche of block ice onto the well deck. Below the waterline, a knobby protrusion in the wall broke open the first six watertight compartments.

Mrs. Walter Stephenson was shaken awake by the impact. She thought immediately of another ominous jolt, six years earlier, just

---

*In 1912 ships did not steer like automobiles. Turning the wheel right (to starboard), actually swung the rudder and the ship slowly left (to port).

before San Francisco came falling down around her. But, no—there were no earthquakes in the middle of the Atlantic. It couldn't be *that* bad.

Passenger Charles Hayes was also awakened by the jolt. He might have wondered, then, what had urged him, just a few hours earlier, to raise his glass and proclaim "that the time has come for the greatest and most appalling of all disasters at sea." But, no—it couldn't be *that* bad.

Within three hours he would be dead.

On the bow, crewman Samuel Hemming had seen a shadow slide by on the starboard side. Walking now among the anchor chains, he was trying to track down a curious whistling sound. And there it was: right between the chains. Something had forced open a hatch cover. Hemming peeked into the opening, into a stiff wind that came up from below and riffled his hair. The air was pouring out of her, a gauge for the volume of water that must be entering far below. It was 11.45 P.M., and Hemming was now the only man on board who understood that it was all so clearly too late.

Lord Pirrie, one of the *Titanic*'s owners, had planned to be aboard for this, her maiden voyage, but had been prevented by a flu-turned-pneumonia. He therefore sent Thomas Andrews in his place to observe the ship's crossing and to make recommendations for improving her.

In stateroom A-36, Andrews had scarcely noticed a distant ripping sound. It did not arouse him, so gentle was the impact. This was a deception. Had the ship rebounded from the iceberg, spilling Andrews to the floor, he would have risen with a look of dread on his face; but the force that threw him down would have, at the same time, been an indication that he was safe, that the hull was strong enough to offer resistance to the blow. Instead, whole slabs of inch-thick steel buckled and popped rivets and caved in, offering no more resistance to the spur of ice than tinfoil drawn over a blunt stick, so most of the *Titanic*'s passengers felt little more than a slight jolt and crunching underfoot, as if the ship had run over a pile of marbles.

With barely a shudder, the *Titanic* had absorbed a concussion sufficient to lift the Washington Monument fourteen times. And so, under the illusion of resilience and safety, Andrews did not stir from his stateroom.

He was surrounded at his worktable by blueprints and handwritten notes and, half-eaten, a loaf of bread made especially for him and sent as a gift from the chief baker. He'd spent most of the day walking the decks with representatives of the firm, interviewing engineers and passengers, retreating finally from dinner to his room. There he worked late into the night, transforming piles of notes into calculations and sketches. His mind sought restlessly to enlarge its outlook on a great science, to conquer new problems, and to achieve an ever-fresh perfection. Taking shape on paper were plans for newer, even more advanced ships...bigger...faster... safer....

And over there, among the plans: reports of improvements still to be made on *Titanic*. One directed attention to a design for reducing the number of screws in stateroom hat hooks. In another letter, amidst technicalities about cofferdams and submerged cylinders in the propeller boss, was a plan for staining green the wicker furniture in the Café Parisien. There was also a suggestion from Second Officer Lightoller to supply the ship's lookouts with binoculars for the return voyage from New York. Frederick Fleet had asked for a pair, only to be told that there were none for him or any of the other five men specially assigned to be "the eyes of the ship." The iceberg was less than a mile away when Fleet first saw it. Visibility that night was so extraordinarily good that stars were cut in half by the horizon before they set. Looking, as he was, straight ahead into the ship's path, Fleet could have seen the iceberg a mile farther—*miles* farther with a pair of binoculars. Even a mile would have given Murdoch nearly three additional minutes to respond. Even fifteen seconds would have been enough. But many things are forgotten during a ship's rush to her maiden voyage. Some common items, because of their very commonness, are overlooked, so the finest ship in the world sailed without binoculars for her lookouts.

The oversight is made large only by hindsight. If the *Titanic* had arrived safely in New York, Fleet's request for binoculars would be forgotten now, seeming no more important than the other reports spread over Andrews' desk…there was serious trouble with the restaurant galley hot press…the coloring of the pebble dashing on J. P. Morgan's private promenade deck was too dark….

Andrews was still writing reports and planning future ships when the captain called for him.

Mary Sloan, one of the ship's stewardesses, had joined a tiny knot of passengers in the frightful cold of the top deck.

"What happened?" someone asked.

"We struck something," acknowledged a tired voice.

Miss Sloan peered over the rail on the starboard side. There was only the cold Atlantic below, as black and calm as a pool of oil. As far as she could see, all the way out to the horizon, there was not the slightest hint of anything the ship could have collided with; to her left was the captain's bridge; to her right, the deck stretching astern, deserted mostly. Behind her the speculation continued:

"Is it serious?"

"Probably not. It didn't feel like much of a bump. She couldn't have suffered any great damage. There may be some leakage, but the pumps can handle it."

"Why has the ship stopped?"

"I expect whatever we hit has scratched off some of her new paint and the captain doesn't want to go on until she's painted up again."

Abruptly, Mr. Andrews emerged on deck, still dressed in his dinner clothes. Ignoring the passengers completely, he walked straight past them and headed purposefully for the bridge. Miss Sloan tried to analyze the expression on his face. There was worry in his eyes. Unmistakable.

It was unlike the man, Miss Sloan thought. It was unlike him to pass people on the ship and not show the slightest interest in them. The thing that struck you about him, next to his Irishman's appreciation of humor, was his warmth toward everyone. When his brown eyes met yours, it was with the look of frankest kindness.

Nevertheless, he seemed changed, somehow. Something about him had been askew all day. It was good to see his pride in the ship as he answered passengers' questions and inspected wooden fittings with his hands; but upon every occasion he'd talked almost constantly about his wife and his little girl, Elizabeth. Sometimes between laughs he would suddenly fall grave and glance over a shoulder in precisely the direction of Belfast.

Then there was that moment when Miss Sloan congratulated him on the beauty and perfection of the ship.

"What I do not like," he replied, "is that the *Titanic* is taking us farther from home every hour."

She looked at him and his face struck her as having a very sad expression.

Presently he was climbing down from the bridge with Captain Smith. A stoker climbed down behind them. His clothes were wet. Without a word, the three men disappeared below.*

No, Miss Sloan tried to tell herself. It couldn't be *that* bad. *Couldn't be.* It was easy to believe so. There was not a whisper of wind, not a single wave slapping against the hull. Indeed, one crewman commented that in twenty-six years he'd never seen the ocean so calm. The *Titanic* lay motionless on the surface, as steady and peaceful as an island in the Atlantic. Miss Sloan felt a sense of solidity, a sense of security.

No, it couldn't be *that* bad.

(Could it?)

No. I won't believe it.

Far below, Thomas Andrews had begun to prepare his mind

---

*The stoker's name was Frank "Lucks" Towers and, though he would survive this night without injury, his troubles were just beginning. In two years he'd be aboard the *Empress of Ireland* when it collided with another ship, opening up a hole in the *Empress*'s side. It would be an unusually hot night, and all the portholes would be open as she rolled onto her side in the St. Lawrence River. In minutes she'd be gone—yet, miraculously, Frank Towers was going to survive—virtually alone. He'd take his next job aboard the *Lusitania*, and would be heard to shout, "Now what!" when the torpedo struck (he'd swim to a lifeboat, vowing every stroke of the way to take up farming). His story was destined to inspire a young writer to script a teleplay entitled *Lone Survivor*. The teleplay was so well received that it paved the way for a series. The writer's name was Rod Serling and the series became the *Twilight Zone*.

for reception of the unbelievable, as he and Smith peered over the companionway into the flooded mail room. The clerks were still at their posts, struggling to save two hundred bags of registered mail containing four hundred thousand letters. They'd dragged the sacks up two decks already, but an unnatural tide pursued them. First to one deck. Then to the other. It seemed to pause for several minutes— then came again higher! Yes—much higher. Soon it would be up to F Deck, and letters now floated in it.

Andrews did some quick figuring: The mail room was in the fourth watertight compartment...the decks were lettered A, B, C, D, E, F, G, from the boat deck down...the ocean was about to reach F Deck...in the fourth compartment...the bulkhead might hold, but...but, no...a sick certainty came over him.

"It's bad."

"But the watertight doors were closed right after impact," said Smith, "all the compartments behind us are sealed. This ship *can't* sink."

"She's made of iron, sir. I'm afraid she can. We should make our way to the other compartments, to see if she will."

The journey forward wound through a labyrinth of fireman's tunnels and steel pipes enclosing ladders. Captain Smith threw open a hatch and found the racquetball court on G Deck running full. Andrews edged past him toward one of the cargo holds, lifted a round hatch cover and poked his head into the number two loading bay. He could actually watch the water climbing up the sides. Fast. It was filling faster than a bathtub with the faucets cocked all the way open. Electric lights still burned below the surface, casting an eerie glow that revealed only dark shapes. William Carter's Renault was down there in the bottom, grotesque and vague.

I'm losing her, he thought as he watched a seam in the wall inch down into the water. Oh, my God. I'm losing her.

Andrews' imprint was in her—all his years of experience. He knew her in and out, the power and beauty of her. He'd been with her

—*losing her*—

from the time of her conception through the long process of planning, designing, building, fitting

—LOSING HER—

He'd watched her grow up, frame by frame, plate by plate, as he'd watched and awaited the birth of Elizabeth. This was *his* ship. *His* child. Born of *his* industrial womb

—*OH, MY GOD*—

and because he knew her so well, as he knew Elizabeth born to him, to lose her was heartbreak.

Andrews moved away from the narrow opening and motioned to the captain. "It's no use. You can see for yourself."

As Captain Smith leaned into the hold, Andrews quietly counted the facts to him: "Water in the fore peak...water in the three cargo holds...water in boilerroom number 6, right behind the holds... water in boilerroom number 5...water fourteen feet above keel level in the first ten minutes, everywhere except boilerroom number 5— which is filling more slowly, but *filling*. We could have snapped off the first four compartments completely, and still she would have floated. But no one ever imagined a two-hundred-and-fifty-foot wound in her side, with the first six compartments filling."

"The pumps can keep the sixth compartment dry?"

"Temporarily. But it won't matter."

"How long do we have?"

"An hour-and-a-half. Perhaps two."

Calmly, Captain Smith asked, "How many people will the life-boats hold?"

"Twelve hundred," Andrews said. And then a strange expression came over his face. "How many are there on board?"

"Twenty-two hundred or more."

"Nooo..."

"I don't think the Board of Trade Regulations visualized this situation, do you?"

Even as the two men spoke, water in the first five compartments climbed toward overflow, dragging the ship down by the bow. During the next half hour, water in the fifth compartment would begin spilling over the bulkhead separating it from the sixth. When the sixth was full, it would spill over to the seventh, and so on.

~ ~ ~

They threaded their way, Smith and Andrews, toward the bridge. Far ahead of the rising water, they passed through the first-class quarters on C Deck. Several passengers were wandering about, but there was no sign that any of them had thought of immediate danger. A man ran past them along the corridor and flagged down a friend. "See!" he said. "*Now* do you believe me?" He held out a foot-long splinter of ice.

Somewhere behind them a steward was taking down the name of a gentleman who had kicked in a door to release a man trapped on the other side.

"The lock was hopelessly jammed," the passenger tried to explain. "The man wanted to come out. He was quite upset."

"There was no cause to damage the property of my company! In the very least you will be expected to pay for a new door. And it is only fair to warn you that you will probably be arrested on arrival in New York."

"See, here! You are addressing a passenger. And you are addressing one very rudely. We'll see, steward, who is in trouble when we arrive in New York."

The two men argued loudly and at length about the broken door, attracting a little knot of onlookers. Neither man, as he hollered, was aware of the infinitely greater damage ending their lives.

Climbing the stairs to A Deck, Smith and Andrews noticed that the stairs themselves seemed somehow out of balance. They *looked* right, but one's feet kept falling in the wrong places. The inner ear perceived what the eye could not: the ship was tilted down toward the bow.

She's also listing to port, Andrews noted. Probably coal had been used mostly from the starboard side, and the weight of coal was now pulling her slowly to port.

As the captain and the shipbuilder emerged from their grim investigation onto the top deck, Andrews recognized one of the stewardesses and went to her directly. Outwardly, Miss Sloan did not believe that the *Titanic* was mortally wounded, but deeper inside there was a feeling that something was about to happen...something...so she'd waited near the bridge for Mr. Andrews to return.

"There has been an accident," he told her. "It would be well, just by way of precaution, to get your passengers to put on warm clothing and their life jackets and assemble on the boat deck."

She read Andrews' face—which had a look as though he were heartbroken. "Is the accident serious?" she asked.

"It is very serious. But keep the news quiet. I don't want panic. Tell them to put on warm clothing. See to it that everyone—*everyone*—has a life jacket. That includes you, Miss Sloan."

He then hurried away to the work of warning and rescue.

Marconi.

Among those who survived, one name would be mentioned with deepest affection and gratitude. If not for his invention, the *Titanic* could not have shrieked her distress into the night, and no one would have suspected trouble until she was listed overdue in New York. Up to this time, lifeboats were simply a means of setting people adrift from sinking ships—a practice from which the word "castaways" is derived. Generally, castaways were destined to wander the sea at the mercy of the winds, until hunger or exposure or storms or some combination thereof killed them. If they were very lucky, they washed up on uncharted islands.

In those days, lifeboats were best described as tools for committing suicide to avoid getting killed...in those days, before Marconi and his wireless.

The *Titanic*'s wireless shack was located twenty yards from the bridge, down the port side of the boat deck. Inside, operators John Phillips and Harold Bride had spent a grueling afternoon tracking down a burned-out relay that, for seven hours, and more, prevented the most powerful telegraph afloat from sending. They were lucky—very lucky—that the transmitter broke down early enough to be repaired before the collision. This was the only good news heard aboard the *Titanic* that night.

The delay, however, had set them back with transmissions from passengers, which included everything from stock-exchange quotations to HAVING LOTS OF FUN. WISH YOU WERE HERE. AL. So new and wondrous was wireless technology that passengers were fascinated—*too fascinated*—by the knowledge that their words could be transmitted across the airwaves from ship to ship to friends and relatives on the mainland. Even without the breakdown, messages piled up faster than they could be transmitted.

Frayed and exhausted, the two men had decided that one of them should get some sleep. "You turn in, boy," said Phillips. "I'm all done with this work of making repairs. I don't know if we'll ever empty the 'In' basket, now. But you turn in, and as soon as you can, come back and relieve me."

Bride took off his clothes, climbed into a berth in the adjoining room, and fell into an uneasy sleep. Background noise kept sneaking into his dreams. There was the ever-present rasp of the telegraph. He was conscious of reading, even in his sleep, what Phillips was sending: traffic matters directed at Cape Race...and there was an interruption from the *Californian,* something about being stopped and surrounded by ice...SHUT UP, Phillips tapped back...SHUT UP. SHUT UP. I AM WORKING CAPE RACE AND YOU ARE JAMMING ME ...Bride heard Fleet's three bells in the crow's nest outside...and then he was aware of waking up and hearing...hearing what?

Gone.

(*Gone?*)

Yes, *gone*. It wasn't a new noise. It was an old, familiar one. A noise that should have been there, but wasn't. The vibration of distant engines carrying up through the ship's frame was felt more than heard. It shook the bones, and it was always there...always there...so Bride had become used to it, had put it out of his thoughts. Until now—now that its very absence had intruded on his sleep.

(*Gone?* Gee, that's funny.)

He shook himself fully awake and heard Phillips sending to Cape Race. Just the usual stuff, Bride noted. More traffic matters.

"Why have the engines stopped?" he called.

"I think we got damaged in some way. Probably threw a propeller. I expect that we shall have to go back to Harland and Wolff's."

"Back to Belfast?"

"Yes."

"Oh, bloody hell!" Bride said, pulling on his pants and bursting into giggles. "I'd hate to be in E. J. Smith's shoes when he tells the Astors and the Guggenheims they're going to be at least a week late getting to New York."

Abruptly, Captain Smith stepped into the shack. "We've struck an iceberg. You had better send the call for assistance."

"What call should I send?" Phillips asked.

"The regulation international call for help. Just that."

Thirty-five minutes after impact, the first distress call went out: DA-DIT-DA-DIT DA-DA-DIT-DA DA-DIT-DIT, representing the letters CQD, the traditionally recognized cry for help.

Almost immediately, the German steamer *Frankfurt* chimed in. OKAY. I MUST CONSULT MY CAPTAIN. STAND BY.

While Phillips and Bride waited, the British liner *Carpathia* answered the call with a question: DOES THE TITANIC KNOW THAT THERE ARE SOME PRIVATE MESSAGES WAITING FOR HER FROM CAPE RACE?

WE NEED ASSISTANCE. THE TITANIC HAS STRUCK A BERG. THIS IS A CQD OLD MAN. COME AT ONCE.

WHAT IS YOUR POSITION?

POSITION 41.46N 50.14W.

WE ARE FIFTY-EIGHT MILES AWAY. WE CAN BE AT YOUR SIDE IN ABOUT FOUR HOURS. SHOULD I TELL MY CAPTAIN?

Just then the *Frankfurt* operator came back on the air with a question from his captain: WHAT IS THE MATTER?

YOU FOOL, Phillips tapped back. WE'RE BUSY HERE. STAND BY.

SHOULD I TELL MY CAPTAIN? the *Carpathia* operator repeated.

YES. AT ONCE.

At that moment, the *Titanic*'s wireless operators still believed in the ship's unsinkable construction. It seemed only a matter of waiting until another ship arrived to take her in tow.

"Won't we be a sorry sight?" Bride asked Phillips. "Won't we look silly? The biggest and classiest ship ever built having to be towed home from its first voyage—probably by some rust bucket!"

Phillips was stricken by the giggles.

THE FRANKFURT WISHES TO KNOW WHAT IS THE MATTER. WE ARE 10 HOURS AWAY.

YOU ARE JAMMING MY EQUIPMENT FOOL. STAND BY AND KEEP OUT.

THE CAPTAIN OF THE CARPATHIA IS PUTTING ABOUT AND COMING HARD.

From five hundred miles away came a call from the *Olympic,* the *Titanic*'s sister ship: WHAT IS THE MATTER?

WE HAVE STRUCK AN ICEBERG AND NEED ASSISTANCE.

Three hundred and fifty miles nearer, rage flared as the *Frankfurt* operator listened to the *Titanic-Olympic* exchange. To British ships the *Titanic* was responding with courtesy. But when a German inquired to help, he was twice called a fool. In a week, a complaint lodged by Germany would attribute the *Titanic* disaster to British inefficiency at sea. In a month, an escalating chain reaction of insults would be flying back and forth across the English Channel.

—YOU FOOL—

It was the birth cry of a growing animosity

—STAND BY AND KEEP OUT—

an animosity that would stretch through a terrible war, fought with all the nightmares that a great science was capable of unleashing

—YOU FOOL—

They'd call it the war to end all wars

—STAND BY—

World War One

—KEEP OUT—

The number, of course, came later.

On D Deck Miss Sloan shouted down a long corridor: "All passengers on deck with life jackets on!"

People were passing up and down on the stairs behind her. The purser was among them, carrying a heavy load of valuables cleared from the ship's four safes. He'd hoped to save them all in one package, on the same lifeboat; but neither he nor the package would ever be seen again.

Opening up a spare room, Miss Sloan began pulling blankets and extra life jackets from the closets to distribute among passengers. She had not, as yet, tied one of the life-clutching jackets to herself.

"Did I not tell you to put on your life jacket?" shouted someone behind her. It was Mr. Andrews. "Surely you have one."

"Yes, but I thought it mean to wear it. It might frighten the passengers."

"Never mind that," he said sternly. "Now, if you value your life, put on your coat and life jacket, then walk around the deck and let the passengers see you."

She then noticed that he was himself insufficiently clad against the biting cold outside, and that he had not yet fastened a life jacket.

The Grand Saloon and the adjoining main staircase were, even by the standards of Victorian England's richest estates, magnificent in their construction. Guilded columns supported a vast framework of exquisite wood sculpture that completely enclosed the winding marble staircase. Carved walnut flowers ran from floor to ceiling. Soon, an unspoken law of the sea would dictate that no ship ever again match the luxury of the *RMS Titanic:* ankle-deep oriental carpets…horse-hair sofas…silk lampshades…crystal chandeliers that hung, now, at an irrational angle.

—at an irrational angle…

Now Miss Sloan could see the evidence everywhere, evidence of a coming catastrophe that had not been apparent when she stood on the deck under the bridge. From high above came a persistent roar. The excess steam from the ship's idle engines was blowing off through a pipe reaching atop one of the smokestacks, making conversation difficult, even below deck. Up the Grand Stairway began a small procession of elegantly dressed men and women, orderly, quiet, and regal. Over each fur coat was tied a white, ghostly life jacket. The emblem of death at sea, Miss Sloan observed.

"If you value your life..."Andrews had said. The horrors were coming, unavoidably. She watched the procession and she knew what it must become, *knew* that all around her the night was shifting from familiar faces and familiar settings into something else; shifting like wax...into a fancy-dress ball in Dante's Hell.

"What signal are you sending?" asked Captain Smith.

"CQD," Phillips replied.

"I've got an idea," Bride said.

"Oh, great," said Phillips. "You've got an idea. *Now* I'm worried."

Bride let out a laugh, and then shot back: "Remember, true genius is no guarantee against dumb ideas. It just means that fewer of your problems cannot be solved."

That remark made them all laugh, including the captain.

"Now," Bride continued. "Why not send SOS. The letters are easy enough for any amateur to understand—even a German. It's the new call. Just approved. We'd be the first to send it—and, who knows? This may be your last chance to use it."

Phillips laughed and changed the signal.

DIT-DIT-DIT DA-DA-DA DIT-DIT-DIT
DIT-DIT-DIT DA-DA-DA DIT-DIT-DIT
DIT-DIT-DIT DA-DA-DA DIT-DIT-DIT

Half as an afterthought, half as a joke, the blips and dashes blazed out over the cold Atlantic.

DIT-DIT-DIT DA-DA-DA DIT-DIT-DIT

Making their appointment with destiny, and laughing as they did so, Phillips and Bride stepped into the history books with the very first use of the SOS call.

5

The Emblem of Death at Sea

"All passengers up top with life jackets on!"

One hundred miles off the California coast, the research vessel *Orca* was trapped near the eye of 1959's most memorable hurricane—memorable, at least, to 17-year-old Bob Ballard, who now attempted to help a man who'd been pitched by a terrible sea from a top bunk. Bob thought the ship would capsize, then.

The man had broken both his legs.

"All passengers muster up top with life jackets on!" came the call from above.

"You get yourself up to the lab," said the ship's research biologist, Robert Norris, as he tied a splint. "I'll take care of your bunkmate."

Bob hesitated.

"He'll be fine. You'd better go."

It was hard going. From time to time the floor seemed about to become the wall, and the wall the floor. Movement was easiest when the ship paused between sways, with down becoming the V between floor and wall. *And the stairs*—"Oh, man—my stomach," Bob groaned. All the crackers in the world didn't seem to help. Norris had told him long ago to toss them overboard and at least spare himself the energy of chewing and swallowing. Coca-Cola was better. It tasted a lot nicer coming up. Even the old salts were sick today. One actually thought he was going to die, and then became afraid that he wouldn't. They were losing a lot of machos on this trip, including Bernard the rat, whom they'd found down on C Deck, pulling himself across the floor on his front paws. Thus far (thus far!) Bernard was the only death attributed to the storm. He was also the only rat in history known to have died of seasickness.

Finally, Bob pulled himself through a hatch and stepped into the lab on the top deck. Norris and the others would be up shortly, he knew—and then the head count would be complete. Bob also knew that the ship was badly damaged. She was taking on more water than the pumps could handle, and she might sink. But Bob had drilled for this very event. He knew exactly where his muster station was, exactly which lifeboat he was to get into, and how to use it. Many things had changed since the *Titanic* died nearly fifty years before. It was legend now: how the ship had carried too few lifeboats for her passengers and crew and how it would have made very little difference had she carried enough because her crew never held a proper boat drill, so boats were still being floated off even as she gulped under. In the boats themselves, the *Titanic*'s sailors had to be shown by women passengers how to row. That, too, was part of the legend. It endured in court transcripts…*"A sailor was pushing his oar about every which way. 'Why don't you put the oar in the oarlock?' Mrs. White finally said to him. 'Do you put it in that hole?' he asked. 'Certainly,' she replied. 'I never had an oar in my hand before,' he explained. The men began arguing over how to manage the boat. One of them snapped at another: 'If you don't stop talkin' through that hole in yer face, there'll be one less in this boat!'"* All the while there shone a light on the horizon, less than an hour away. The light belonged to the *Californian*. It did not move, for her wireless operator was asleep and never heard the SOS. The men who slept at Pearl Harbor were paragons of preparedness by comparison to those on and in and near the *Titanic* that night.

But many changes had been instigated by the incredible events of April 15, 1912.

Oh, yes. Many changes indeed.

There were enough lifeboats on the *Orca* to accommodate everyone aboard, and then some. Inflatable rafts would be dispatched automatically to the surface if the ship sank—backups for the lifeboats. All-night radio vigils on ships at sea and listening posts on land assured that the *Orca*'s SOS was heard. And now the cavalry was on its way. A Coast Guard cutter was hurrying to *Orca*'s side; but it was many hours distant. Coast Guard helicopters were on call; but the winds would not allow them to fly until the hurricane moved off, sometime tomorrow, and the *Orca* might be gone by then. Yes, but the boats and rafts could float, even if they were swamped by waves, even if they were battered to pieces. And each one carried a radio beacon. It's all right, Bob decided. The helicopters would find them.

"Thank God for the lifeboats," Bob said.

And then he remembered a rumor he'd heard about the Coast Guard. It was said that every April 15 they sent a ship or a plane to drop a wreath over 41°46′ N, 50°14′W.

It was no rumor.

The U.S. Coast Guard's International Ice Patrol owed its creation to the loss of fifteen hundred souls on a cold April night. But to Bob Ballard the story remained an interesting myth, a welcome distraction, as he looked out across the warm lab into a rain that drummed against the windows as if fired from cannons. Beyond the rain, on the deck, a lifeboat waited in its davits. Bob tightened his life jacket, hoping for the best, preparing for the worst.

A lifeboat in its davits…the image was to haunt Bob for the next twenty-seven years—right up to the moment he landed on the *Titanic*'s B Deck.

6

Killing Joke

Now for close on twenty minutes the SOS hissed out in every direction at the speed of light as Phillips and Bride felt the floor tilting...tilting...tilting. It dipped toward the bow with the relentless perceptibility of the minute hand of a large clock.

"I don't know much about watertight compartments," Phillips said. "But I'm beginning to think we're in a tight pickle."

"You think we'll be having sand for breakfast?"

"I'm afraid so."

"I've got an idea."

"Uh-oh. Look out, everybody. Bride's got an idea."

"The boat's got a hole in it, right?"

"Right."

"So, make another hole."

Phillips's nose wrinkled "—another hole?"

"To let the water out!"

That broke the ice, as it were. Phillips chuckled, and the two operators continued saying many funny things to each other.

~ ~ ~

A terrible shiver spread through Thomas Andrews as he stripped off a lifeboat cover and helped Mr. Murdoch clear away the lines to the davits. He barely noticed violinist Jock Hume brushing against him as he hurried aft. Poor Mr. Hume. The ship's band was underpaid even if the White Star Line wasn't eventually to withhold three-quarters of their agreed-upon fee for the maiden voyage, on the premise that they'd wind up playing only through the first half of the outbound leg. Their entire earnings for this trip would not add up to the cost of replacing their uniforms, and their widows would be billed for the loss of the uniforms. Mr. Andrews heard a voice: "Perhaps we'd better cancel our morning swim," joked one passenger to another. The gentleman was referring to the *Titanic*'s swimming pool—the first ever built into a ship. Presently the little joke didn't seem very funny. The pool was located on F Deck, in the sixth watertight compartment. The bulkhead between the fifth and sixth compartments went only as high as E Deck. Andrews knew that if he could do magic, if it were somehow within his power to extend the bulkhead just one deck higher, to D Deck, and to guarantee that the barrier would hold, water could never spill over into the sixth compartment and the sea would not now be up to the pool-room ceiling.

7

The Weeping Dolphins

Chet Ballard gripped the rail with aggravated impatience for arrival of the bus carrying his son. He wondered, as he stood on a dock at Scripps Institute of Oceanography, if Bob, under the circumstances, would ever go near the water again.

It had been difficult getting him there in the first place. Who would believe that the man *Omni* magazine would one day call "the real Captain Nemo, risking his life to explore virgin territory," was, as a child, afraid of the water?

Chet was reminded achingly of Redondo Beach. Whenever he'd had a Saturday off, he used to bring the two boys there. He started them playing in the sand near the base of an old wooden stairway on the upper beach. Eventually he coaxed Bob and Dick down to the edge of the sea, but a wave came up and wet their feet and sent them shrieking and running for the stairs and, try as he did, Chet could not get them to follow him again into the wet sand.

One day he got the idea of building sand castles with them near the stairs, and then gradually building mounds and walls lower and lower on the beach. As the summer drew on, the castles encroached on damp sand, but Bob was still a little scared, and the castles remained above the highest water. The boys had shovels and buckets, and they loved to run in the sand—*and in the sand only*—looking from time to time down at the water, as if checking to make sure it wasn't coming for them.

Finally, Chet decided the day had come to be a little devious. He began the morning with his usual above-the-highest-water castle, and then announced, "Well, boys, we gotta have a wall around this castle." He started the wall downhill, keeping his back to the tide, which was coming in. He backed the wall into the wet sand, and his sons eventually joined him; but they ran away the moment a wave threatened to touch their feet. Chet stayed...and stayed— stayed until water surged around him and his wall.

From on high, Bob and Dick watched their father.

"Oh, you know, this isn't too bad," Chet called up from the tide line. "And, gee...Hey! You know what? We need another wall over here, you know."

It did not occur to Bob to ask why they "needed" a wall there. At four years old, one does not stop to think that Daddy could be devious. It was just a fact: the wall was needed. So he went to work. After three more weekends Bob and his brother were building castles in the wet sand with Daddy. Oh, for quite awhile they'd continue to yell when a wave came up and made their feet wet, but soon their behavior was quite the opposite, and Chet found himself having to say, "Now, look, fellas. People *can* go too far in the water...."

Presently, Chet wondered if he'd sent Bob too far too soon. Wasn't there something a little bit crazy about sending a seventeen-year-old kid out to sea on an expedition? No, Chet decided. Not at all. For better or for worse, the boy had to find his own way. He'd come home one afternoon and said he wanted to be an oceanographer, and it just so happened that Chet's work with preliminary design of rockets, in what was eventually to become the Minuteman Missile program, brought him into contact with all sorts of Navy personnel, including Dr. Roger Revelle, who headed Scripps Institute.

"I've got a boy," Chet told Roger. "He's a sophomore in high school and he indicates that he is interested in some kind of oceanographic work. And I'm not really up on that field. I don't know how to advise him."

Roger said he'd be very happy to talk to Bob and, as it turned out, he took an immediate liking to the boy. They talked for a whole afternoon about the ocean, and Bob's future in it. Then Roger gave him an application for the National Science Foundation's summer trainee program, designed especially for high school kids interested in oceanography. The month of July was spent in the institute's labs. In August they sent Bob out to sea, where the hurricane had overtaken his ship. The details were sketchy. Two people were very badly injured...Bob was not one of them (thank you very much) ...the Coast Guard had to go out and rescue them, get them off the ship...which was said to be sinking...they'd sent helicopters ...Oh, boy. What a way to get a first taste of oceanography! Would the boy ever be willing to take a second taste?

The boy was certainly willing.

"Wow! Absolutely incredible!" Bob said as he stepped off the bus. "I've got to go out there again. *Got to!*"

"You enjoyed it? Hurricane and all?"

Hurricane and all. If anything, the storm added spice to the danger of Bob's dreams. He figured, if he could go through something like that and survive—then, what the heck! He'd be happy to spend the rest of his life on the sea, and under it.

In a week he was sailing with another Scripps expedition, off the coast of Baja, where strange upwellings were hoisting nutrients from the bottom and creating an oceanic garden. The place became a feeding ground for whales, and Bob marveled over them.

In a year, he was a summer "gofer" on North American Aviation's proposal to build a small, deep-diving submarine for the Navy. At that time, North American was devoting more and more of its energy to Chet Ballard's rockets, and to something called "the space race," while a man named Joseph Shea raved on and on about building a steel compartment able to orbit the moon, or some such craziness.* A result of this was that North American lost the submarine contract to General Mills, the people who make Cheerios. The Cheerios people sold the contract to Litton Industries in Minneapolis, who eventually built the submarine and christened it *Alvin*.

There followed four-and-a-half years in Santa Barbara, where Bob immersed himself in college life, and pursued a physical science degree. "The prettiest part of the world is up there, in Santa Barbara," says Bob. "Up there, where the rugged Pacific pounds into the rugged landscape—and that gorgeous interaction between them: the strength of the sea and the strength of the land...I like that a lot. Seeing that, feeling it, I began to learn that I was not so interested in the surface of the ocean as I was in the floor of it. I wanted to go where the ocean meets land, whether it's on the shore or on the bottom. I didn't get a big thrill out of going out to sea and looking around and seeing nothing but water all the way out to the horizon. My mind was down there. All the time it was down there. I didn't think about the surface. I thought about the volcanoes beneath me. So, it was the surface of the Earth that fascinated me, not the surface of the ocean. I knew that was what I wanted to study—forever. At least, I thought I knew it...until a couple of professors decided that I was not scientist material. I ran into a head-on collision with them. But that has been my fate all my life: of either alienating someone or having them like me. I can remember

---

*There was also, at that time, an undersea race. The American bathyscaphe *Trieste* was a hollow steel ball suspended from a buoyant bag of gasoline. In 1960 this undersea balloon descended almost six miles into the Challenger Deep of the Mariana Trench. Don Walsch and his crew almost got killed on that one. They reached the bottom and saw a flatfish. No one had expected to find life there. As they wondered what a halibut, of all things, was doing in the deepest part of the ocean, there came a pinging sound, followed by a crunch. The spherical cabin was caving in under two hundred thousand tons of water pressing in from all sides. "But they made it back alive," says Bob Ballard. "They did it. It was sort of neat: the space race was over under water before it even started. They went to the deepest spot right off and nailed it and that was that. So it wasn't a race with the Russians; so you had to have another reason, you know—'Why are we going down there?' And that was healthy because it wasn't a quest for depth. Suddenly it was a quest for knowledge that became a reason for sending people into new worlds."

one particular geology professor who didn't like me defocusing my energy into student government, into basketball and volleyball and tennis and girls. He was determined to make me a better academic and I didn't want to hear of it because I wanted to live—to really live as well as learn. And he started laying down ultimatums and I proceeded to disobey and he deliberately lowered my grades over that—simply to show me that he had the power. That was a critical point. Here was an individual who was trying to shape my life while I was trying to shape it myself and he almost turned me away from science. In my junior year at Santa Barbara I was very close to changing the whole course of my life. I was going with a girl and I was engaged, and then *that* whole thing exploded right in the middle of this professor's attacks and threw me off course, sort of disoriented me for six or nine months. I spent the summer of 1964 studying business administration at UCLA. I was at a crossroads then. But I decided to finish my degree in physical science, while simultaneously applying everywhere I could to get away from California. I wrote to Woods Hole; but they had no graduate program in oceanography. They were, at that time, just a research lab. University of Hawaii's Institute of Geophysics accepted me in midterm. That was my ticket out, so I just went. I jumped on a plane. I can remember not knowing where I was going. I'd never been to Hawaii. I didn't know anything. I was sort of lost and disoriented. I'd followed a fixed course all my life, and now the future was nothing more (or less!) than infinite possibilities."

The future began to gel almost the moment Bob stepped off the plane. Robert Norris, with whom Bob had sailed on the *Orca*, had a brother who worked at Hawaii's Cetacean Research Center, located in the Sea Life Park. Bob rented a Honda 50 and drove out to the park from Honolulu. There he met Karen Pryor, daughter of Phillip Wylie, the science-fiction writer, and daughter-in-law of Sam Pryor, chairman of the board of Pan American Airlines. She told him that Ken Norris had left for the day and that she ran the place. "Perhaps I can help," she said.

"Well, I'm looking for employment, actually. I'm studying oceanography at the university and I hope to have a job while I go to graduate school."

"Have you had any experience training animals?" Karen asked.

"Horses. I used to train horses; but nothing serious."

"Come outside," she said.

Karen led him out to a large tank filled with water. She had someone bring Bob a swimsuit, and said, "Jump in the tank."

He put on the suit and jumped in. Within seconds he was aware of two discomforting things. First, dark shapes had materialized at the far end of the tank, moving busily to and fro beneath the water and, second, a pair of fins was coming straight at him. Bob had been a scuba diver since high school, and fins meant sharks; but he knew that this was a cetacean research center—which meant whales and dolphins, and Karen did not appear to be the type who would throw a young man to the sharks. He swallowed hard, and tried to quench his innate fear of fins. Those were dolphins, no doubt about it. He let them swim around him and he started to relax. Three minutes later he was discovering that dolphins loved to have their necks rubbed just under the chin. They wouldn't leave his side.

"You're hired," said Karen. "Report here at nine o'clock tomorrow morning. You're a dolphin trainer, now."

"For almost two years, while I went to graduate school, I lived a dual life," recalls Bob. "Front stage, we performed dolphin shows for the public—which is where I learned a lot about speaking in front of people, because I had to. Backstage we did research for the Navy.

"We were, at that time, working on open ocean release: training dolphins to plant and retrieve objects, particularly where deep diving and speed were called for. And these animals…it was…a strange experience…like meeting a Martian. If you're ever going to work out a way of communicating with extraterrestrial species, you ought to begin with dolphins because their world and the way they move within it is more alien than Mars. The dolphins and whales are highly developed—I won't say intelligent, I'll just say highly developed—creatures that don't have any arms or legs or written language or tools. And they live in a three-dimensional medium and move freely throughout three-dimensional space. It's a strange world, compared against the two-dimensional streets and sidewalks and floors we are confined to and—they must think in strange ways.

"I'd love to find out what really goes on inside a dolphin's head. Some people believe they communicate the sonic images of other animals to each other—the shape of a school of fish, for example, and whence it comes, and how far away it is. If that is what their squeals and clicks are all about, then they're communicating information, mere facts as opposed to thought. I don't know if it would be very exciting to me personally to unravel how they know 'that's a tuna over there.' What I want to know is what they think about it.

"There seem to be voids in dolphin thought. I'd demonstrate for them how I wanted a certain object moved on the bottom of the tank. Some of those demonstrations were simple enough for a dog to follow and repeat; but they seemed incomprehensible to the dolphins. I sometimes felt like I was working with a really smart artichoke. I'd actually have had better luck with a dog on certain tasks. I'd walk away feeling as if I had a creature with parts of its brain missing, and in their place were other parts I'd never heard about. I couldn't evaluate what I was dealing with. My contact with them convinced me that they had talents that were very advanced and unique. But, when you stop and think about it, so does a fly.

"I remember a species called *Steno redarensus,* the rough-toothed dolphins, really tough characters. They'd attack you, work you over, break your arms and legs. They're really hard, that species. They run around with whales and are thought to be deep-diving dolphins. For that reason the Navy had selected them for our particular research program. But they had a problem with those animals in that, among other things, after you'd spent months training them, when you finally brought them into the open sea for a test they had a tendency to run away."

(So long, and thanks for all the fish!)

(Oh, yeah? Good riddance—bitch!)

"The bottle-nosed dolphins were more cooperative. Once you released them, they'd stay with you. But the rough-toothed ones were very unreliable. When I arrived at the park they were down to two. One animal was named Kai. He was a male toughie. He had scars all over him when they caught him in a noose and pulled him out of the sea. He was weeping when they brought him on deck. The other one, the one I worked with, was a very young female. She was crying also, when they caught her, and they named her Ho, which means 'to cry' in Hawaiian.

"So I began working with Ho, whom they wanted trained as a backup for Kai; and it turned out that Kai ran away.

"I then found myself in a really intense program to get Ho on-line. I'll never forget that. We worked around the clock. I spent eight hours a day in the water. I really got into that animal on a human-to-dolphin level. It was a pure, personal level of me showing Ho what I wanted her to do, and Ho reaching a level where love and affection were the primary motivating tools in the training. Rewarding her with fish—eventually that didn't even enter into it. Screw the fish! She couldn't be bothered. It was really love and affection and mutual caring. I worked hard with that animal, and got her out to sea for her dives; and she did not run away. It was very, very strange. I really loved that animal like a human would love a human. There was an awkwardness and a scariness about that feeling. I looked into another creature's eyes and saw affection looking back at me, much beyond any affection I've ever seen in the eyes of a devoted dog. It's one thing to look into the eyes of a creature and have their eyes stare dully back—it's quite another thing to realize they're looking back at you and asking questions of themselves. My God!—to actually see it looking back; and that's what I saw because with dolphins your primary communication loop is eye contact. You're looking at each other and they're trying to understand, and you're trying to communicate, and you're trying to understand!

"Strange...

"I will carry it with me for the rest of my life, because it was an experience that...sort of unhinges things.

"Ever since, I've wanted to reach a point in my life where I could have a dolphin or a pair of dolphins live with me. I'm a builder.

I've been building my house for fifteen years. I love building and someday I'm gonna have a house that they can swim through—you know, canals through the house.

"Alienness...total alienness...Just imagine spending eight hours a day with Ho, month in and month out, and reaching a level of one on one, a unity of feeling that—*no one else in the world*. You're so intent on getting this animal ready that there's nothing else in your life but that animal, and you're the only thing in its life because it's isolated. That's it. Period.

"I've never been that close again—to anyone."

8

A Unity of Feeling

EXCERPT FROM THE MEMOIRS OF COMMANDER LIGHTOLLER,
SURVIVING SECOND OFFICER OF THE R.M.S. *TITANIC*

It is difficult to describe just exactly where that unity of feeling lies, between a ship and her crew, but it is surely there, in every ship that sails on salt water. It is not always a feeling of affection, either. A man can hate a ship worse than he can a human being, although he sails on her. Likewise a ship can hate her men, then she frequently becomes known as a "killer."

9

Humanity

By now, Thomas Andrews understood that the ship meant to kill him. He felt no desire to fight it. Absolutely none. What he felt was a calm resignation to the fact. He would help wherever he could, for as long as he could. He would make no attempt to enter one of the boats. He would not even fasten a life jacket to himself.

"You men had better move out of here," Andrews called from a companionway. "Get out of here. Soon."

Below him, on a turbine motor, workmen clambered as if on a cliff. He remembered seeing that motor lowered in place, hanging like a giant Kragan in chains. And these same men had put it there …his men…

Oh, my God. I'm losing them…losing my men…"One evening," began an entry in Mrs. Andrews' diary, "my husband and I were in the vicinity of Queens Island, and noticing a long file of men going home from work, he turned to me and said, 'There go my pals, Helen.' I can never forget that tone in his voice as he said that, it was as though the men were as dear to him as his own brothers. Afterwards, on a similar occasion, I reminded him of the words, and he said, 'Yes, and they are real pals, too.'"

"How long?" asked Chief Engineer Bell.

"Little more than an hour," said Andrews. "She'll continue to dip forward until eventually the propellers rise out of the water and that wall becomes the floor. All this machinery is going to break loose. You'd better be out of here by then."

"We'll try," said Bell. "But the *Titanic* needs lights. And power for the electric davits. And telegraph, too. We'll stay as long as we can."

It was a splendid gesture—but little more. The men were needed here only in case the machinery broke down. The odds were that it would continue to run flawlessly without them—certainly for the next hour or so. What use to stay with the machines? What would be saved? To remain here and keep watch over turbines was certain destruction. Far away below the boat deck, there was no chance of a dive and a swim to a lifeboat or a piece of floating debris. Soon there would be no hope of climbing up in time to reach the sea; yet engineers could be found this night to guarantee that the electricity flowed until the turbines broke loose and left them.

—We'll stay as long as we can—

They wouldn't give up. During the coming hour and a half, the stubborn persistence of the lights would have a calming effect on people crowding near lifeboats, and they would throw a tingle into Andrews' blood, making him even more proud of the men who kept watch below deck and—who knows?—made life-saving, last-minute repairs. (Who knows?) No one from the generator room would ever return to Belfast, ever again.

—We'll stay as long as we can—

Andrews grabbed the first rung on a ladder and began to climb. "Good luck, Mr. Andrews," called a familiar voice. He stopped. It was Archie Frost. Almost two years ago, during a gale, Andrews had climbed up eighty feet of scaffolding to rescue Archie, who had gone up to secure two loose boards. Archie wasn't in trouble yet, Andrews had judged, but he would be. The man was terrified. Archie remembered being ordered down from the scaffold. When he protested, Andrews explained that married men's lives were precious, so he should leave. Then Andrews himself stayed behind and took the risk. It did not occur to Archie until he was out of the wind and safe that Andrews' wife was expecting a baby. He'd been at Andrews' side ever since. He hoped to one day repay the man, to one day make him proud.

"How are you?" Andrews asked.

"All right, sir," was the reply.

"How is it, Archie, that you always like to be beside me?"

"Ah, sir, it is because you carry up so well."

Andrews turned away and ascended the ladder. Tears did not come easily to him; but as he climbed, he wept.

10

Infamy

Within the ship, the library was empty and ominously silent. Lamps still burned brightly, lighting elegant lounges and armchairs and writing tables planted about. It was hard to believe that only a few hours earlier the chairs were filled with people. Over there, near the bureau, a child had broken in noisily on her father's conversation with two ladies, demanding that they take notice of a porcelain-headed doll clasped in her arms. Of this group, only the doll would ever be seen again. And over there, through the broad, brass-framed windows, Mr. Hoffman had been seen just before dinner, playing in the hallway with his two baby boys. He was said to be devoted totally to them, never absent from them. In an hour he would hand the boys over to First Officer Murdoch. He'd kiss them goodbye as they were lowered into a lifeboat, and then, without any fuss, he'd step back and disappear into the crowd—forever. His name was not Mr. Hoffman. He had abducted the children in Nice, and was planning to raise them in America under an assumed name, where their mother, his former wife, could never find them.

Presently, in mahogany shelves flanking one side of the room, hundreds of books leaned forward in their restraints. The restraints creaked. Among the books was a little-known science-fiction novel written fourteen years earlier and placed in the ship's library as a grim joke. It was about the wreck of a fantastic luxury Atlantic liner called *Titan*—bigger and faster and more beautiful than any ship that had existed in 1898. The author, Morgan Robertson, had imagined a ship like the *Titanic* in almost every detail, including the three large propellers, the twenty-four lifeboats adequate to save but a few of her two-thousand passengers, and the claim that lifeboats weren't needed because the ship was unsinkable. While trying to cross the Atlantic in record time, the *Titan* struck an iceberg during her maiden voyage and sank on a cold April night.

Robertson's novel had detailed events of the past few hours with spine-chilling faithfulness. It also detailed events that had not occurred this night; but would.

If you searched the *Titanic*'s bookshelves carefully, you might have found Robertson's latest work. Again, he'd written about futuristic machines: airplanes far beyond the kitelike spit-and-glue flimsies of 1912. They had sleek bodies and low-lying wings. They carried bombs in their bellies, and machine guns, and a great world war would be fought in the air…plagues of iron locusts…setting whole cities afire…the war would begin on a December morning, when planes swarmed out of the Rising Sun to riddle American harbors in Manila and Hawaii.…

Unable to sleep, Harriet Quimby had come out to the airstrip and stood, now, alone in the dark with the machine she hoped—*hoped*—would carry her across the English Channel. The prospects for a morning launch looked good. The sky was exceptionally clear. Stars normally too dim to be seen by unaided eyes shone so intensely and seemed so thickly clustered that portions of the sky contained more points of light set against black space than the backdrop of space itself.

Oh, yes, Harriet decided. Good weather tomorrow.

Running a hand over a wooden propeller, she prepared herself for the lonely flight—for a trial by water. In these early days of aviation, the chances of Harriet dying tomorrow were better than fifty-fifty, and she knew it.

As history would have it, she'd survive her trial. But history would also forget her, while the crossing of the channel made by Louis Bleriot was hailed as front-page news, and lived on as one of aviation's most celebrated achievements.

Harriet Quimby, though she was flamboyant and beautiful, though she was one of America's first woman journalists, and America's first woman aviator, was doomed to obscurity because the weather was clearing a path for her on the morning of April 15, 1912. On April 16, every paper would carry the same headline; but it would have nothing to do with aviation. Another name was to dominate the world's news—*Titanic*.

11

A Family Tradition

The Ballards were pioneers. All the way back to the eighteenth century—pioneers.

They came from England near 1750...by 1800 they were in Kansas.

As the twentieth century opened, Bob's grandfather was appointed sheriff of Wichita. He didn't keep the job very long. He and two deputies were killed in a gunfight with cocaine peddlers. Chet Ballard was only five years old when he saw his father for the very last time. Seven years later his mother died, and he was sent west to Montana, to live with Uncle Masterson, great uncle of the famed lawman Bat Masterson. The Mastersons were homesteaders, and Chet Ballard grew up to become a cowboy in Stillwater Valley—which was considered by almost everyone except Chet to be one of the most beautiful places in the world. He just couldn't see it that way. He saw himself as "the kid," being passed around from homestead to homestead. There was no love. He damned near froze to death there.

Chet escaped through his intelligence. He went off into a new thing called engineering, beginning with the development of processing equipment for Mobil Oil's Augusta refinery, and moving on to aircraft. By the time World War II had died away, he was a test-flight engineer with a taste for rockets and screwball airplanes that looked more like boomerangs than bombers. He'd pushed the Ballards farther west by then—to Muroc Air Base in California's Mojave Desert. He was one of the men behind "*The Right Stuff.*"

Bob Ballard's earliest recollections were of being out in the middle of nowhere, in the desert, with *things* streaking overhead—the first jet airplanes. He grew up with memories of giant tortoises, coyotes, and rattlesnakes, and he'd always wonder what became of Muroc. "You dumb idiot," someone would eventually tell him. "Muroc is Edwards—Edwards Air Force Base, where they land space shuttles."

On March 10, 1967, Bob placed a long-distance phone call to his father. He and his bride had just driven cross country to Woods Hole, where the Navy had sent Bob to join a team of geologists and engineers who were carrying a three-man submarine called *Alvin* through a transition from merely going down and up safely to going down and up routinely. It was similar to the goal men had toiled to achieve with space capsules, but only six weeks earlier, North American Aviation's *Apollo 1* spacecraft had bloomed into roaring hellfire on Pad 34, killing astronauts Gus Grissom, Edward White, and Roger Chaffee, and proving that exploring a deep range—whether it be outer or inner space—was anything but routine.

"So," Chet Ballard asked from across the continent, "how are things in Massachusetts?"

"Fine," Bob said. "All the major geologists here are from Hawaii—from the same graduate school I went to. So I've been welcomed as a good guy. I've fallen right in with them, through this quirk of being stationed here by the Navy. And *Alvin*...she's beautiful! A beautiful machine—but, but what's happening with you, Dad? What's happening with Apollo?"

"A lot of firings, that's what's happening. A real witch-hunt. Joseph Shea is out. He practically started the Apollo program, and they just tossed him out. I've had a talk with General Phillips. I'm afraid they want me in there."

Bob knew that his father dreaded being assigned to Apollo. But it seemed inevitable. He'd worked on Project Navaho, an early cruise missile design that the Air Force had canceled. But before the program died, it had spawned newer, more advanced liquid-fuel rockets, used now in Apollo. The Apollo people wanted him, but Chet was too busy for all that moon nonsense. He was chief engineer on North American's Minuteman Missile program. He had three thousand men in his department, and a budget that exceeded one million dollars a day and

"—How bad does it look, Dad?"

"Not so good. Phillips seems to think I can do anything. He wants me in the moon program. He said he doesn't like the way things are going over there. In essence, at least as I interpret it, NASA has too much influence on the division. They were pressuring this guy, Joseph Shea, to rush the program, to put schedules ahead of safety. And he never told them to shut up."

Poor Roger Chaffee, Bob thought. Chet had come home one day after meeting all three of them—Grissom, White, and Chaffee—at a Minuteman launch. Chet was unimpressed with astronauts. He liked technical talk, but astronauts were not chosen for technical ability. Nice guys, but generally boring. He'd look at them and say, "You do your thing, I'll do mine." But Roger Chaffee was different. He loved technical details. He wanted to see every part of the rocket, and to meet the people who built the parts. He was utterly fascinated. If anyone deserved to stand on the moon, it was Chaffee.

But the moon was not for Chet. If there was any way humanly possible, he'd steer clear of the race between Apollo and Zond, the Russian moonship. "I hope I can get away with it, Bob. Really, what I did is I went over there to the space division for a couple of days with about three of my key people. I left them there and I get together with them one day a week.* That's it: one day a week. I want to keep it that way. Two jobs—you can't do either of them."

"Is Apollo really that bad?"

"It's that bad. First of all, they're incredibly overworked. I met a guy who said he hasn't had dinner with his wife in over a year. Secondly, when I went over there, I found out by talking to people

---

*Twenty years later, one of them was still there.

that NASA directed North American to do thus and so, and in reading minutes to old meetings I learned of times when North American said, 'No. Do thus,' and NASA said, 'No. Do that (and hurry up about it!).' You see, Minuteman has links with the Air Force, but the Air Force doesn't run *me*."

"But getting to the moon...we need to beat the Russians."

"We need to have Minuteman, too. But why the hurry to beat the Russians to the moon? The reason I want to be on Minuteman, as opposed to Apollo, is that I am firmly convinced that the United States has to have Minuteman. *Has to have it*." Chet said no more on the subject. He was briefed once a month on what was going on in Russia, to the best of his country's ability to know that sort of thing. He'd decided that until we got a few hundred missiles built, we were in real danger of waking up to a nuclear Pearl Harbor.

"Son," Chet said, changing the subject.

"Yes?"

"I'm mighty proud of you."

"Thanks, Dad."

"Take good care of Marge. She's your treasure. And remember what I've always said: be your own boss. Own your own life."

Bob thought about that for a moment: Own your own life.... His father couldn't do that; but it had been such a grand journey, from branding cattle to building rockets. For two centuries, his family had spread west, and now Bob was the first to go back east. But he wasn't really going back. Woods Hole was a frontier town, a jumping off point to new worlds. No, he didn't go back. You know what he did? He went underwater, to continue a family tradition of pioneering.

~~~~~~~~

12

Popping the
Superman Balloon

~~~~~~~~

EXCERPTS FROM A CONVERSATION
WITH ROBERT BALLARD
Research Vessel: *Melville*
Expedition: *Argo*-Rise
Date: Saturday, December 15, 1985
Time: 7:00 A.M.
Place: Somewhere over the East Pacific Rise

ROBERT BALLARD: I always felt that space was a defocus. I don't know if, as far as wowing and zapping people, *Argo* and I can ever beat a walk on the moon; but I'm sure going to give space a run for its money (if you find an intelligent octopus on, or in, Titan, then all bets are off). I feel that the most important thing to come out of the space program is the view that it gave of the Earth from afar. It popped what I call the Superman balloon. I had grown up with Superman, like all kids my age, and there was this planet called Krypton, and Superman's people screwed up their own planet and blew it up—

CHARLES PELLEGRINO: That's not how Krypton was destroyed!

BALLARD: Well, it blew up, you know. I mean, it was—he escaped its destruction and he came to Earth, and we grew up into the space age thinking we were all going to be like Superman, that if the experiment went awry we were going to escape Earth and colonize the solar system. We were going to swim in the canals of Mars and grow tomatoes on Venus and all that sort of stuff—and it was our manifest destiny as humans to leave Earth. I felt that the closer we looked at the other planets of the solar system, the less attractive this concept became. Mars is more like the moon than the Earth.

PELLEGRINO: Yeah, and Venus makes hell look like Club Med.

BALLARD: And Jupiter! We've always known Jupiter was bad. It's more like the sun than a planet. And then there was that unforgettable view of the Earth—this beautiful, living emerald suspended in a black velvet void of nothingness. And we saw that the Earth was finite. The space program provided us with an opportunity to look in the mirror and see ourselves, and that mirror was the view of Earth from the moon. All of a sudden we saw—really saw—that it's finite. Don't mess it up, please. There's very little of it. And it isn't very pretty anywhere else. We live on the Earth in a potentially parasitic, terminal situation. We could kill the host. We could blow it up. We could pollute it. We almost did that. Thank God it's got resilience.

PELLEGRINO: Yes. The Earth looks so small out there. From hundreds of miles up you can distinguish ship trails and jet vapor streams over the oceans. You can see our impact even though you are very far away, and a world that from the ground feels solid and indestructible, begins to look fragile.

BALLARD: I want to make sure we don't kill the oceans. We don't breathe oxygen from redwoods. We breathe it from plankton. Space instilled in us this consciousness: that we need to protect the Earth. That knowledge is embedded in our subconscious now, whether people recognize it or not. I don't look to space as a frontier of importance other than a spiritual importance.

PELLEGRINO: Oh, it will eventually provide materials for Earth. We can bring metals down from the moon—just whip them up into metallic foam and drop them down through the atmosphere. The foam will actually float on the ocean.

BALLARD: Just what we need: more crap floating on the ocean.

PELLEGRINO: Power production is going to be a very big thing. We're working on that at Brookhaven. It looks like we'll one day be able to tap thousands of times the U.S. energy budget from the moon and Mercury—clean energy for all humanity. It's raining soup out there. We are just beginning to learn how to build soup bowls.

BALLARD: The point is that I don't see space as a frontier anymore. I see the ocean as the frontier. I see the space program becoming militarized heavily and I see it lesser and lesser as being our spiritual release than it was when we landed on the moon. That was a tremendous human undertaking. It was one of the finest things the human species has done. But it's been done. Going to Mars will be great, but lesser.

PELLEGRINO: But there *are* frontiers in space—whole new ones. We're almost certain that Saturn's moon Enceladus has an ocean of liquid water under the ice, and probably Jupiter's Europa. There may even be hydrothermal vents down there. We can do both, you know: we can explore the Pacific, and we can look at the new oceans we're finding in space. Those vents, and the oases that thrive near them; don't you see it? New worlds. Life. You've shown us what we can find out there.

BALLARD: But you see, it's a question of how much money do you spend to satisfy that interest. I think humanity is obsessed with that question: Is there life anywhere else? Even though, statistically, it's a certainty, is it worth twelve gross national products to find bacteria or worms in a moon of Saturn?

PELLEGRINO: It won't cost anywhere near that much. We're talking about sending robots, not people, with all their expensive life-support requirements. Part of the reason I'm here is to get a feel for what conditions our machines will have to operate under. *Argo* and *Jason* are merely ancestors to what we hope eventually to send to Enceladus and Titan and Triton. And it can get very cheap if you do it with the Canadians and the Chinese and the Russians—if you split the cost with them. Also, international cooperation in space might decrease tensions on Earth. Who knows? We just might discover our common humanity out there. It sure beats the hell out of a space weapons race.

BALLARD: It won't stop the weapons race. It won't, so you can dream on. But when you're dreaming on my tax dollars, then I want to comment and criticize. When I worked with dolphins I learned one thing: the guy who said, "The universe is not only stranger than we have supposed, it is stranger than we can suppose," was absolutely right.... Who was it who said that, anyway?

PELLEGRINO: I don't know.* *(*J.B.S. Haldane)*

BALLARD: It doesn't matter. You don't have to go poking around Saturn to be wowed and zapped. There's strangeness enough right here on Earth. Look, now. Look down where *Argo* is. I'd like to see a little more money put into exploring the ocean, on the grounds that it's reachable. It does have life! It *is* a mystery and a wonderment.

PELLEGRINO: The oceans are a window—a window through which we can begin to see the rest of the universe. Look at Neptune. There's a world circling it, a world called Triton. Stoff and I said years ago that it might be covered with a nitrogen ocean. And now, University of Hawaii has used radar to find that ocean. *Voyager* is going to be there in 1989. We may see a world very similar to our own Earth. But nothing will be as it appears. The continents will be ice. The glaciers will be methane. And if, by any chance, carbon and hydrogen have become life, the water that flows within the tree trunk will be liquid nitrogen.

BALLARD: Look, I understand the need...our love of space. It's that total expansiveness, it's that release. Okay, I understand that, and we'll continue doing that—but the budgets! The amount of real *cash* going into underwater exploration is minuscule compared to the budget of NASA. Woods Hole operates for a whole year on what it costs NASA to launch the Space Shuttle just one time.

PELLEGRINO: Money and resources aren't so scarce as they are mismanaged. We live in a country whose people spent twenty times NASA's budget buying cocaine last year. So don't tell me that the money doesn't exist. And yet the average person on the street could look at Woods Hole's annual budget and say, "What good does that do us? So, big deal, there are hydrothermal vents on the East Pacific Rise and, big deal, these people over here say there may be hydrothermal vents in a moon of Saturn that I can't go out at night and see anyway."

BALLARD: But the point is, from a very practical point of view, we have, as a nation, been explorers. It's the pioneering spirit of America. If you're crowded, move on. We had a release mechanism: send them west—mostly misfits and youth. It was a relief valve. My family was part of it. I got a good dose of cowboy in me, and by that I mean a freer spirit. I feel I'm more of an explorer than a scientist and I think my gravitation toward technology is more representative of an explorer's interests. Explorers tend to be more interested in how the hell they're going to get there. So I bring in the experts to build the machines, and to make the machines do what I want them to do. And then I bring in the scientists and I show them the bottom. We all get wowed and zapped, and some of you guys go back into the world and communicate what you have seen, or dream of seeing more of the same on other planets. It's fine. I have no bones to pick. But I am an explorer—

PELLEGRINO: Who is always wanting to see something new.

BALLARD: Yes. And pushing a frontier.

PELLEGRINO: I want to get inside Europa. That's the one that looks most accessible. The ice is thinnest, there. We just let a reactor get very hot and use the ice to cool it. It melts its way down, capping the hole behind it and carrying two descendants of *Argo/Jason*. And we can only guess what it looks like down there. That's what's so fantastic. When we get that first picture of the inside, even if it's just water and a ceiling of ice, it will be a whole new picture, an explosion of new information.

BALLARD: Well, an explosion of the spirit.

PELLEGRINO: Well, it will put my brain in overload for a few seconds as all this new information comes flooding in. Nothing matches that in the world.

BALLARD: That's right! Look, I said I have no bones to pick. I'm ready to buy a ticket on the Space Shuttle, if they ever start selling seats. But you can guess what part of the Earth I'll be looking at.

PELLEGRINO: The blue part.

BALLARD: You bet. Now, speaking about looking around in space, how did your Halley search go last night?

PELLEGRINO: Not too well. The sky was very clear, but Halley's Comet is still too far away from Earth, still too dim to be seen without some kind of magnification, and the vibration of the ship's engines makes small objects impossible to see through binoculars. But just wait till January. The *Challenger* will be going up with special scopes just for Halley. And then an international fleet of robot spaceships is going to fly right through Halley's head. The view is going to be tremendous—far better than anything you'll see from Earth.

BALLARD: Sounds like sour grapes to me.

PELLEGRINO: Well, it would have been nice to see the comet. But it was still the most beautiful night I've ever seen, up there on the bridge, looking out and seeing nothing but stars all the way to the horizon. I've never seen the stars so bright. It was like sitting on the floor of heaven.

13

And the Stars Did Speak

EXCERPT FROM THE MEMOIRS OF LAWRENCE BEESLEY,
A SURVIVING PASSENGER OF THE R.M.S. *TITANIC*

First of all, the climatic conditions were extraordinary. The complete absence of haze produced a phenomenon I had never seen before: where the sky met the sea the line was as clear and definite as the edge of a knife, so that the water and the air never merged gradually into each other and blended into a softened horizon, but each element was so exclusively separate that where a star came low down in the sky near the clear-cut edge of the waterline, it still lost none of its brilliance. As the Earth revolved and the water-edge came up and covered partially the star, the upper part continued to sparkle as long as it was not entirely hidden, and threw a long beam of light along the sea to us. And each star seemed, in the keen atmosphere, to have increased its brilliance tenfold and to twinkle with a staccato flash that made the sky seem nothing but a setting made for them in which to display their wonder. They seemed so near, and their light so much more intense than ever before, that fancy suggested they saw this beautiful ship in dire distress below and all their energies had awakened to flash messages across the black dome of the sky to each other, telling and warning of the calamity happening in the world beneath. That night, the stars seemed really to be alive and to talk.

14

Like a Coffin Long and Narrow

Overhead, the smokestacks were shutting down. As the last of the venting steam died away from a tolerable roar to a whisper, and then to nothing, an unnatural calm settled over the *Titanic*. The engines were cold now, and the ship sat on the sullen black mirror of the Atlantic as steady as a rock on the shore. The passengers were similarly steady. There was no jostling or crowding. No panic or commotion. Quite the opposite: there was a peacefulness about the place. One could not have imagined them standing quieter if they had been gathered in a church.

Harold Bride delivered a handful of Marconigrams to Captain Smith, then decided to take a quick tour of the boat deck. Stepping out from the bridge, he headed aft along the starboard side, passing under a brass placard that warned:

THIS DOOR FOR USE
OF CREW ONLY

It occurred to him that he was not officially a member of the crew. Wireless technology was so new that it was considered to be little more than a novelty—a toy for wealthy passengers. To be allowed on the bridge was therefore an unusual privilege for a man no more vital to the *Titanic*'s operations than a pastry chef or a calisthenics instructor. He was grateful for the privilege, for the sudden importance that was assigned to him.

Bride stopped near the gym, on the starboard side, and peered over the rail with first-class passenger J. R. McGough.

"The air has a strange odor," McGough observed.

"Yes," said Bride. "As if we were in a clammy cave."

"And the water! There isn't a ripple. Even on a small lake you'd see a ripple."

He was right, of course. An ocean wasn't supposed to behave like this. It was creepy, yet at the same time soothing. The Atlantic was as calm as quarry water. Reflected stars burned in it, and reflected meteors, too. Harold Bride had never seen so many falling stars. Sometimes they trailed long running sparks and incandescent smoke. Other times they streaked down in twos and threes. The brilliance of the sky only intensified the blackness of the water, making it seem much farther below the rail than it actually was. Add to this the ship's complete lack of motion, and the combined effect was a wonderful sense of buoyancy and security.

"We are safer here than in one of those little boats," said McGough.

Harold Bride knew better. He'd been to the wing bridge, and things looked pretty grim from up there. He had watched the portholes just under the ship's name disappear into the sea. They still glowed under the cold, green water. Spooky...very spooky.

"—Bride?"

Bride turned, hearing Murdoch's voice and thinking the first officer had called him.

"Put the brides and grooms in first," Murdoch continued, ignoring Bride completely.

Three pairs of newlyweds entered boat number seven. The rest of the small group milling around seemed to be expressing McGough's sentiment. They were hesitant about leaving the light and warmth of the *Titanic* for the cold, lonely sea. It seemed so much safer on the deck.

McGough was looking over the rail when Murdoch grabbed him

by the shoulders and gave him a push saying, "Here, you're a big fellow. You can row. Get in that boat!"

"B-but, but—" He tumbled in, then looked around and discovered empty seats in every direction.

"Any women or children?" Murdoch called.

No answer.

Christ! Murdoch thought. If we're going to start lowering boats, we might as well put people in them. "Any men?" he asked.

Bride gave it a passing thought. But he shook the thought away. There was work for him in the Marconi shack.

"Anyone?"

The French aviator Maréhhal stepped forward.

Bride turned away from the rail and prepared to leave. Across the deck, through the large gymnasium windows, he could see instructor T. W. McCawley showing passengers how to work out on the mechanical horses and camels while they waited for the boats. The machines were said to copy the motions of real horses and camels with astonishing faithfulness. For the moment, the people inside seemed more interested in exercise machines than in lifeboats. If they'd bothered to look out a window, they could have seen Murdoch ordering the first boat away: number seven, capacity sixty-five, occupancy twenty-eight.

John Jacob Astor was in the gym. Bride watched him through the windows. He was sitting on a bench with his wife, pulling a life jacket apart and showing her what made it float. J. J. Astor was the richest man in the world. He could easily have bought the *Titanic* ten times over—yet, in little more than a half hour, he would be powerless to secure a place in a measly little lifeboat.

So much for the tour, Bride decided. He blew warm air into his hands and headed for the first-class entranceway. It was the quickest shortcut to the Marconi shack. From somewhere far away came a pleasant melody on violin, cello, and piano. It was ragtime, lively and hot.

Oh, goody! Music to get drowned by, Bride thought, and then hurried away.

15

Camp 4-H Sings

No one knew for sure where the song came from and no one really believed that such lyrics could be invented by children.

Oh, they built a ship Titanic
to sail the ocean blue
And they thought they had a ship
that the water wouldn't go through

This much was certain: all through the spring of 1912, the ballad became a chant for diabolical schoolboys.

It was on its maiden trip
when an iceberg hit the ship
It was sad when the great ship went down
BOOM—BOOM—BOOM

It appeared simultaneously on opposite coasts of the United States. It was like that. It traveled fast.

Uncles and aunts
little children lost their pants

It was sad when the great ship went down
BOOM—BOOM—BOOM

Seemingly out of nowhere the words came...and stayed. Three-quarters of a century later, the song would still be a favorite at 4-H Club summer camps for children.

Irish people came aboard
with very little dough
so they put them down below
where they'd be the first to go

At 12:45 on the morning of April 15, 1912, Thomas Andrews was having a terrible time filling lifeboats on the port side. A girl wanted some belongings from her room, so she jumped out of number eight. Two ladies argued that number six looked prettier, so they'd just as soon wait.

"Ladies, you must get in at once. You cannot pick and choose your boat. Get in. Get in. Don't hesitate."

Four first-class passengers climbed into one of the half-empty boats, bringing with them two valets and a dog. It occurred to Andrews that there were no steerage passengers about. Where are they? he wondered. It's getting late.

—so they put them down below—

Oh, God, it's far too late—

—where they'd be the first to go—

—to save them from their fate!

Husbands and wives
little children lost their lives
It was sad when the great ship went down
BOOM—BOOM—BOOM

16

Scared to Death

One day in 1934, *Alvin*'s ancestor, the Beebe-Barton bathysphere, was lowered over the side of a ship off the coast of Bermuda. It was a hollow steel ball on a string, little more than an *Alvin*-type crew compartment minus all its motors and batteries and flotation equipment. Huddled inside was William Beebe, the world's first oceanaut. He tried to shrug off memories of the bathysphere's unmanned deep dive, when it had come up full of water—the result of a hairline fracture in the hull—and the pressure inside was so great that the hatch flew across the deck as if shot from the mouth of a cannon. Stowing the memory in favor of new astonishments, he called on the phone for more line to be let out, and inched his way into the deep wilderness.

The only other place comparable to these nether regions must surely be naked space itself, thought Beebe as he watched fish-shaped things with fangs and running lights gathering outside his porthole. In the distance, three glowing triangles circled round and round ...round and round..."Yes," he said. "Far beyond the atmosphere, in the blackness of space, the shining planets, comets, and stars must be closely akin to the world of life as it appears to the eyes of an awed and frightened human being in the open ocean a half mile down."

He descended into night on a warm, bright afternoon, probing barely beyond the limit of the sun's rays, and that first dive was less than a training exercise for a modern *Alvin* pilot—and let me tell you something: he was scared to death.

Bob Ballard's early *Alvin* dives were in a chain of dead volcanoes located some eight hundred miles east of New York. None of them came within a half mile of the ocean surface, though most of them stood more than two miles high.

In the summer of 1968, the Navy wanted to survey the mountain tops; so, one sunny morning, Bob Ballard and *Alvin* pilot Larry Schumaker cast off the mooring lines and slipped under. About thirty feet down, the pressure outside had doubled. Bob looked out the view port and saw a lion's mane jellyfish veiled in streamers of tentacles. A white-tip shark patrolled beyond. He noticed a puff of churning excrement in its wake. Eating and excreting, each creature contributes to the snow of nutrients that falls to the bottom. Eventually they contribute their own dead tissues. Bob understood that almost half the sediment covering the slopes of the seamounts was actually the skeletons and waste products of plants and animals living in the water above. But how fast did the sediment accumulate? he wondered. An inch every thousand years? An inch a century? No one knew. Truly no one.

Alvin dropped through the water at barely more than a foot per second. The water pressure doubled and tripled, then tripled again. The light outside faded gradually from green to deep blue to violet. It was like a sunset coming on unnaturally fast. Just fifteen minutes into the dive, the world outside was blacker than a mineshaft. Larry switched on the dull red cabin lights. Two minutes later and two hundred feet deeper, the fireworks began. Animals of the middle depths, agitated by *Alvin*'s wake, protested in flashes of green and yellow and red. Bob could make out no details. As *Alvin* fell, they appeared only as upshooting lights. He knew what they were, though. Hanging in the water on the end of a string, William Beebe had time to observe the lights close up, and to sketch the creatures they belonged to. They looked like images in the mind of a depraved, seagoing Dr. Seuss. Some appeared to be all head, with fangs like swords. Other creatures had bags attached to them, in which fish three times their size writhed. The bags were expandable stomachs. Monsters, Bob thought. He remembered seeing the drawings as a child and being frightened by them; but they were monsters that he'd never really found. Few of them were more than three inches long. It would probably scare the crap out of you if you were a minnow, but as a human Bob wasn't terrified of a three-inch hatchet fish.

The echo on *Alvin*'s sonar indicated that the bottom was only two minutes away. At an altitude of two hundred feet, Larry pulled a lever that released some of the ship's ballast. An inch-thick steel plate fluttered down into the night. Their descent slowed. A row of buttons was punched, and floodlamps blazed on. In the spray of lights Bob watched the ocean floor coming up at him. Beyond a radius of about forty feet everything became shadowy and vague before fading off into absolute black. The only light was the light you brought with you. Cauliflower billows of sediment churned under the lamps as Larry pumped propellers—a quick final adjustment—and then landed *Alvin* on a gentle mountain slope more than a mile below the surface. A tan fog surrounded the ship. The swirling particles dissipated quickly. They simply blew away on a light breeze of cooler water seeking the foothills.

As the fog passed, it unveiled a loose mud that stretched in all directions like fresh-fallen snow. It was far from being fresh-fallen, however. The "snow" was many feet deep and probably millions of years old, and it had footprints in it. Long, meandering trails were everywhere. Some of them led to purple, rocklike things nearly a foot long. They were sea cucumbers. They grunched along the substrate, sucking in the snow, drawing off whatever nourishment was in it, and then depositing the rest behind them.

Larry kicked on the motors and *Alvin* was airborne again. Skimming low over the sea cucumbers, they began their uphill flight, toward the summit of the volcano. More trails moved into *Alvin*'s hemisphere of light. It was frustrating not to be able to see beyond that hemisphere. Bob likened the view from *Alvin* to standing with your toes against a tree, viewing in detail the nature of its bark. The observations only had significance if you'd determined beforehand the type of tree you were looking at and its relationship to the rest of the forest.

Larry saw something strange looming up ahead. He slowed down, hovering for a time over what looked like a field of bomb craters. Most of them had large round boulders in their centers.

"Meteors?" Larry guessed. "Nah! Can't be. But those boulders seem so out of place here."

"I think I've got it," Bob said. "During the last ice age—some twelve thousand years ago—huge glaciers bulldozed the land, scouring the Earth and picking up rocks. The powerful grinding action of the ice smoothed and rounded the rocks, as it carried them slowly to the sea. There, icebergs broke off from the glaciers—just as they do now in Greenland. The icebergs melted and dropped their boulders. These rocks might have come from various parts of North America that were covered with ice.

"Icebergs?"

"Yes. I think that's it."

"Icebergs…" Bob trailed off. Icebergs…

(She's out there, Bob. Don't you feel her? Out there, waiting in the dark.)

As they neared the top of the volcano, Larry sighted an outcrop of rubble coated with manganese. He landed in it. Using *Alvin*'s robot arm, he cracked open some of the rocks and found that they were white beneath the black metallic covering. The outcrop was coral. A whole reef had lived here. It lived in the sun; but now it crumbled in silence in the absolute black of the deep sea. A short way up the slope, Bob guessed, had existed a beach, and beyond the beach a tropical rain forest. Several million years ago, before the Pleistocene ice ages, this place had looked like Bermuda: a huge seamount breaking the ocean surface. Since then, it has subsided under its own weight. It need only have sunk inches per year to reach its present depth. What was once a tropical paradise was now an extinct volcano capped with dead coral. It occurred to Bob, as he looked at the manganese-encrusted fossils, that the same fate awaited Bermuda and Hawaii.

Six hours passed.

Alvin hovered over a vanished forest—over the closest thing anyone had found to...to what? To a myth?

It was time to return home. More steel plates dropped away, fluttering down like leaves over...over Atlantis. The top of the volcano receded and soon the cold and the dark gave way to an undersea dawn. The robot arm outside Bob's view port became a shadow outlined against voilet-gray. A minute later it gleamed under a strengthening blue. The ship sailed up and up and up, breaking suddenly into the warmth and brilliance of a New England afternoon.

Sometimes it got funny.

The swordfish fight was a funny one. Swordfish are fairly territorial creatures—but no one understood how territorial they really were until *Alvin* threatened one. The ship dropped down two thousand feet onto the Blake Plateau, under the Bahamas, and what the crew took to be a large rock lying on the bottom came suddenly to life. *Alvin*'s portholes were glowing like eyeballs. The swordfish went straight for the eyes, hitting the seam between a Plexiglas window and its support, and wedging its sword in the vessel's skin. The animal actually impaled itself in the submarine and began shaking violently.

The crew got worried and cut the dive short, popping up to the surface with a seven-foot-long fish stuck in *Alvin*'s eye.

They ate it.

Other times it got scary.

On October 16, 1968, Ed Bland was taking *Alvin* out for a dive to the seamounts. He stood inside the sail atop the spherical crew compartment. The submarine dangled from the support ship *Lulu* like a giant sea creature in chains.

Lulu was aptly named. She was essentially two pontoons held together by a bridge. Living quarters were in the pontoons, and to move from your bunk in one pontoon to the galley in the other pontoon, you had to cross the bridge. In rough weather, waves broke and sprayed all over the bridge, which was largely unshielded and about as wide as a six-lane highway. To get across dry, you had to time the waves. You learned a lot about nature's wave patterns on that ship, whose unusual construction prevented her from pitching and rolling like most ships. She rocked in a figure eight instead. Sailors who had spent years getting used to pitch and roll got sick almost the moment they stepped aboard *Lulu*. It also worked the other way around. The figure-eight veterans were destined for terrible bouts of seasickness when *Alvin* was eventually transferred to a normal support ship.

Ed Bland's first indication of trouble was a peculiar tilt backward and to the right...*jolt!*—He's aware that a cable has snapped—*Alvin's* nose pitches up fifty degrees—there's a terrific load on the starboard forward cable—*Snap!*—and here we go!—The sub dunks down forty feet—It's dark outside, and strangest of all: there is time to sightsee—Ed's brain has switched automatically into overdrive, taking every possible measure to help him live—All pain receptors have been cut off—He sees a flood leaping down at him through the open hatch—It's also spurting up through seams in the floor, because the sail is meant to fill with water during a dive—leave it airtight and it squashes like a beer can—He sees bubbles outside the Plexiglas window—He hears them hiss—His brain is snatching up every image, every sound, pulling in all the information it can get, spreading it out on the floor of his skull and analyzing the pieces for a way out. His mind is crowded with so many new experiences that a second is stretched to the outermost limits—He lives in a nether world of slowed time—his eye pauses at a crack in the Plexiglas. He ducked as the cables snapped. His head must have hit the front of the sail—The flood is drifting in—falling down into the hollow sphere at his feet—He's jerked by the ankle—*Two men down there!*—they are scrambling up—no time for anything else—up—up—abandon ship—*Clunk!*—three, maybe four seconds have passed—*Alvin* has popped back up to the surface—But…no…not quite—It's too dark outside—He's under the forward portion of *Lulu*—the forward portion is decked over and the submarine has surfaced under the deck—The deck completely covers the hatch on the sail—*no exit!*—and keeps the sail partly submerged—and lets water spurt in to fill the sphere—Three men crowded in the sail—no way out and sinking lower every second—If the sphere can be kept from filling, the sub can't sink—can't sink—The sphere has a hatch—Close the hatch!—Ed kicks it down—Shit!—It won't go down!—A cable is stuck in the hatch—The fall did more mischief than he'd thought—His mind doesn't want to believe that this is really going to happen: he is going to lose his ship, perhaps even his life—And now there is sunlight—The captain!—The captain has kicked *Lulu* forward and brought *Alvin* out from under the deck—The two scientist-passengers scramble out the top of the sail—Ed notices, as he clambers up after them, that there have been no words—no cursing aloud—no cries for help—*no words at all*—and the sail settles lower and lower—Ed jumps off and swims away—his brain is taking it all in—taking all of it—for five full seconds he listens to water lapping at the sail and tumbling in with an awful sucking sound—in those five seconds the sail vanishes—but he's safe, and he knows it, and his brain shifts out of overdrive…As time begins to speed up again, Ed becomes aware of a hot knot on his head…and notices that his ankle appears to be sprained…He's jerked up by the shoulders…It's a diver fitting a lifejacket under him…He's come from *Lulu*….

"Are you all right?"

"Yeah. Fine. But I'm afraid I've lost *Alvin. I've lost my ship.*"

"What a mess," recalls Bob Ballard. "*Alvin* was lost and our whole deep submergence program went through quite a crisis because we were experiencing cutbacks in what little government funding we had. This was the high-tide mark of the Vietnam conflict and the country was running out of money. We were being "Proxmired" to death. It was an evil time. There was a whole mentality, a division between the Department of Defense and the academicians, that began cutting off sources of funding to the academicians. There was this distrust that had developed between the military and the scientists—a by-product of Vietnam that would take fifteen years to heal.

"The Navy said, 'Do we really need submersibles, particularly ones that get lost on the bottom of the ocean?'

"Somehow, a decision was made to go back and get *Alvin*—which was quite an operation."

On Labor Day, 1969, the deep-diving submersible *Aluminaut*, built by Reynolds Aluminum, broke open *Alvin*'s sail and hooked a crossbar into the open hatch atop the sphere. A ship on the surface then hoisted *Alvin* from her resting place—one mile down on the edge of Hydrographer Canyon. Nearly a year had passed. Ed Bland's lunch was found to be soggy but edible. Water near the canyon was refrigerator cold. Aside from minor salt corrosion of *Alvin*'s outer hull, everything appeared to be in pristine condition...until *Alvin* hit the air. That's when a very strange thing happened. As the sub dried, it began falling apart. Salt had crept, at high pressure, into the spaces between every microcrystal in *Alvin*'s aluminum frame. Metal that had seemed solid only a few hours earlier crumbled into grayish-white flakes. Portions of the outer hull were suddenly no more resilient than a child's sand castle.

Still...a surprising amount of equipment was salvageable. The ship's batteries hadn't even lost their charge. The propulsion motors, which were encased in flexible boxes of oil to keep the ocean out during a dive, were still usable. So was the sphere, the stern propeller, and the hydraulic pumps (as a matter of fact, the hydraulic pumps would still be in *Alvin* sixteen years later).

"And here's where things got crazy," says Bob Ballard. "After we went out and recovered the sub, after we did all the cleaning up and rebuilding, the funding from the Navy to *Alvin* was cut off. And that's where I really started to become involved. That's my pathway into the early development of science programs for *Alvin*. We needed time to transform *Alvin* from an engineering toy to viable technology. It took five years—five years of fighting for every penny, fighting to keep *Alvin* alive a month or even a week longer, just so we could prove its worth.

"In its early years, the sub was used out of context. It was used to find things. When you can see only forty feet ahead of you, it's very hard to find things. *Alvin* is great after you've found a ship-wreck or a hydrothermal vent and you want to go in for a close look; but it's a lousy search mechanism. The development of good side-scanning sonar mapmakers and robots—now *that's* a proper search mechanism. Those systems have given us useful maps. In the early days of *Alvin* you had a very crude map and you'd dive and you'd look out the view port and you'd look at your map and you'd throw the map away. It didn't bear any resemblance to what was actually out there and you'd have to ad-lib, and ad lib science is bad science. And we wanted to know more about plate tectonics—and we understood that to really get proper use out of a deep-diving submarine, you needed to ask the right questions about what you wanted to look at, and then send *Alvin* down only to those places where a detailed look via human presence was required. All of this led up to something called Project FAMOUS, when *Alvin* really came into its own.

"After 1969 we began weaning this tool away from its military or-igins, to where it arrived in 1974 as a true research tool sponsored more and more, as time went on, by the National Science Foundation—which eventually took up eighty percent of the funding.

"Yeah, 1974 and Project FAMOUS—which stands for French-American Mid-Ocean Undersea Study—was our World Series. Then the whole world was looking on and I was terrified—not about the dives themselves, although there is always risk, but about the sci-ence. We had finally convinced the scientific community that the deep-diving submersible was a creditable tool and the National Sci-ence Foundation had laid out several million dollars to explore the antics of the live Earth along the Mid-Atlantic Rift Valley. We had to prove our contentions. Up to this point, many scientists thought that the use of deep-diving submersibles would never amount to anything scientifically in relation to the cost expended—about twenty thousand dollars per day for a support ship and crews' salaries and all the rest. We were diving on the axis of the mid-ocean ridge, thought to be the origin of the sea floor.

"It was exhausting—sort of like being a symphony conductor, orchestrating ships, French and American submarines, scores of people. All the machines and all the people were tuned to do something. There was the brass section, the woodwinds—they all had to do it right. And we had to make them do it.

"And, God bless, we did it.

"And let me tell you something: I was scared to death."

17

The Eye of the Hurricane

EXCERPT FROM THE LOG OF CHARLES PELLEGRINO
Research Vessel: *Melville*
Expedition: *Argo*-Rise
Date: Tuesday, December 24, 1985
Place: Somewhere over the East Pacific Rise, with 1.7 miles of water below

No submersible can lay claim to an evolution as long as *Alvin*'s. State-of-the-art equipment is being added continually. When its twenty-year-old robot arm and hydraulic pumps are replaced sometime next year, nothing, not even a single wire, will remain of the vehicle that was originally launched in 1964.

Alvin now faces its greatest challenge: *Argo/Jason*. Even when everything is working to 100 percent perfection, *Alvin* spends only 25 percent of its on-site time gliding over the bottom. Even with technical difficulties plaguing our *Argo* mission—including an avalanche of volcanic glass that put the robot out of commission for a full day—90 percent of our time over the East Pacific Rise has been spent photographing lava fields and mapping a continental spreading center.

And then there's Bob Ballard, *Argo*'s creator. Well, he's not the creator, actually. He's not the man who invented the robot, or even the one who built it. He doesn't know a damn about microchips. But he infects the people who do. He infects them with his vision and he lures them aboard, to build the machines that will go where he wants them to go and do what he wants them to do. He infects everyone around him. He's the eye of the hurricane.

And it all adds up to one hell of a storm.

"These guys are so goddamned talented that I feel embarrassed being in the same room with them," says the storm's eye. "They're like a breeder reactor, now. And it's going critical."

Sure. Step into the *Argo* van anytime and you can see the result of a dozen Ballard-infected engineers: *Live from the bottom of the Pacific*. I remember Bob telling me how he grew up in an aerospace family, how his house was a meeting ground for engineers. Although he's not an engineer, he knows they don't bite. They don't scare him. "An engineer is an interesting piece of machinery," he says. "An engineer is a nonthreatening person. You give engineers a problem and they calculate the answer. I like engineers as humans more than I like scientists. They don't have the ego. They're more predictable.

"That doesn't mean you don't need scientists; but if you live with them day after day, they wear you out.

"I'm the only full-time scientist in the *Argo/Jason* group and that's just because I'm the ultimate consumer, so to speak. I'm the Ralph Nader of the operation. I love science. I love the pursuit of anything and the pursuit of truth is very noble. I think of science as a game of *Clue,* where the butler did it in the library with a candlestick. And the game is: Can you figure out the truth with the minimal amount of information? That's what science is.

"I think truths are inevitable. If the apple hadn't fallen on Newton's head, it would have fallen on someone else's head a few years later. What a scientist pursuing truth does is precipitate something earlier than it would normally happen. He accelerates it. He's a true catalyst. A catalyst precipitates a reaction but is not consumed by the reaction. They live on to be catalysts again. I'm a catalyst that doesn't necessarily care whether my catalytic properties are used in science, in commercial areas, or in the military.

"And the military doesn't really care if I build an *Argo/Jason* system to serve science, okay? If I elected to do a sophisticated analysis of lava fields and service the scientific community, that's my problem. The military just wants to be able to find things and look at them up close—you know: *things*—wrecked Russian submarines or things that fall out of the sky. Look how much stuff we put into space that goes splash right off the pad. They want a lot of those things back and you've got to find them. That's what *Argo/Jason,* from a military point of view, is all about: if we can find a hydrothermal vent or the *Titanic,* we can find anything."

From Bob's point of view, *Argo/Jason* is all about diving his brains out, in *Alvin,* for nearly twelve years, and then, in 1979, finding himself under scrutiny for tenure at Woods Hole. The tenure procedure is always rough. It's a do-or-die sort of thing and a lot of good people are told to die—

(*Go away! And stay there! And don't come back!*)

—and Bob thought there was a good chance he'd be told to die. So he began to prepare himself and his family for the possibility. During the year-long process, he went away. He knew that there would be a lot of meetings about him that he was not involved in. Things would be happening behind his back. So he went away to Stanford to teach for a year, and there the "what ifs" began creeping up on him: "What if I don't get it? What if I *do?* What next? Do I go back to Woods Hole and jump back inside the submarine and do what I've been doing all these years?"

When he worked out the mathematics of it, he'd been going out to sea about four months a year for twelve years and he'd seen one-tenth of 1 percent of the mid-ocean ridge and—hell!—what do you do with tenure? Go out and spend the next ten years looking at another tenth of one percent?

(You're insane!)

(I know—Heh! Heh! Heh! But I've got tenure!)

Bob didn't think anyone could completely eliminate the excitement of making a dive in *Alvin*—especially if it was one's first dive. There was something particularly adrenaline-flowing—a sense of peril, a sense of "What am I doing here?" and "Wow!"

So people will always want to go down in submersibles, he guessed. But after you've done it for twelve years, it's gone—no more adrenaline. It's like professional football. Sooner or later your knees start to go.

He still liked to dive, but it was becoming more and more a nine-to-five job. Bob figured that you could overdo anything—go to Yellowstone Park everyday, for example, and eventually you'd get sick of going there. It would still be a beautiful drive in and out of the park, but after twelve years you'd stop looking out the window.

(So? What if you *do* get tenure? What are you going to do?)

(Find a more efficient way of looking at the sea floor, that's what!)

Up to this point, Bob was hired on a year-by-year basis. He could only think in terms of one-year projects, but if he got tenure…he could plan a future…for the first time in his professional career he'd be able to think in the long term, to think of fantastic things—

(Bob sketched a picture of a little robot hovering over a lava pillar…another showed it descending the *Titanic*'s Grand Stairway… *Argo*… *Jason*…Jason and the Argonauts… *How's that, Senator Proxmire? I'm gonna dare you to give me a Golden Fleece Award!*)

—but *Argo/Jason* was clearly a ten- to fifteen-year thought, and one can't have those thoughts—one won't be taken seriously if one does not have the security to endure.

That's what tenure's all about.

"So, in 1980, with tenure in hand," says Bob, "I began to assemble engineers to rough out this whole concept, to figure out where to put each nut and bolt. My job was to concept it and raise the money and then to take it to sea. Even then, I understood that *Argo/Jason* might eventually put *Alvin* out of business. What's ironic is that I spent so many years of my life dedicated to making *Alvin* into a good tool, making it into my entire life. I was really an *Alvin* advocate. What happened is that since 1967 we've had a changeover of people. The people who work with the sub today don't remember my years of dedication to *Alvin*, and they view me as an enemy of *Alvin*.

"I'm not attacking *Alvin!* I'm trying to build a future capability, and it's really made me sad where I'm—I'm viewed as an enemy of *Alvin*. My God! I love that submarine! I've put so much into it, my heart and my soul. But none of these new *Alvin* people remember that. They weren't around when we were fighting the battles to raise funds and save *Alvin,* and now I'm perceived as this bastard who threatens *Alvin.* How do you threaten a piece of machinery? They think *Alvin*'s threatened? *Alvin* doesn't give a damn about anything!

"I don't think that technology would care if a better technology came along and replaced it. It's sort of funny, how people protect a piece of technology. What's to protect? Y'know, it's metal and rivets and a lot of plastic. I mean, do you really want to protect an Atlas Agena booster? You put it in a museum and you say what great things it did. Good luck to anyone who thinks they could have kept people away from the Space Shuttle. I mean, the Atlas was incredible in its time, when it carried John Glenn into orbit, but it was replaced by Apollo. And then Apollo was replaced by the shuttle. I don't think Apollo rolled over in its grave because of that. So, it's sort of funny, how I've gotten myself into this situation by believing that *Argo/Jason* is the technology that needs to be concentrated on and that maybe thirty years from now you'll put on a helmet for a wide-screen, 3-D, color robot's-eye view of the ocean's bottom—and maybe thirty years from now *Alvin* will be rendered obsolete by the helmets—but I believe that telepresence *is* the future technology. I believe that in the long term manned submersibles are doomed. And I *do* believe it. Now, when is that going to take place? I don't know. Maybe 2010. But it's inevitable.

"I also believed it when I said, in 1970, that manned submersibles were the only way to explore the mid-ocean ridge. At the time it was true. It was sort of like the only way to cross America at one time was by covered wagon. I wouldn't say that today.

"It's been argued that if someone wanted to become an oceanographer, and then learned that his version of a dive would be sitting in a room looking at a TV monitor, or maybe someday wearing a helmet, he'd be pretty disappointed. Okay, so we'll squeeze his head and bounce him down in *Alvin* and then have him go to work. It's sort of like being in the Antarctic. A new-comer will complain, 'What do you mean I'm going to be in a Winnebago the whole time? I want to go out!' Fine. Put him out in the deep freeze for thirty-seven seconds and then put him back in the Winnebago.

"I have nothing against submarines. Some people claim that I hate submarines. I don't hate them. I love 'em. It's sort of like you left home and got married so someone concludes that you must therefore hate your mother.

"No, I love my mother; but I love my wife, too. It's the same thing with manned submersibles. I moved away with *Argo;* but I love *Alvin*. That little machine will always have a very special place in my heart.

"I just wish I could make them understand. I still love *Alvin*."

18

A Pilot's Story

"Captain" Kirk McGeorge first read about *Alvin* when he was a child. Years later, while operating small submarines for an oil company, he heard reports of Bob Ballard's descent, in *Alvin,* to sulfide oases on the East Pacific Rise.

"I only dreamed of being part of it," he remembers. I wished I could be one of those people. Now I have my dream."

Kirk is one of the newest members of the *Alvin* team. When I met him first, in November 1985, he was hammering a mock-up of a new thruster together from Maxwell House coffee cans and plastic buckets. The assembly would later be nailed to a broomstick, then rotated back and forth on *Alvin*'s after section to verify that the real engine, when it became available, would have enough clearance on the starboard side. Coffee cans…this was certainly a long way from the mock-ups I'd seen used in the space program. Mock-ups for the lunar module and the Space Shuttle were, from outward appearances, indistinguishable from the real thing. Carved from wood in excruciating detail, they displayed every screw, every label, every knob that the final item would have. Even the silver-plated connectors were in place.

They must have cost a small fortune.

Of course, money is much tighter at the Deep Submergence Laboratory than in the space program. Looking at Kirk's mock-ups drove home the message that every *Alvin* dive was a miracle. How, I wondered, would you go about building a Space Shuttle out of coffee cans?

There are other differences between the probing of inner and outer space. While many astronauts are trained engineers, the engineers and mechanics who actually build and maintain the Space Shuttle are never astronauts. Their end reward is to stand on the ground and know that something they built is carrying people into the far sky. It's just the opposite with *Alvin*. Every mechanic who joins the team automatically goes into pilot training if he's not an oceanaut already.

"There's a nice policy here," explains Kirk. "It goes like this: You better build it right, because you're going to pilot it. That keeps people who are working on the thing honest. We want to have confidence in our ship—to know the ship will work. And that's the way it should be, I think."

Working with *Alvin* is, to Kirk, like stepping into heaven. On his previous job, he piloted an industrial submersible off an exploratory drill ship. His supervisors were displeased whenever his attention turned to fish—which was often impossible to avoid. How could you ignore an octopus snaring a fish and dragging it down into a hole?

One day he was sitting on the floor and krill shrimp—thousands of them—started swarming around his floodlamps. The world filled, out there, with frantic criss-crossing traffic.

"I've never seen such a dense cloud of them," he radioed up. "You can't even see through them!"

A blizzard of flailing bodies swirled about him. And then fish appeared in the swarm, sharp-toothed, racing, and snapping. Severed legs and periopods floated and—oh! What was that? Something *really* fast. Like a lightning strike. Bigger fish lanced down—seemingly out of nowhere—striking the smaller fish—

"It's turned into a feeding frenzy—going on right in front of my eyes."

"I'm not interested in that sort of thing," an irritated voice called down from above.

Kirk said no more about it. His superior did not like to hear the pilots expressing interest in anything other than rocks and platforms—in anything other than the very structures that were part of the drill program. Kirk shrugged. They just didn't care about what was living down here.

When he emerged onto the surface, he was warned, once again, to stop talking about fish.

But how do you do that? How do you stop talking about fish when you're on the bottom and you come across an orange hardhat that someone dropped overboard, and as you unfurl the robot arm and move closer to retrieve it, it sprouts wings and flitters away? No one has any idea what the creature was. No idea at all.

Kirk was reprimanded for "wasting" film on it.

"It was a problem," says Kirk. "The different companies that hired the drill ship would have these executive types listening to what's going on down there. And it cost so much money to send us there that they wanted us to be concerned strictly with their drilling equipment, and all these cements they were pumping around on the bottom. Anything else was just irrelevant.

"It's kind of a shame, because a lot of us who were piloting the subs were very interested in the biology end of the game. And we felt that the company executives were trying to limit our imaginations. So, that's why I was always dreaming of coming to Woods Hole and *Alvin*. Here, if we see something interesting, everybody wants to know about it. Yeah! That's the reason we go down to the bottom, to discover new things—beautiful things. Here they want to learn about the ocean rather than take everything they can out of it.

"How many people are as lucky as I am, to have a life-long dream, and to have it come true?"

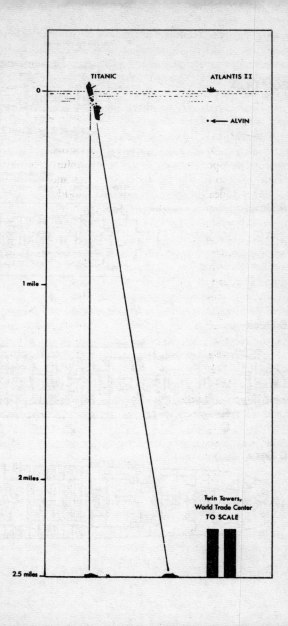

Boat Deck

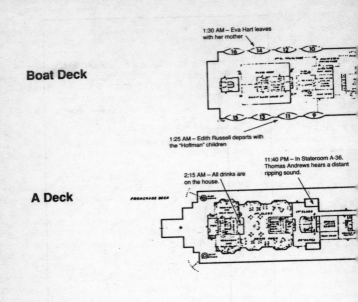

1:30 AM – Eva Hart leaves with her mother

1:25 AM – Edith Russell departs with the "Hoffman" children

A Deck

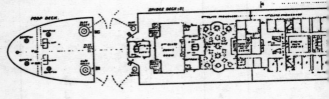

2:15 AM – All drinks are on the house.

11:40 PM – In Stateroom A-36. Thomas Andrews hears a distant ripping sound.

PROMENADE DECK

B Deck

C Deck

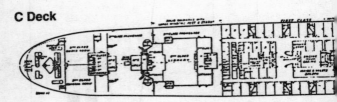

The band gathers as boats are lowered. Harold Bride hears them playing a waltz at 2:12 AM.

Marconi shock

2:05 AM – Samuel Hemming jumps overboard.

2:05 AM – Thomas Andrews sends Mary Sloan away on the last boat. Charles Lightoller refuses a seat.

12:50 AM – Quartermaster George Rowe fires the first rocket.

12:40 AM – Card sharps start a rumor.

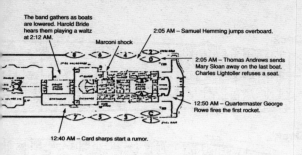

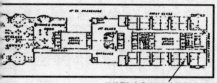

11:40 PM – In Stateroom A-11 (this is where the jewels are).Edith Russell hears a loud bang and watches a wall of ice glide past her window.

11:00 AM, July 14, 1986 – Ralph Hollis, Dudley Foster and Robert Ballard land in <u>Alvin.</u>

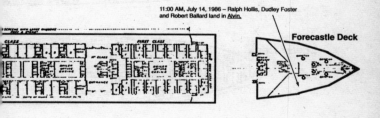

Forecastle Deck

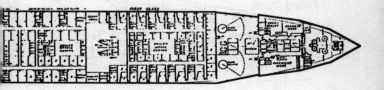

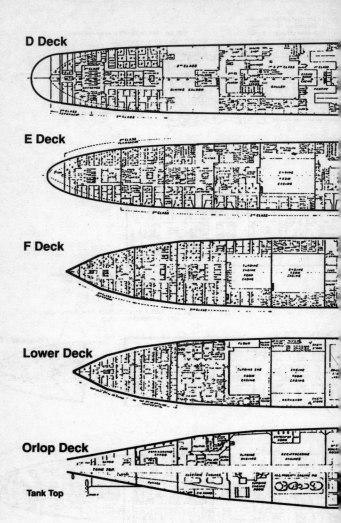

D Deck

E Deck

F Deck

Lower Deck

Orlop Deck

Tank Top

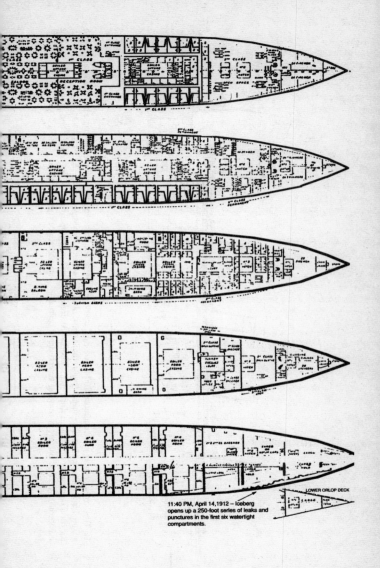

11:40 PM, April 14,1912 – Iceberg opens up a 250-foot series of leaks and punctures in the first six watertight compartments.

LOWER ORLOP DECK

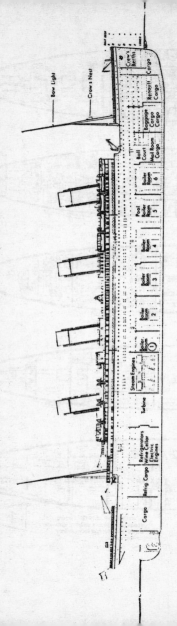

1. This cross section of the almost-900-foot-long *Titanic* is adapted from plans for her sister ship *Olympic* (the original plans for the *Titanic* went down with shipbuilder Thomas Andrews' stateroom). Vertical partitions running several decks deep divide the boiler rooms, mail rooms, cargo holds, and so on into watertight compartments. At 11:40 P.M. on April 14, 1912, an iceberg opens up a series of leaks and punctures in the first six watertight compartments.

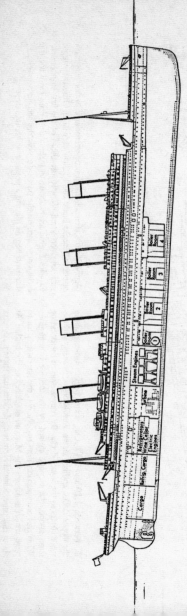

2. At 1:20 A.M., an hour and forty minutes after the collision, water begins to slop over the top of boiler room number five and into boiler room number four. Up to this point, the damaged compartments have filled slowly, for the accumulated surface area of the leaks and punctures measures no more than twelve square feet. But now the openings through which the anchor chains run have been pulled below the surface, exposing another twelve square feet and doubling the rate of the *Titanic*'s filling.

Soon cargo bay doors and windows will dunk below the surface, opening hundreds more square feet to the sea. If the watertight doors sealing the compartments had been opened by this time to allow the ship to sink on an even keel, only twelve square feet would remain open to the sea during the next six to eight hours, and the *Titanic* would still be floating when the first rescue ship arrives. On the top deck, Edith Russell is, at this time, preparing to leave in boat number eleven, just forward of the fourth smokestack.

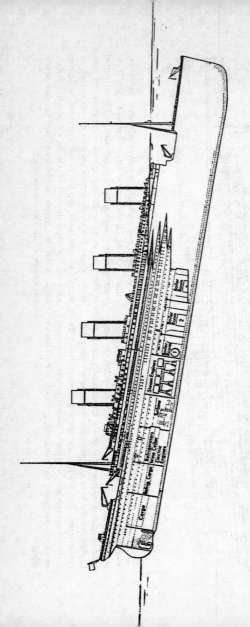

3. Between 2:10 and 2:12 A.M., water begins running along the upper decks, spilling down ventilators, stairwells, and elevator shafts to the lower decks. By comparison to the flooding from above, the seepage caused by the iceberg is negligible. What this cross section does not show is the liner's ugly list to port, which immerses the Marconi shack before the bridge. At about this time, Samuel Hemming decides that there really isn't plenty of time after all, and jumps overboard. Junior telegraph operator Harold Bride kills a fellow crewman. Officers struggle with an overturned lifeboat just ahead of the first smokestack. Charles Lightoller is about to make a desperate swim for the crow's nest and, on the port side, near the second smokestack, the band begins playing a popular waltz, its last song.

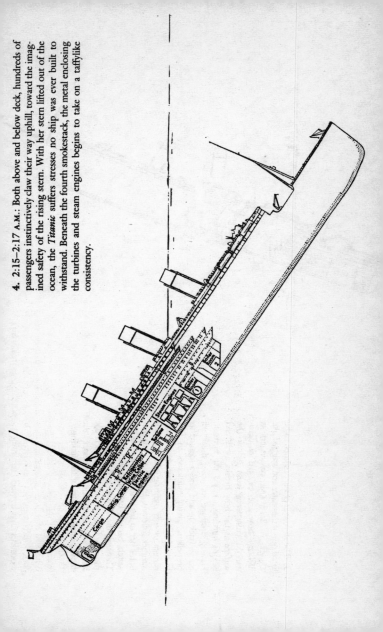

4. 2:15–2:17 A.M.: Both above and below deck, hundreds of passengers instinctively claw their way uphill, toward the imagined safety of the rising stern. With her stern lifted out of the ocean, the *Titanic* suffers stresses no ship was ever built to withstand. Beneath the fourth smokestack, the metal enclosing the turbines and steam engines begins to take on a taffylike consistency.

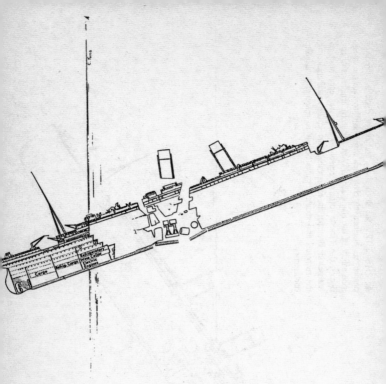

5. The stern was never designed to be lifted out of the water and wagged like a stick. At 2:18 A.M., passengers in lifeboats hear a series of thick detonations emanating from below the surface as the bow breaks away and begins hurtling toward the bottom. Having dropped its nose, the stern buoys back up and settles toward its propellers, giving witnesses in lifeboats the impression that the *Titanic* is miraculously righting itself. In boat number fourteen, Eva Hart's mother holds her in her arms, not letting her watch, because Eva's father is aboard. Thinking the *Titanic* is coming back, she now loosens her grip and lets the child look, and she witnesses the most gruesome part of the sinking.

6. At about 2:23 A.M., within five minutes of breaking loose from the stern, the *Titanic's* bow has fallen two and a half miles, striking bottom at close to forty miles per hour. The *Titanic's* nose buries itself more than sixty feet deep in the sediment. As inertia (the continued, forty-mile-per-hour downward motion of the ship and the funnel of water that trails behind it) takes over, the sediment will hold the nose as if embedded in glue.

7. Below the bridge, inertia breaks the *Titanic's* ribs, bending and tearing her skin. Looking like a torn accordion, the *Titanic's* ruptured hull will be interpreted by Jacques Montlucon, a member of the 1987 French expedition to the wreck, as being the result of an explosion at the surface, and perhaps the real reason the liner sank. A problem with this theory is that the rupture is large enough to drive a freight car through and the *Titanic* could not have floated with such a wound anywhere near as long as she did. Essentially, the ship has been halved at the surface, and is halved again upon contact with the bottom. With her nose held fast in the sediment at an odd angle, her continued downward momentum snaps her in two. Less than a second later, the downblast hits. Once the bow comes to a complete stop, the water following behind it at forty miles per hour continues pushing toward the bottom at forty miles per hour. It strikes like a tidal wave. The bridge and open decks aft are stamped flat, as if by a stupendous detonation directly overhead. The well deck cargo cranes are slammed down, rails and lifeboat davits are uprooted and tossed overboard. The steel roof of the officers' quarters is kicked in, its walls bulldozed out. Billowing away from the center of the ship, the blast swings the anchor crane forward on the forepeak.

8. 2:20–2:24 A.M.: The severed stern section floats for nearly two minutes, rolling onto its side before it disappears at 2:20 A.M. Once below the surface, the last of its air soon escapes and the weight of engines and turbines quickly levels the stern out. She then begins to pick up speed, carrying with her immigrant families whose passage to the top deck has been barred, and the (French and Italian) kitchen staff, who were herded into rooms on E Deck aft and locked in.

9. 2:23–2:24 A.M.: Though the bow has a two-minute lead, the stern reaches bottom at almost the same time. The bow falls to the bed of the Atlantic at nearly forty miles per hour. The stern crashes into it at somewhere between fifty and seventy-five miles per hour. If you imagine a tidal wave striking a skyscraper at sixty miles per hour, you will have some idea what the downblast against the stern must have been like. At the center of the blast, decks compress down upon one another and the outer hull wrinkles like an aluminum can being squashed. Hammered deep into the Earth, pieces of the stern actually explode away, Cargo cranes, rails, and davits, which had remained anchored to the deck all the way down, are torn loose by the rush of water. Just forward of the aftermast, the only crane still rooted to the deck curls down over the starboard side. The poop deck is pried up and peeled backward on itself. Seventy-five years later, Robert Ballard would comment: "To me, this is hallowed ground. It really is a special place. It's a devastated piece of wreckage. You'll never raise it. You'll never want to do anything with it but put a wreath on it—which is what we did."

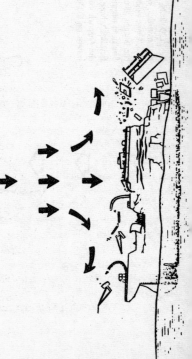

19

Introducing Jacques Cousteau, Tom Dettweiler, and the Canadian Mafia

In the summer of 1975, as the first fighting erupted between Christians and Muslims in Lebanon's resort city of Beirut—as American astronauts and Soviet cosmonauts prepared for a rendezvous and docking in space—Tom Dettweiler attended classes at the University of Miami. During his evenings he tended a museum gift shop. Being a student of oceanography, he did not fail to recognize Captain Jacques-Yves Cousteau as he entered the shop.

Oh, wow, Tom thought. Do I tell him I'm studying oceanography? Do I tell him he's been an inspiration to me since I was a kid? Oh, no—he must have heard that a thousand times before. The last thing in the world I want to do is make an ass out of myself in front of the world's best known explorer.

So, Tom watched quietly as the captain examined a display of necklaces draped over a large piece of blue coral.

(*a large piece of blue coral…*)

"This is terrible," Cousteau said. "A terrible thing."

"What?" Tom said.

"Look what you have done. This is endangered. And you have killed it!"

"I—I…We aren't *selling* the coral. I—it's just for display."

"That makes no difference. It is dead now. What is the difference?"

"Let me explain," Tom protested. "The coral was collected on the beach. It was not live coral that someone took from a reef."

Cousteau's face softened a little, but he was not about to let up. He was upset, and Tom had the misfortune of being the only person in the shop that evening. He made an easy target. "People do not respect the sea these days. You take everything out of it, and you put sewage back into it. Parts of the Atlantic that were clear water only ten years ago are dark now. All the way in the middle there are dark lumps of oil floating. Do you not realize that the sea has a life of its own? Tiny plants near the ocean surface use the sunlight and make most of the oxygen we breathe. You must respect them. You must respect everything about the sea. It is the most precious thing we have. We need it to survive, but it doesn't need us…" he trailed off, looking thoughtfully at the coral.

"…The sea lived four-and-a-half billion years without *us*," he said, and then walked away, leaving Tom in a dark mood.

The next day, after a tour of the university, Cousteau stepped into one of the marine biology classes and gave a guest lecture. As he spoke, his gaze fixed, from time to time, on the seat occupied by Tom Dettweiler.

The lecture passed. Tom departed as quickly and as quietly as he could for the cafeteria and, when he sat down with his lunch tray, he was immediately joined by Cousteau. Tom's first reaction was to analyze the expression on his face. Within a second he sensed that this was going to be a friendly visit. The net of wrinkles around his eyes showed concern, but no traces of anger.

"I want you to know that I realize you were not the one at fault. You really did not take the coral from a reef, did you?"

"No," Tom said. "Nobody killed the coral."

"I apologize for…as they say, coming down on you. You were just an innocent."

The stiffness in Tom's back abated a little, and his admiration for the captain went up a few notches. "It's okay," he said. "Forget it."

"You study oceanography, do you?"

"Sure. I've always loved the sea."

Cousteau's face crinkled in fatherlike pride. "What would you like to be doing in marine science?"

"Ocean engineering, primarily. My hopes are just to simply get into the ocean world…" Tom's eyes became uneasy and sad. He was part of that era in which the ocean became very romantic—and Cousteau had romanticized it—and young students had flocked to the marine sciences, and were learning, now, that there were not enough jobs for them, not even for a small fraction of them. "I'm just hoping there will be jobs for marine engineers when I graduate."

"You work with electronics?"

"I *love* electronics. I'm heavily into the electronics side of it. I love gadgets."

"Gadgets and electronics. That's what I like. Always I have been kind of a tinkerer. We must talk."

And they did talk, through lunch, about the future of oceanographic instruments—about robots and computerized sailing ships, about all the wonderful things that Tom would see in his lifetime—and how he would fit into them. And when the meal was through, the captain put out his hand and said, "You really do love the sea, I can tell. Who knows? We could be working together in a few years. Just…I hope you will keep me in mind."

Tom shook his hand. "I'll keep you in mind," he said.

Tom did keep Cousteau in mind. In 1979 he became the second American to be hired full time aboard the research vessel *Calypso*.* Captain Cousteau appointed him science officer and electronics engineer. He spent most of the next three years exploring the Great Lakes, the St. Lawrence Seaway, the Canadian Maritimes, and the North Atlantic. Some regions were so isolated that they'd remained essentially unchanged throughout history. It was in one of those cold, isolated regions on the Gulf of St. Lawrence that *Calypso* sailed

---

*The first was a helicopter pilot, who had been working with Cousteau since 1974.

into a winter squall. The ship was taking a tremendous amount of spray on the topside, which froze and accumulated everywhere, much the same way layers of calcium accumulate on a pearl. But this particular pearl, as it grew, was in real danger of tipping over. The only thing preventing this was the sheer weight of water accumulating below deck—which spilled in through cracks in the hull. It was anybody's guess which would drag *Calypso* down first: the weight of water below, the weight of ice above, or both. The entire crew, including Captain Cousteau, was out on deck hammering and shoveling ice, fighting to keep *Calypso* afloat. Tom noticed that Cousteau had brought cameras. He'd shove a slab of ice overboard, then pause to photograph the desperate efforts of other crew members, most of whom were, like *Calypso* itself, coated with ice. Tom had no doubts that, were they all to drown that day, Cousteau would have kept on filming even as the deck glided down into the wash. He was just that way.

As it turned out, the ship was saved, but she was terribly battered, and every electrical contact below deck was coated with and corroded by salt. *Calypso* had to anchor at the nearest town, for several weeks' repairs

"It was fun traveling through the Canadian Maritimes," recalls Tom. "We had a reputation for liking to drink beer—which preceded us in all the little towns. Oh, yes. It was fun…picture this town that never had anything really happen in its life and all of a sudden *Calypso* is docked down at the end of the street! We'd go out to the bars and immediately be recognized because we were the only strangers in town, so they knew who we had to be, and then the tables would fill up with beer that everybody had bought us—clearly more than anybody could handle. We had a pretty good reputation.

"We always liked the small towns. But the big ones were…crazy. Every time the boat pulled into a large port, we attracted crowds. And we kept hearing the same questions over and over: 'Why does the boat look so small? It looks bigger on television.…Is it *really* made of wood?…How did you get your job on *Calypso*?…How can I get a job on *Calypso*?…Can you put in a good word to Jacques for me?…'

"At that point we might have been working for a couple of months at sea and all we wanted to do was get off the boat, hit town, and not be asked these questions. You'd have to literally jump off the boat, run through the crowd, and get out of there. There was a point, though, when we started to play games. I'm afraid Captain Cousteau's son, Jean, was one of the instigators. We would jump off the boat, run through the crowd, and then sneak back into the crowd and stand there shouting these same dumb questions at the captain and the others as they tried to leave. And they'd get mad at us because our silly questions merely prompted more of the same from the people standing beside us.

"It was always strange when we'd get off in a town. And of course you'd all be tired of each other after living together on a ship day after day. So you'd go off on your own separate ways, but by ten o'clock that night everyone inevitably drifted into the same bar, because you'd find the first place you could, and after a while you'd ask people where they'd recommend going after that, and of course the final place is always the best place in town and by ten o'clock the whole crew would be together again.

"Sometimes it got *really* strange. One night, up in a Canadian town called Sept-Iles, this guy came up to us while we were at the bar and asked in a sort of broken French if we were from the *Calypso*. We invited him to sit with us and we started joking around with him. He seemed like a nice guy. Told us that his name was Jocelyn and that he was the head of the local Mafia.

"Well, we thought that was a joke and we started really giving this guy a rough time, really kidding him. We asked him who he had to mug to get that ugly coat he was wearing. And the guy…he didn't laugh. He just got up and went to the bathroom. And then the barmaid came over to us and said, 'Look guys, he's serious. He's the local Mafia. You don't fool around with Jocelyn.'

"When he came out he sat down with us again. And, well…we'd had too many beers to know any better, so we put our arms around him and continued to kid around. Finally, he said, 'Okay, guys. 'Cause I like you, I'm going to let you go.'

"'Okay,' I said. 'Sure. Fine.' And we all burst into loud laughter.

"The next thing we know, Jocelyn is gone and there's this big gorilla standing behind us, who can't speak English at all. It was obvious that he was there to break our faces, but we couldn't stop laughing. And then we started calling him 'Dogface.' And because he didn't know what we were calling him, we *kept on* calling him Dogface, and razzing him real bad and I guess he realized he wasn't going to get anywhere with us, so finally he held up his drink to us and said, 'Merry Christmas'—which must have been the only English he knew because it was about three months before Christmas.

"By the time we got back to *Calypso*, the local police were there advising Captain Cousteau not to let us off the boat for the remainder of our stay. And that's where we stayed, half-fearing a bombing of *Calypso*, and keeping a lookout for big black limos."

Cousteau's expeditions were confined primarily to the top two hundred feet of the ocean—a region Bob Ballard refers to acidly as "the Cousteau layer." More and more, each passing year, Tom Dettweiler's interests turned to deeper, darker reaches.

Then, in the fall of 1983, Ballard invited Tom aboard the Deep Submergence team. He dangled an irresistible carrot in front of Tom's nose. "Come to Woods Hole," he said. "I'm going after the *Titanic*."

20

The Crash of Two Worlds

April 15, 1912

"Now, men, remember you are Englishmen. Women and children first."

Miss Sloan was helping a woman passenger put on her life jacket when she heard his voice again.

"Ladies, please be quick. Please get into the lifeboats."

She was learning to love Thomas Andrews that night—to love him for his bravery and his unselfishness. It seemed to her that he was there—there—and everywhere; looking after everyone except himself. He neither wore nor carried a lifejacket. He hadn't even paused to throw a warm coat over his back—which was perhaps just as well. Despite the freezing temperatures, he was drenched in sweat as he toiled with Second Officer Lightoller to lower the boats.

Andrews' bravery was not uncommon. Samuel Hemming knew better than to stand around watching lifeboats go down half-empty and assume that he would be safe on the *Titanic*. He knew that the unsinkable ship was dying. And he'd known it even before Thomas Andrews, as he stood in the shadow of the berg and listened to water-displaced air bleeding out of the holds. Hemming understood that he was taking a terrible risk when he stepped out of boat number six—one of the first boats down on the port side—to tend the falls. Lightoller had ordered him away in the boat. Unnoticed, Hemming disobeyed orders and snuck back on deck.

"Someone for that after-fall," Lightoller called.

Hemming was there. "Aye, aye, sir! All ready."

"Why aren't you in that boat?" Andrews asked quickly.

"Ah, sir. There's plenty of time yet. Plenty of time."

Without another word, Andrews helped Hemming feed out the line and lower number six away.

When Harold Bride returned from the bridge, he heard Phillips sending directions to the *Carpathia*. Phillips turned, looked Bride up and down, and laughed. "Don't you think you should put on some clothes?"

Bride looked down and noticed that he was wearing only his pants, his slippers, and a half-open overcoat.

"No wonder I'm so cold," Bride said, then walked back to his bunk and began putting on warm clothes—the warmest he could find. The air outside was absolutely freezing. And the water was colder still. And he understood that in an hour he'd probably be swimming in it. He pulled open a drawer. Then another.

—*Shit! Where the hell did I put my wool sweater?*

"A-ha!" He found another overcoat and—Bad! It's not only cold outside, he realized. It's freezing in here, too. Something must be wrong with the electric heaters. He brought the overcoat out to Phillips and slipped it over his back.

Phillips continued sending.

"How far away is the *Carpathia?*" Bride asked.

"Still a couple of hours."

"That's not good."

"I know. The slant of the floor keeps getting worse. What did you see out there?"

"She's sinking by the head and they're putting people off in lifeboats. Water will be lapping at the ship's name very soon, if it isn't already."

"The wireless is getting weaker," Phillips said. "Could be trouble in the generator rooms. I hope *they're* not taking water already."

Just then, the *Olympic's* wireless operator chimed in, wanting to know his sister ship's latest status.

"Tell him it's definitely fish for breakfast for us tomorrow," Bride said, trying to sound comical.

"Sure," Phillips said, and tapped it out.

"Or vice versa," Bride added.

Phillips did not laugh. The mood for jokes was leaving him as he began to ponder the sixth ice warning that had come nearly two hours earlier. It came from the *Californian*. They had tried to tell him they were stopped and surrounded by icebergs and— *God forgive me,* Phillips thought. I told them to shut up . . . we hit the iceberg a half hour later . . .

—*God forgive me . . . God forgive me . . .*

—SOS . . . TITANIC . . . POSITION 41.46N 50.14W . . . REQUIRE IMMEDIATE ASSISTANCE . . . COME AT ONCE . . . WE HAVE STRUCK AN ICEBERG . . . SINKING . . .

Quartermaster George Rowe continued his watch on the after bridge. He'd felt the bump. He'd seen the berg—close enough to reflect brilliant white light back at the ship. In seconds it was gone, lost in the dark astern. Gone, except for "the whiskers 'round the light"—millions of little icy needles that swirled around the floodlamps and sparkled in rainbow colors.

We've had a close brush with an iceberg, he guessed. Very close. But if anything important is going on, surely they will call me from my post.

He kept watch, and forgot about it, while the rest of the ship forgot about him.

An hour passed. Rowe saw no one, heard nothing. And then there was a lifeboat drifting below him on the starboard side. He lifted the phone and rang the bridge.

"What is it?" demanded a nervous voice at the other end.

"There's a lifeboat afloat on the starboard."

"Who are you?" The voice had shifted from nervous to incredulous.

"Quartermaster Rowe," he replied. "I'm on watch on the after bridge. Is something wrong? Are you aware there's a lifeboat in the water?"

"Yes. Something is wrong. Come to the bridge right away. And bring some rockets with you."

Rockets! Distress signals...Rowe climbed down from the after bridge, pulled a boxful of rockets from a locker, and ran for the bridge. He was the last crewmember to learn that the *Titanic* was dying.

It was almost 1:00 A.M.

September 1, 1985

It was almost 1:00 A.M. on the Grand Banks, that portion of the Atlantic where the Labrador Current and the Gulf Stream turn east and merge. The mixing of cold and warm water creates one of the world's most spectacular plankton blooms—a midocean pasture known also for some of the world's best fishing.

Aboard the research vessel *Knorr*, both Bob Ballard and Tom Dettweiler had retired from the *Argo* control room for some much needed sleep. It had been a particularly exhausting expedition, this French-American search for the *Titanic*. There were tremendous highs and lows...abnormal magnetic readings that turned out to be geologic formations...protrusions on the bottom that turned out to be sand dunes. The French research vessel *Le Suroit* had been crisscrossing the target area since June, using a new deep search sonar. According to plan, the French would find the ship. The Americans would then send down their robots to document the find. When the Americans arrived on August 9, more than eighty percent of the target area had been searched without success. *Argo*, fitted with its own sonar equipment, was low~red to the bottom, doubling the search effort. By August 20, Ballard began to suspect that they might have chosen the wrong target area—actually missed the *Titanic* by a hundred miles or more.

Shipboard morale was particularly low this morning. *Argo*'s cameras and sonar had shown days and days of just flat sand on the bottom. And then, yesterday, the printout from the side-scanning sonar had indicated a shadow, something sitting on the floor. It was just the right size for the *Titanic*. Morale soared—but minutes later, as *Argo* moved in with her cameras, it turned out to be merely a pile of rocks, and elation turned immediately to extreme depression—depression that deepened with the understanding that the 150-square-mile search area set aside by Jean-Louis Michel and Jean Jerry as the most likely to contain the wreck was running out. In only four days, *Knorr* and *Le Suroit* would have to leave the Grand Banks. Just four more days. That's as far as the funding went.

During that first hour of September 1, 1985, *Knorr*'s cook, Johnny, stood alone in the dark on the stern, fishing there, and feeling sorry for the scientists.

He remembered his first meeting with Tom Dettweiler and the *Argo* team, right there on the stern, just before they steamed out of Woods Hole. Cooks, by tradition, never get involved in the expedition. But Johnny had been reading the publications that came out of the oceanographic institute, and what he read fascinated him.

"Boys," he said, "I've heard about this new piece of equipment they've got called *Argo*. They say it's a camera sled, and that it carries video equipment down to the very deepest ocean. I think that's tremendous, that you can accomplish something like that."

"Johnny," Tom said pointing. "Turn around. You're leaning against it!"

"You're kidding. That's it?" he said, running his fingers over a meshwork of steel. The mesh covered the whole thing, like skin. "What's all this grillwork?"

"Just a grille," said Tom. "The *Argo* is basically a cage with a fin on top. If we bang into a pile of rocks, the cage protects all the equipment inside."

Johnny saw little steel canisters with deep, thick lenses in them. He guessed correctly that they were pressure-tight compartments for cameras and other equipment. Clear, soft plastic veins ran between the cylinders. There were wires in the veins, soaked in oil.

"What are these for?"

"Pressure compensation," Tom explained. "We can't just run electrical wires directly into the cylinder, because high-pressure water would push in around the sides of the wire and flood the cylinder. So, you see that knob on the end of the cylinder, the knob the wires run out of?"

"Yeah."

"Well, that's a connector. We have male and female pins anchored inside to carry the electricity across from the wire into the cylinder. And the little hollow space where the pins meet is enclosed by rubber O-rings, which act as seals to keep the water out—but, so the seal doesn't have to do much work, we let the ocean squeeze oil into the space, making the pressure inside equal to the pressure outside. That's what that oil is doing in there inside the plastic veins. As *Argo* goes down, the water squeezes the plastic and forces oil into the connector through a little valve. The only thing we really have to watch for is that a rock or something doesn't smash through the grille and open up the veins. If oil bleeds out and seawater seeps in, where the wires are, we can short out the whole system."

"That's one fantastic piece of work," Johnny said. "Absolutely fantastic."

But all the ingenuity in the world didn't seem to be helping now. No. Not tonight, Johnny decided. No cries of excitement had come from that big blue box chained to the deck, from which the scientists were controlling both *Argo* and the ship, leaving the crew with very little to do. He'd heard no hopeful conversation in the galley, where he sat with the scientists at every opportunity, and asked them many questions. No, there was none of the optimism of three weeks before. The cruise was almost over, on the verge of failure, and everyone knew it.

Johnny pulled in his line. No catch tonight—which was unusual for the Grand Banks. A dozen feet away, *Argo*'s tether moved noisily up and down on its winch, fishing for bigger game.

He stowed his gear and made for the blue box. He'd never been in there before, and it seemed he wouldn't have many more opportunities. As he stepped through the door, the clock on the wall clicked forward to 1:05 A.M. Someone looked up and said, "Hi, Johnny." But save for those two words there was utter silence in the room.

The place looked to him like the bridge in that movie, *2010*. TV screens everywhere—all displaying the same landscape, dusty and bland.

Five...ten...fifteen seconds passed, and then Johnny noticed a dark letter C in the middle of the screen. Just opposite the crescent was a shadow in the shape of a large comma. He realized that he was looking at a circle—more, it was a cylinder turned on end.

"Whaa..."

During the next fifteen seconds, the object drifted to the bottom of the screen, and *Argo* swung twenty feet closer. The resolution improved.

"That looks like a part," announced a calm voice at the data logging station.

"That's big..."

Giant rivets drifted into view—

"Look at it," said someone with curious detachment.

—three stoking doors—

"Whew..."

"*Christ.*"

"*It's a boiler!*"

"*BOILER!*"

"*LOOKS LIKE A BOILER!*"

"*—YES! YES!*"

"*FANTASTIC! ALL RIGHT!*"

"What do we do now?"

Someone punched a button. A telescopic view flashed up on the screens. The craftsmanship was unmistakably turn of the century.

"We better get Ballard."

Everyone turned around, looking at each other, then at the screens, then at each other. No one wanted to leave the room. No one wanted to miss what was coming up next.

They turned around, and there was Johnny the cook. And Johnny said, "Don't anybody move. I'll get him!"

"It was really nice," Tom Dettweiler recalls, "that he had an opportunity to play such a role in the thing, to be the one who actually broke the news to Ballard. And it was funny, too, because Bob had just gotten into bed—and he threw on his jumpsuit and practically ran over Johnny's back and was downstairs in seconds. He looked at the screens and said, 'Yep. That's it,' and then ran outside.

"I was in one of the staterooms below deck, and awoke to a loud bang. The door was almost literally thrown off the hinges. It slammed against the bulkhead and scared the shit out of me, and all I heard was, *'We got it!'*

"I jumped out of bed and my roommate, Emile, jumped out of the top bunk, practically on top of my head. We were throwing clothes on in the dark and finally Emile stopped and said, 'Who was that?'

"'That was Ballard,' I said. And we knew from his excitement that we had indeed found it. We were up in the *Argo* van in thirty seconds, probably, and sure enough the boiler was up on the screen and the high was just unbelievable."

It was a high that ebbed, however, as the minutes drew on...as Tom became aware that the goal of a lifetime had suddenly been reached, and realized that he did not know where to go beyond that point...as a quarter-mile-long strewnfield inched by on the screens.

There were things—just things on the bottom—that had spilled out when something snapped and cut the stern loose from the plunging, twisting hulk. The resulting scatter was a sampling from every walk of life—ivory pots...cut-glass windows from the second-class smoking rooms...bedsprings and chamber pots from steerage quarters...bottles of ale and stout—pressure-compensated by corks that merely pushed in an inch or two against fluid that had already been corked under pressure. The contents may still be drinkable, though unaged in the intense cold...lumps of coal...a wine glass...a workman's tools...a silver platter...personal effects that immigrants brought aboard at Queenstown, dreaming of infinite possibilities in a land most of them would never see...and finally the bow, and that place between the anchor chains, where Samuel Hemming had found the air escaping. The hatch door was still open.

Every piece of wreckage brought the disaster back to Tom. He would constantly relive it through the next four days, even in his sleep.

Something leapt up from the bridge, up to where the cold stars burned, and then the stars were gone—extinguished in a concussion of light and shadow. Hundreds of upturned faces flashed out pallid white. When their eyes adjusted to the blaze, they discovered that their field of vision was improved enormously. The water sparkled for miles around. Lifeboats could be seen on it. The huge smokestacks and tapering masts were illuminated by a shower of white stars that sank slowly down the sky. In that cave of man-made light, minds, too, were illuminated. Everyone understood the message of the rocket without being told: the ship was calling for help from any steamer, any fishing boat—anyone who was near enough to see.

Thomas Andrews no longer had any difficulty persuading people to enter the lifeboats. Each went away with an ever-increasing number of passengers as it became evident that what appeared to be warm and bright and omnipotent—the *Titanic*—was in fact overwhelmingly frail.

At 1:30 A.M., Andrews heard a gurgling noise that sent the blood draining from his face. He hurried forward to investigate, and saw the well deck vanishing into the sea. The wash made whirlpools around the forward cargo cranes, and near the base of the foremast from which Frederick Fleet had sighted the berg. Andrews tried to separate the sounds that reached him—objects sucking and dragging and collapsing under the weight of water—the outrush of air—the hiss of rockets—a woman's shriek—a cheery, ragtime tune...far away aft, a ten-year-old boy climbed over a rail and jumped in boat number fourteen. An officer dragged him screaming to his feet.

"Please, mister. I won't take up much room. Ple-e-ease! Let me stay!" His voice was high and squeaky.

The officer thrust a gun in the boy's face, saying, "This boat is for women and children only. You're old enough to be a man!"

"No-ooo! No! NO!"

"I give you just ten seconds to get back onto that ship before I blow your brains out!"

The boy left.

At about 1:40 the first gunshots were heard. "Get away from here! Get away from here!" an officer warned. "If any man tries to get in that boat I'll shoot him like a dog."

Moments later, on the opposite side of the ship, Murdoch fired his pistol in the air to stop a rush on number fifteen.

At 1:45 Lightoller threw open the cover to one of the last lifeboats and found a group of men huddled on its floor. "Get out of here!" he shouted, drawing his revolver on them. "Cowards! I'd like to see every one of you overboard!"

They crawled out. Lightoller motioned a woman forward. She entered the boat without hesitation, asking her husband to please come with her. "No," said her husband. "I must be a gentleman."

Elsewhere, four men jumped into a boat as it was being lowered. One of them was Dr. Hugo Frauenthal. He weighed almost three hundred pounds without the two life jackets he'd tied to himself. He impacted against a woman passenger, breaking her ribs and knocking a child unconscious as he bounced off her.

As the raft known as "Collapsible D" prepared to cast off at 2:00 A.M., Miss Sloan watched Lightoller standing in the boat and helping ladies across a wide gulf. The *Titanic* had taken an ugly list to port, and Collapsible D hung away from the deck at a crazy angle.

Thomas Andrews came striding up the deck waving his arms and giving a loud command: "Get in. There is not a minute to lose!"

Miss Sloan stepped back a little way from the scene, and Andrews recognized her.

"Why aren't you in that boat?" he asked.

"All my friends are staying behind. It would be mean to go."

"It would be mean for you *not* to go. You must get in." He took her by the arm and led her to Lightoller. It was a long way across to the boat—scary. If Andrews were not beside her she would have walked away, but the command of the man, who for nearly two hours she had seen working so fiercely that his clothes were literally bathed in sweat, persuaded her to take Lightoller's hand and jump across.

"You go with her, Lightoller," said Andrews.

Lightoller jumped back on deck. "Not damned likely!" he shouted, and worked the davit.

Collapsible D was the last boat down on the davits. Two more collapsibles remained aboard, but they were stowed upside down on the roof of the officers' quarters abreast of the first smokestack. Time was running out. Water now slopped halfway up the white superstructure of the bridge. The deck seemed to shiver and from somewhere came a crashing noise resembling a million pieces of china breaking. At the Grand Stairway the forward-leaning chandeliers had dimmed to an ominous red glow. In the half-dark, the water gleamed obsidian black as it crept up the stairs. Horsehair sofas floated in it.

In minutes the sea would be up to the first smokestack. There was no time to unlash the last two boats, push them down to the deck, and load them in the davits. They'd have to be floated off as the bow went under.

With Collapsible D gone, quiet returned again to the *Titanic*. Most of the people began walking toward the imagined safety of the stern—which appeared to be rising out of the water as the bow buried itself deeper in the Atlantic's skin. Rarely have human eyes looked upon anything so hopeless as the empty falls dangling from the *Titanic*'s every davit head.

~ ~ ~

The empty lifeboat davits—that's what brought Bob Ballard to shivering and tears. *Argo* glided over the decks and the picture of the davits was like a punch in the stomach…*Bang!* He never expected the *Titanic* to hit him emotionally. *That,* he was unprepared for. Suddenly it just came screeching out of the dark—*Oh, my God…This was supposed to be archaeology—nothing more. It was a disaster that was partially put to rest more than seventy years ago and it just came like a freight train roaring back into the present. And there were the davits…empty…hanging there with no boats. That's what all the people who died saw. They must have stood there looking at those davits, looking for lifeboats—and they're all gone!*

SOS…TITANIC SINKING BY THE HEAD…WE ARE ABOUT ALL DOWN …SINKING…

Harold Bride tried to tie a life jacket over Phillips's back. Phillips wouldn't slip his arms through the straps. He was too busy with the telegraph key. The message went out through his fingers—DIT-DIT-DIT DA-DA-DA DIT-DIT-DIT

—a despairing, electronic shriek in the night.

Phillips let out an acidic laugh. "Maybe you should look out and see if all the people are off in the boats, or if any boats are left."

Bride stepped outside. The water was close up to the boat deck now. People had begun to jump in and swim away, fearing that the ship might create a giant whirlpool and draw them after her as she dove under. Thomas Andrews had pulled a mahogany door from its hinges. Bride watched him throw it overboard to three men struggling in the water below. It wouldn't make any difference. They needn't fear drowning. Within twenty minutes the cold water would stop their struggle. Andrews began throwing deck chairs and cushions down to the swimmers—anything that would float. There was something almost humorous in that useless gesture—but Harold Bride did not laugh at the shipbuilder. He was only doing his best.

Bride was attracted to a commotion on top of the officers' quarters. A dozen men were having an awful time trying to push a collapsible raft down to the boat deck. He climbed up and helped them shove it to the edge of the roof.

"All ready, sir," called someone from below. Lightoller, pushing beside Bride, seemed to recognize the voice.

"Hello, is that you, Hemming?" said Lightoller.

"Yes, sir," was the reply.

"Why haven't you gone?"

"Oh, plenty of time yet, sir," he said cheerily. "Here. I'm passing up a block and tackle. I've got the lines working nicely. Push her down to the boat deck and we can lower away."

"Forget the block and tackle! We're going to leave the raft on the ship and float away."

Not the brightest move in the world, Hemming judged. For a start—just for a start—smokestacks wide enough to accommodate railroad cars would probably be toppling every which way as the ship continued to tilt forward. He had no desire to be anywhere near the *Titanic* when that happened. He lowered himself down a fall and swam to a solitary lifeboat that seemed intent on staying at the *Titanic*'s side, keeping her company till the very end. Two other men swam to the boat and were hauled in with Hemming. A barrel splashed down nearby. It was followed by a deck chair.

"It'll be bigger things than that aiming for our heads in a few minutes," said Hemming. "We'd best row away a little bit, and come back for swimmers when it's all over."

Bride gave a final shove, and the raft slid down a hastily constructed incline of oars to the deck. It landed upside down. He looked longingly at it for a few seconds, listening to escaping air cut off by a gurgle not very far away. He ran back to Phillips.

"The power is pretty low," Phillips said. "How do things look outside?"

"She can't have many minutes left. The last raft is gone—"

Just then the captain came into the Marconi shack and said, "You can do nothing more, look out for yourselves."

Phillips looked up for a moment, then returned obsessively to his work.

"You have done your full duty!" Smith shouted. "I release you. Abandon your cabin." And then he was gone.

Phillips did not budge. So long as there was electricity and the cabin remained above water, he would cling on.

Bride went into their bunk and gathered all their money together. He glanced out the door and saw a fellow crewman trying to slip the life jacket off Phillips's back. Phillips did not notice, as he tapped off two "V's"—the last word anyone heard from the *Titanic*. The clock on the cabin wall clicked forward to 2:10. Bride came out kicking and swinging at the intruder. He had murder in his eyes, as he recalled the example Phillips had set, sticking to his work, trying to save what men might save, while all around the world was coming to pieces. And then enter this—"Bastard!"

Bride grabbed a length of steel and struck the man on the head. He dropped to the floor, and Bride clubbed him to death right where he fell.

"What the—"

"That man doesn't deserve to die a decent sailor's death!" Bride explained. "Drowning's too noble for him."

The lights dimmed, winked out, then came on again. "Come. Let's clear out," Phillips said.

Bride had kept the wireless book entered up, intending to take it with him when he left the Marconi shack for the last time, but water surged into the room and erased all such thoughts. In a second it was ankle-deep. In six seconds it was knee-deep. As the two operators ran out, a metallic groan carried down through the roof. One of the smokestacks was shifting restlessly in its bed.

Up! Up! The only way was up! They climbed on top of the roof. Phillips began walking aft, past the crystal dome of the Grand Stairway, toward the lofty strains of a popular waltz called *Songe d'Automne*. Bride watched him disappear into the night, and then the music ceased abruptly.

Bride ran toward the first smokestack, where the last raft had been. He was surprised to find the raft still there, and men still struggling to move it off the ship. They were trying to swim it off— upside down.

"Be British, boys! Be British!" That was Captain Smith's final order. Legend has it that he went down with his ship; but Harold Bride saw him dive into the water just before the bridge vanished. Someone else saw him swimming out there, trying to aid a child. No one ever saw him again.

Utter confusion. Too much was happening. An officer fired his revolver and a man fell at his feet. The officer was up to his knees in water. He gave a military salute and then put a bullet in his head. *Jesus! My Jesus! Was that Murdoch?*

No time to think. The sea washed over Harold Bride. The raft came with it. He caught hold of an oarlock and was swept with the upturned boat over the starboard side. He saw Lightoller swimming away—toward what, he did not know.

Ahead of him, Lightoller could distinguish the empty crow's nest in the glow of the mast light. The shock of the freezing water had kicked the breath out of him, and something appeared to be tugging at his feet, trying to pull him under. The crow's nest was now level with the water—if he could just grab on, just for a few seconds...the nest slid under. Grab onto anything and that will be your fate, Lightoller warned himself. *She'll drag you down with her.*

And she did seem determined to drag him down. As better judgment took sway over blind instinct, the ship inched forward and gulped him under. He went down against a vent in front of the partly submerged first smokestack. It was an intake, designed to face forward into the ship's glide path and scoop air down to the furnaces. There was a grille over the scoop, and he found himself splayed out against an iron net with uncountable tons of water rushing past him into the shaft. Instinct was again in command. His fingers curled around the grillwork as the bow pulled him deeper...deeper...the pressure built in his ears...and he'd have drowned there, clinging to that grille, if not for a blast of hot air that shot up through the ventilator and flung him to the surface. He barely had time to clear his lungs and suck in new air before he was pulled down again and glued against the grille.

She's toying with me—the bitch! THE BITCH!

With renewed determination he thrashed and kicked—once he even thrust himself a couple of feet forward—but he was drawn irresistibly back—

—BITCH!—

—BITCH!—

—Bi...

—His struggle abated. An unlikely calm swept over Lightoller as he gave in to her. Down...down...he was beginning to lose interest in everything when she let him go—spat him out like so much garbage.

There's bigger prey for her...all those passengers...and Andrews! She'll get Andrews...

Ascending air and planks of deckwood nudged him back to the surface—and as a wonder—right alongside the overturned raft. He grabbed on. He felt he had to put more distance between himself and the ship—*had to*—but he could not draw his eyes away from her. It was hypnotic. Her lights still burned, and there was something dreadfully beautiful about her. She exuded a tangible vapor that spread with lazy speed and hung in distinct layers only a few feet above the sea. Dirty steam was gurgling out of vents at the feet of the first two smokestacks. Dozens of people swam in the mist. And someone shrieked in it. It sounded at first like a man, but the noise spiraled up and up and up without pause. It was hard to believe that human lungs and vocal cords could sustain such a cry. Lightoller felt as if he were moving through one of the pictures he'd seen of the River Lethe in Dante's hell.

—*Yes. Oh, yes. She'll get Andrews. The poor fool, he loves her*—

She was pivoting around a center of gravity located just behind the second smokestack. If the bow angled down 1 degree, the stern angled up 1 degree. Four blocks away the rudder and propellers were climbing into the air. Three blocks away, in the gentlemen's lounge on A Deck, men in evening clothes were still playing cards on tables that slanted 20 degrees. Their way of coping, it seems, was to impose a mental gag order on themselves and keep busy. The bartender tried by staying at his post and minding the store. He felt the ship tilt forward and down another degree. A glass threatened to slide off the bar and smash itself. "All drinks are now on the house!" he announced.*

"I'll just have a little splash," someone said.

The *Titanic* continued to settle nose first into the ocean. Loud thuds mixed with a rumbling roar carried through the mist to Lightoller and Bride. Something groaned and popped. It was a sound you might imagine inch-thick steel plate making if you could cut it open and peel it back with a giant can opener. The noise was muffled and distant-sounding, as if it came from beneath the surface. She held Lightoller spellbound. She was awesome and obscene. She was fascinating and violent. She was horrible and wonderfully dramatic. The mist threw a glare of backscattered light on her. She glowed red, standing out of the night as though she were on fire.

The stern groaned up there—*up there*—where it had no business being.

"Now, there's something you don't see every day," said Harold Bride, just before the first smokestack tore loose and plunged into the water. The top of the thing shot down barely two yards from the overturned raft, churning up a giant wave that carried the raft a hundred feet, and more, from the *Titanic*. Bride and Lightoller scrambled atop the raft's underside. Several other men climbed up with them. They noticed suddenly that there were far fewer swimmers in the water. Many had been under the stack.

And the sea tugged at her, eating up the gymnasium and the second smokestack and the roof of the first-class lounge. Aft of the third smokestack, the ship continued to rise in frightful majesty. As she did so, her iron frame took on a taffylike consistency between the third and fourth smokestacks. The stern was never meant to be lifted out of the water and shaken like a stick.

Now the fourth smokestack broke away, and a two-hundred-foot length of ship stood motionless and almost perpendicular in the water, looking like a tall building, roaring and rattling as engines, boilers,

---

*The "bar" was actually a room separate from the gentlemen's lounge, and not the typical bar Americans had come to know. Passengers sitting at tables ordered drinks from a "bartender" or steward, who then prepared them "off stage" and brought them out.

and turbines tore loose from their beds. The lights snapped off, and then she let out an awful grating sound that was partly a vibration, partly falling furniture, and partly a chorus of metallic snaps. Seen now only as a dark shape against the stars, she suddenly picked up momentum in her plunge. There followed a long, high-pitched shriek of bending, breaking iron—and then silence.

A kerosene lantern on the flagstaff drifted up amongst the stars, and showed the stern to be settling from ninety to thirty degrees.

"That's impossible," said someone on the overturned raft. "She's floating back again."

"No, not floating back," observed another. "Probably two-thirds the length of the ship is already hundreds of feet below us, and hurrying to the bottom. She broke in two, and the afterpart is floating back."

"Can it stay afloat?"

"No, that's wishful thinking."

As indeed it was. The forward section of the afterpart—more than half of it—dangled below the surface. It was flooded completely and pulling for the bottom. Air pockets in the uppermost part of the wreck shrank with each passing second. It was 2:18 A.M. What was left of the *Titanic* would not last another two minutes.

She rolled slowly, smoothly onto her port side, drifting toward the raft and threatening to take it with her if she made a whirlpool. In the dim light of the flagstaff lantern, a man could be seen hauling himself over a rail. He then ran along the actual side of the ship, toward another man who was descending along the six-story rudder. The rudder drew a knife-edge shadow across the backdrop of space. As Lightoller and Bride watched, a star rose behind the rudder...then another...then three...then ten.... She seemed to be picking up speed as she slid down. The towering silhouette diminished to the shape of a large rock on the water, then to an outcrop of coral, then to a lone kerosene lantern. Then it was gone.

Thomas Andrews drifted just a few feet below the surface. He never did fasten a life jacket to himself. Streamers of green light penetrated down—the glow of the aurora borealis. His face was pale, without detail.

Harold Bride noticed no whirlpool as the ship glided under—not the least bit of suction. Through some miracle he had been spared. He was exhausted and freezing, but he told himself that the horrors were over. His fellow castaways on the overturned raft found planks of deckwood floating. "Oars," someone suggested. "We can use them for oars. We must row to keep warm, if nothing else."

They snatched up the planks and began rowing—toward the worst horror of all.

September 5, 1985

Tom Dettweiler stood alone in the sunlight on the fantail of the *Knorr,* sipping coffee and taking in sounds of water slapping against the ship's hull, of the robot's two-and-a-half mile tether vibrating in its winch, of the mysterious airplane that had been circling for more than an hour. The plane had no identification markings and refused to answer on the radio. Bob Ballard had suggested that it was taking a navigational fix on the *Knorr,* and thereby on the *Titanic,* directly below.

Near this very spot, Tom knew, Harold Bride and Charles Lightoller and the others had clambered atop an overturned raft. He tried to understand what it must have been like.

According to one survivor's account, "There was no indication on the surface that the sea had just closed over the most wonderful vessel ever built by man's hand; the stars looked down just the same and the air was just as bitterly cold. There seemed a great sense of loneliness when we were left on a small boat without the *Titanic.*"

But that sense of loneliness was merely a few seconds respite. It was false, and it put a shiver through Tom's spine to imagine the sound that rose around Harold Bride as he sat atop the raft. They say it was the most horrible thing ever heard by human ears.

It was the sound of a thousand throats crying out with the same pain. The sea was so frigid that at first contact the water felt like knives. Tom Dettweiler knew that if he stood in this place on that cold April night of 1912, he would have found himself right in the thick of it—the wails of terror and suffering, the gaspings for breath. To stand on a dry deck and imagine a thousand swimmers within a couple-hundred-foot circle of the *Knorr*—where the *Titanic* had been—and then to imagine only one overturned raft in the vicinity …the world tilted irrationally…in no time at all there were thirty-two people on the raft…water splashed over Bride's clothing…then it splashed over his head and he was pinned down under someone and he had to breathe whenever he could…get…out of here…have to get out of here…swamped…sinking…thirty-two paddled away …turned their backs on the thousand…listened to their pleas….

It must have been awful.

It must have been fucking horrible!

And then came dawn…and silence…and mountains of pale ice in every direction. The sunlight revealed one dead on the raft. It was Phillips.

…and the world tilted irrationally…. No television or radio programs reach over the curve of the Earth to a ship in the middle of the ocean. No satellites bother to beam HBO or MTV to such desolate places. If you want to watch TV on the *Knorr,* you are confined to the ship's video-tape library—*A Night to Remember* and *Raise the Titanic* had been popular mainstays…until September 1. On a research vessel you are normally cut off from the world. Your only news comes from merchant ship traffic and occasional satellite phone calls. Today was different. Every passing communications satellite seemed to be aimed at the *Knorr*. Merchant ships held their traffic and listened to *Knorr's*—and the word went outward and outward: "Somebody found the *Titanic*."

The world seemed to be taking it as good news. You couldn't take it that way after you'd imagined yourself surrounded by all those moaning people—like locusts on a midsummer night. Tom guessed that the rest of the world viewed the *Titanic* as something that had gone into a deep realm never to be seen again. Now that realm was suddenly accessible, just like the moon—which people had looked at for hundreds of centuries, and then, in 1969, it was covered with footprints. The moon will never be the same again. Neither will the deep. Though places deeper than the *Titanic* had been visited twenty-five years before, the abyss was only now conquered. Already it was in the media traffic: "If they can find the *Titanic*, they can find anything." The *Titanic* had been lost. It had been a needle in a haystack to many people, rightly or wrongly—and now we were in a new era.

Opening the doors to a wilderness was one thing. Living with the *Titanic* was something else.

The men and women aboard the *Knorr* were experiencing something else.

As the ship prepared to leave on the afternoon of September 5, a mist began to form over the site. Bob Ballard came running down from the radio room, where he'd just broken into tears and hung up on Tom Brokaw. Looking astern, where the *Titanic* had been, he whispered, "Goodbye."

He wept. And wept. And wept.

21

The Disappearance
of Robert Ballard

> And if you gaze into the abyss, the abyss gazes also into you.
> —*Friedrich Wilhelm Nietzsche*

September 5, 1985

No one expected the *Titanic* to have an emotional impact. She just wasn't supposed to. She was merely iron and brass and wood—but she had an impact nevertheless. What happened aboard the *Knorr* was surely the strangest display of human behavior in the history of marine exploration. Almost from the moment the first picture of a boiler turned up on the screens, there came a trauma that had never been felt on Earth before.

It was indiscriminate. It ran in parallel through both French and American members of the team. Bob Ballard likened it to "a kind of nervous breakdown." Someone else called it "the Medusa effect." If you were part of the scientific party, if you looked at the pictures and let yourself touch the *Titanic* too intimately, then she got you. She was like that. She was severe. She was sneaky.

Bob Ballard, who up to this point had considered himself a public scientist—

("pop-culture scientist," said his detractors)

—found himself withdrawing from the media. What the hell are you doing? he asked himself. Cutting off a satellite link with NBC television? Hanging up on Tom Brokaw? Did that make sense? Any sense at all?

Wandering the decks of the *Knorr* that day, it was easy to believe people were grieving over the death of a close friend. But no one was mourning, actually. Or, at least, they shouldn't have been mourning—not for a ship, not for men and women who had been lost seven decades ago. It didn't make sense. Somehow the past had come unstuck. It slipped into the present and caught them by surprise. It caught them all.

April 18, 1912

A mist began to form over lower Manhattan as forty thousand spectators crowded along the Battery. Scores of tugboats, steamers, and yachts went out to greet the rescue ship *Carpathia*, with her 705 survivors.

Among the spectators was Jim Speers of *The New York Times*. The order from his boss was simple and direct: "Get all you can. We must especially have the *Titanic* wireless man's story, if he's alive."

Easier said than done, thought Speers. City officials had roped off the Cunard Line's Pier 54. Police were ready to baton-charge the press, if requisite, to prevent them from crushing in around exhausted survivors. Speers recognized an inventor friend in the crowd, a man who was well known to the public and who might be especially welcome aboard the *Carpathia*. He decided to stick with him.

From the mayor's tug, a dark shape could be seen moving in the mist near the Statue of Liberty. It was 8:30 P.M.

"Liner ahead," called the tug's lookout.

The shadow veered slightly as it edged past Liberty Island, revealing a single smokestack.

"It's the *Carpathia!*" the captain shouted, and then hit the ship's siren. The tug whooped and screamed. Another boat followed the example, answering with its bells. A second joined in, then a third—and then the toots, bells, and whistles of fifty boats blazed out across the harbor. The sound rippled through the sea of people along the Battery, and was met by their outcry.

As the ship crept up Ambrose Channel the very Earth itself added a voice to the bedlam. No novelist could have created such a scene and gotten away with it. It was too dramatic an end to the *Titanic* disaster. A reader of fiction could not be expected to suspend disbelief, so it would never be written; and yet it really happened. A storm came on seemingly from nowhere, bringing with it horizontal rain blown with the violence of a hurricane. From the sky came continuous vivid lightning—which blended undetectably with the magnesium explosions of photographers' flashbulbs. It was accompanied by a heavy, rolling thunder that drowned out the wails of fifty boats.

Survivors began streaming onto the *Carpathia*'s decks. They found a boat trailing alongside. It was full of newsmen, and they were waving fifty-dollar bills.

"Jump overboard!" called one of the men. "We'll pick you up."

Lightning and magnesium furnished the infernal scene with sporadic illumination, revealing lifeboats hanging in the *Carpathia*'s davits. Several flashes showed them to be slightly too big for the davits that held them. One flash illuminated six more boats stacked on the forward deck. Another flash drew a deep sigh from the newsmen. They were the *Titanic*'s lifeboats.

Aboard the *Carpathia,* Harold Bride was missing all the commotion. He'd been in the Marconi shack for three days. Following Phillips's example, he clung now to the ship's telegraph, tapping out updated lists of those saved, plus private messages from survivors. He guessed that a hundred messages remained to be sent. He'd hoped to finish before the ship docked; but there was simply no time and he was bitterly disappointed. He imagined a hundred people out there, awaiting word that a loved one was still alive. There was nothing to do except carry on, to soothe as many as he could, all the while ignoring incoming queries from newspapers. His receiver buzzed endlessly. Every paper in the country was trying to reach him. But the survivors came first. He saw himself as their only link to friends and home. He couldn't care if it was President Taft calling on the telegraph. He'd ignore him just the same. In fact, he'd already done so—repeatedly.

As he tapped, Bride's mind snapped back, from time to time, to what he'd later describe as the most exciting night he could ever have asked for. It ended with a rosy dawn, and Venus on the horizon, rising ahead of the sun and gleaming out there long after all the stars had faded. The planet was brilliant, but even more brilliant was the light reflected off the mountains of ice that rose in every direction as far as the eye could see. Fantastically chiseled, sparkling in a billion points of backscattered sunlight, they were… *beautiful*. One of Bride's companions on the overturned raft was awed by the knowledge "that those same white mountains, marvelous in their purity, had made of the just ended night one of the blackest the sea has ever known."

At the feet of the bergs, the ocean was strewn with oak cabin fittings, mahogany drawers, a large fragment of the Grand Stairway that had floated up from somewhere far below, deck chairs, cork from ruptured bulkheads, cushions, a cello, and bodies in lifejackets. Falling smokestacks had caved in the skulls of many swimmers, pressed their faces into ribbons of curled flesh.

And over there, washing up against one of the larger bergs, a woman had an infant locked in her dead arms.

And the ice itself—it did not belong there. Lightoller had mentioned that he'd crossed the Grand Banks many times, but had never seen a field of icebergs before. Something unusual, perhaps a quirk in the solar constant, had sent warm air into the Arctic, producing an extremely mild winter in the north and causing glaciers to melt and crumble at a psychopathic rate. The scene that greeted Harold Bride and Charles Lightoller on the morning of April 15 belonged to the polar regions, not to the Atlantic's middle latitudes, and certainly not in April.

"Never before has there been known to be such quantities of icebergs floating down with the Labrador Current," Lightoller had said. "In my fifteen years' experience on the Atlantic I have never seen anything like this—not even in the South Atlantic, when we used to sometimes go down as far as 65° south."

And Lightoller could see only a tiny part of it. The field slipped below the Earth's horizon and out of view—twelve miles wide and seventy miles long. No one in command had anticipated such unusual conditions, so they drove ahead at full steam, trying to meet a schedule, and perhaps even to set a world speed record. There was no way the *Titanic* could have passed through that field without hitting something. The wonder is that she penetrated all the way to its heart.

By the time the steamer *Carpathia* nosed around the corner of an iceberg about four miles away, many standing on the overturned raft were wondering how much longer they could stay afloat. The rising sun had stirred up a morning breeze and the sea turned suddenly choppy. Every time the raft swayed, the bubble of air beneath their feet let out a burp. Their little island was sinking. Fist-sized chunks of ice washed around Lightoller's knees. He kept the raft trim by having the men lean this way and that; but it was exhausting work, and it was cold, and the waves were not about to let up. Depression was beginning to gnaw at them. It bit so deep that even the sight of the *Carpathia* could not buoy their hopes. They expected to be in the water, freezing or frozen by the time anyone on the ship spotted them. They expected nothing but death.

Bride watched six of the *Titanic*'s lifeboats rowing toward the *Carpathia*. Hopeless, he thought. We're so near, and so bloody damned far.

Lightoller then thought he saw a lifeboat coming toward him. He fished around in his soggy pockets—which were bristling stiff with ice—drew out a whistle and blew.

In the lifeboat, Samuel Hemming looked around and saw what appeared to be a group of men standing on the tip of a smokestack. Terrified at the thought of the dead *Titanic*'s smokestack floating toward them, several of those in the boat with Hemming wanted to row away. Hemming put his head over the gunwhale and looked along the water's edge. "It's not a smokestack," he announced. "It must be a slab of ice. Not that it matters what they're standing on. They need our help."

"Ship ahoy!" Lightoller called.

"Aye, aye, sir!" shouted Hemming.

Lightoller recognized the voice. "Hemming. Is that you?"

"Yes, sir," was the reply.

"Come over and take us off!"

"Plenty of time for that, sir. Plenty of time."

Harold Bride never heard the crowd at Pier 54. He did not feel the ship docking. He was barely aware of the thunderstorm outside. Tapping away in the *Carpathia*'s Marconi shack, he failed to notice *New York Times* reporter Jim Speers and his inventor friend stepping into the room.

Speers was shaken by what he saw. Bride looked thin and sickly, and he did not move. Only the electric spark dancing under his fingers indicated that he was alive. His frostbitten feet were wrapped in bandages and towels, and were propped on a chair. And there had been weight loss, Speers could tell. A hand that only a few days ago must have been wiry was now merely stringy. The skin had drawn back so tightly over the temples that the bones of his cheeks and brow protruded hideously, making deep shadows under his eyes. The eyes themselves had a spiritual look, a look such as people have in a religious painting.

Bride's hands looked as if they wanted to shake, yet his morse was swift and unerring.

"That's hardly worth sending now, boy," said the inventor.

Bride suddenly looked up and felt shock run through him like a live wire. "Marconi!" he gasped.

The Nobel laureate shook his hand warmly, taking special care not to squeeze.

"Mr. Marconi," Bride said. "Phillips is dead. He stood his ground until the crisis had passed, and then he collapsed, I guess."

~ ~ ~

September 9, 1985

It looked almost like a reenactment of the *Carpathia*'s arrival in New York, except for the brilliant New England afternoon, and the helicopters buzzing over the *Knorr*'s masts. Hundreds of reporters and film crews jammed the pier in front of Bigelow Laboratory. Scores of cabin cruisers, yachts, and little power boats swarmed around the *Knorr*. Whistles whooped and screamed.

Bob Ballard wondered what the powers that be at Woods Hole must be thinking. They had not been particularly excited about him going after the *Titanic*. They'd predicted that a carnival atmosphere would surround the adventure, and they didn't know how he would handle it—and right now *he* didn't know quite how to handle it. Guests were to be welcomed aboard the *Knorr* immediately upon docking—admirals and that sort of thing. And television interviews were scheduled. They wanted him on *Good Morning, America*. They wanted him on the *Phil Donahue Show*. But he'd find himself turning them all down. And he couldn't figure out why.

And there was that message from his mother: "You've done a lot of good science; hope you survive the *Titanic*."

Bob wondered. His bosses had seen more negatives than plusses in the expedition—right from the beginning. Now they'd have to deal with one reporter who'd walked through a plate-glass window at the institution and was threatening to sue, and another who was threatening to publish the addresses of the *Titanic* explorers when they went out on another expedition (so thieves would know their homes were empty) if they continued to deny her interviews.*

Bob had to give his supervisors credit: they didn't try to stop him. They gave him enough rope to hang himself; they let him proceed. And that says a lot about Woods Hole, he decided.

When all counsel was advising them that it was not in the best interest of the institution to let one of its scientists follow his instincts, Bob had to tip his hat. They might not have gone out of

---

*Bob Ballard and his team did continue to deny her interviews, and she did carry out her threat.

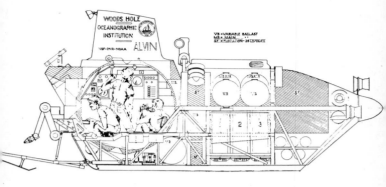

Inboard profile of Woods Hole's inner spaceship, *Alvin*.

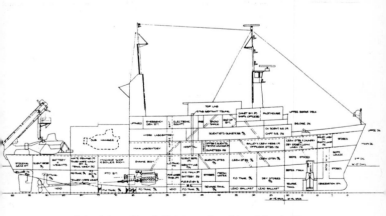

Inboard profile of *Alvin*'s mother ship, *Atlantis II*.

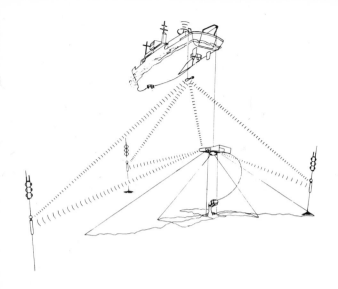

Above: The *Argo/Jason* robot system as conceived by Robert Ballard. *Argo,* *Jason*'s garage, is able to fix its exact position on the Earth within a few inches by "talking" with three sonar transponders dispatched to the bottom, and also with a sonar receiver dangled from the mother ship, which in turn "talks" to a global positioning satellite. The outer cone shown projecting down from the robot indicates the area covered by *Argo*'s sonar imaging equipment, and the three inner trapezoids (projected on the bottom) show the view provided by *Argo*'s 200,000-ASA cameras, which are essentially capable of seeing in the dark. If a particularly interesting object turns up in *Argo*'s down-looking cameras, *Jason* is sent in for a close up view. Equipped with robot arms, it can even collect samples. **Below:** Profile of the fifteen-foot-long robot *Argo,* showing the placement of its 200,000-ASA cameras and other components.

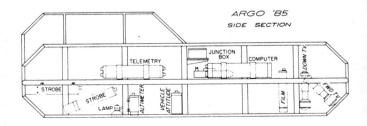

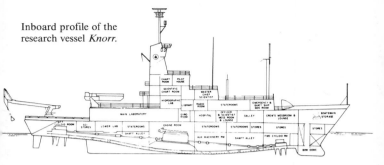

Inboard profile of the
research vessel *Knorr*.

In November 1985, *Alvin* was dismantled and overhauled for one of its
seemingly perpetual updatings. One of the most interesting things about the
loftiest of technology's achievements—and *Alvin* is one of them—is that such
machines are almost entirely handmade. *Alvin*'s titanium skeleton is seen at
the right. At the left, mechanic/pilot Kirk McGeorge sits atop the three-man
crew compartment, built to operate in an environment of 6000 pounds per
square inch, which is equivalent to the thrust coming out the back of a space
shuttle engine at lift-off. The sphere withstands such force by equalizing
pressure on all sides. Nevertheless, *Alvin*'s titanium crew compartment
shrinks a fraction of an inch by the time it reaches its maximum operation
depth of 2.5 miles, and the only things keeping the foot-thick Plexiglas
windows from being squeezed out like watermelon seeds between thumb and
forefinger are precisely cut angles that allow them to sit in beds of constricting
titanium. (PHOTO BY THE AUTHOR)

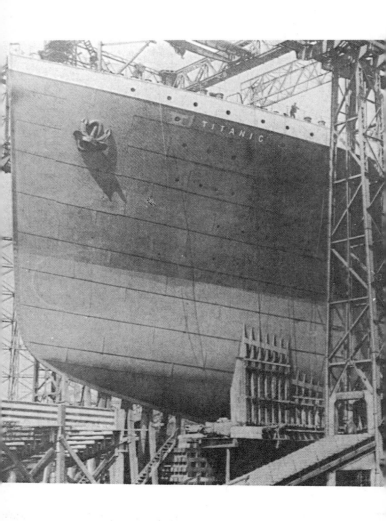

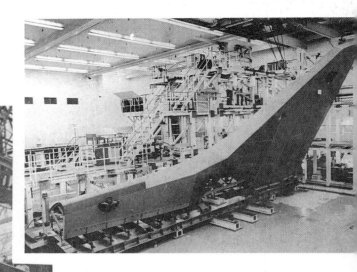

The Royal Mail Steamer *Titanic* and the Space Shuttle *Challenger* are seen in their cradles. Seven decades after the *Titanic* disaster, as civilization ascended into a new ocean, escape systems were removed from space shuttle blueprints. Escape systems weren't needed, it was said. Although her sister ship, *Columbia*, had flown with ejection seats for her pilots, *Challenger* was destined to become the first crewed rocket to be launched under the same code that had led to the mathematical discrepancy between passengers and lifeboat seats on the *Titanic: each ship its own lifeboat*. On January 28, 1986, an ice storm hit Florida. Ignoring ice warnings, the *Challenger* sailed without lifeboats. (*TITANIC* PHOTOGRAPH FROM THE AUTHOR'S COLLECTION; *CHALLENGER* PHOTOGRAPH BY THE AUTHOR)

Three generations of pioneers, left to right: *Argo*, oceanaut Robert Ballard, and rocket pioneer Chet Ballard. (PHOTO BY THE AUTHOR)

A wooden block inaccessible to boring mollusks dangles intact at the end of the davit for Collapsible D, the last boat sent down on the *Titanic*'s davits. Near this spot, shipbuilder Thomas Andrews and Second Officer Charles Lightoller refused seats in Collapsible D, just fifteen minutes before the liner went down. (PHOTO BY ROBERT BALLARD)

Alvin poses in front of its support ship, *Atlantis II*, during prelaunch operations. (PHOTO BY THE AUTHOR)

Dispatched from *Alvin*, the robot *Jason Junior* pokes a finger of light into the officers' quarters on the R.M.S. *Titanic*. (PHOTO BY ROBERT BALLARD)

Small enough to be contained in most living rooms, *Alvin* returns to its garage on the *Atlantis II*'s stern during the 1986 Panama Basin Expedition. (PHOTO BY THE AUTHOR)

Former *Calypso* Science Officer Tom Dettweiler (left) and University of Rhode Island volcanologist Haraldur Sigurdsson are seated in the *Argo* control van during Expedition *Argo*-Rise in December 1985. From this room the movements of both the robot and the research vessel *Melville* are directed, leaving the scientists in control and the ship's crew with little to do except worry about the scientists. (PHOTO BY THE AUTHOR)

Just before the pilot empties *Alvin*'s flotation tanks, divers perform a final prelaunch check and remain on hand to assist if an emergency exit becomes necessary. (PHOTO BY THE AUTHOR)

Above: In September 1985, the deep-sea robot *Argo* transmitted this fuzzy image of anchor chains and brass bollards on the *Titanic*'s foredeck. On July 14, 1986, the submersible *Alvin* made the first manned *Titanic* landing, in the upper right-hand portion of this picture. (PHOTO COURTESY OF WOODS HOLE OCEANOGRAPHIC INSTITUTION) **Below:** Scraps of broken iron, lumps of coal, a dish, and a mysteriously untarnished silver tray litter the *Titanic* debris field in this 1985 reconnaissance photo. In the summer of 1987, a French expedition recovered the silver tray. (PHOTO COURTESY OF WOODS HOLE OCEANOGRAPHIC INSTITUTION)

The *Titanic*'s starboard anchor is draped in iron stalactites. (PHOTO TAKEN ABOARD *ALVIN* BY ROBERT BALLARD DURING THE 1986 *TITANIC II* EXPEDITION)

Stalactite formations, the secretions of iron oxidizing bacteria, drip down over the *Titanic*'s portholes. When he first encountered the ship, its portholes reminded Robert Ballard of the eyeless sockets of a skull. (PHOTO COURTESY OF WOODS HOLE OCEANOGRAPHIC INSTITUTION)

Above: Iron stalactites stream down a wall outside an officer's cabin. A particularly beautiful one hangs from a lamppost once occupied by an imploded light bulb. (PHOTO COURTESY OF WOODS HOLE OCEANOGRAPHIC INSTITUTION) **Below:** An unbroken porthole looks out on iron stalactites. These curious drip formations crumble easily. They are mostly empty space (like sponge or Styrofoam), and appear to represent little actual mass wasting of the *Titanic*'s iron. Intact bedsprings in the debris field between the liner's two halves lend support to this view. When *Alvin* pilots went down to the *Titanic* with Navy officers (leaving Robert Ballard behind on the surface) they conducted the first crude structural tests on the hull—essentially hammer blows—and concluded that the inch-thick steel plates are still quite sound. A 1987 French expedition conducted more extensive tests and arrived at the same conclusion. Already there is serious talk about raising the 400-foot-long bow section. (PHOTO COURTESY OF WOODS HOLE OCEANOGRAPHIC INSTITUTION)

Above: Throughout the ship, iron oxidizing bacteria have created mournfully beautiful stalactite formations, such as these seen near the Marconi shack, streaming down from an electric winch that handled lifeboat davits on the *Titanic*'s port side. The iron stalactites are reminiscent of formations commonly seen in caves, except for being a curious hybrid of natural and man-made lines. (PHOTO COURTESY OF WOODS HOLE OCEANOGRAPHIC INSTITUTION) **Below:** In July 1986, the robot *Angus (Argo*'s ancestor) snapped this reconnaissance photograph of damage on the *Titanic*'s port side, astride the opening to the second smokestack. On the morning of April 15, 1912, during the first seconds of contact with the ocean bottom, a length of downblasted iron (visible in the center of the photograph) punched a hole through the roof of the library. A 1987 French expedition to the *Titanic* retrieved a leather satchel containing bank notes that were still readable. Since books of the period were, like bank notes, printed on rag paper, volumes in the library may be in similar condition—including Morgan Robertson's novel about an "unsinkable" ship named *Titan* that struck an iceberg and sank the first time it sailed. (PHOTO COURTESY OF WOODS HOLE OCEANOGRAPHIC INSTITUTION)

Above: Directly beneath the bridge, two cargo cranes were slammed down, one on top of the other, by a downblast of water that continued pushing for the bottom after the *Titanic* had ceased to fall. (1985 *ARGO* PHOTO COURTESY OF WOODS HOLE OCEANOGRAPHIC INSTITUTION) **Below:** The effect of downblast is illustrated in this picture of the demolished roof over the Grand Stairway. Fragments of the roof are still in place precisely where they were kicked down, meaning that the damage seen here could not have occurred at or near the surface (because the fragments would have been hoisted up into the ship's slipstream and lost during a forty-mile-per-hour, two-and-a-half mile fall through water). Once the liner stopped descending, its slipstream punched down much like a tidal wave impacting against a skyscraper. Not only is the roof collapsed, but the iron wall that supported it has been bulldozed out. (1985 *ARGO* PHOTO COURTESY OF WOODS HOLE OCEANOGRAPHIC INSTITUTION)

Stalactites drip from two bollards, which were used to secure mooring lines on the *Titanic*'s starboard bow, near the place where Ralph Hollis, Dudley Foster, and Robert Ballard first landed on the *Titanic*, at 11:00 A.M., July 14, 1986. (PHOTO COURTESY OF WOODS HOLE OCEANOGRAPHIC INSTITUTION)

A copper kettle from one of the *Titanic*'s kitchens lies in the half-mile-wide debris field. Despite the passage of seventy-five years, the copper has not tarnished. As a general rule, as objects are unappetizing to wood-boring mollusks and scavengers or to iron-oxidizing bacteria, they remain untouched, making the bed of the Atlantic almost as timeless as the mountains of the moon. The bottom is strewn with leather suitcases, gleaming silverware, carpetbags, items of clothing, even edible cheeses and bottles of wine. In most bottles, the corks merely pushed in an inch or two because the bottles had already been corked under pressure, so the wine is still drinkable—as proved by a 1987 French expedition— though unaged in the intense cold of the deep ocean. This copper pot, incidentally, was recovered by the French *Titanic* III expedition. (PHOTOGRAPH BY ROBERT BALLARD DURING THE *TITANIC II* EXPEDITION)

Six-year-old Robert Spedden (whose family survived the *Titanic* disaster intact) spins a top in front of a large cargo crane on the first class after-Promenade Deck's starboard side. (PHOTO FROM THE AUTHOR'S COLLECTION) In July 1986, the deep-sea robot *Angus*, operated by explorer Tom Dettweiler, snapped this picture of the same cargo crane. When the *Titanic*'s stern crashed down on the floor of the Atlantic at sixty-to-eighty miles per hour, the funnel of water that had been trailing behind it punched down with all the force of a tidal wave. The crane, which was stowed facing inboard, was caught in a downblast emanating from the center of the ship. It was simultaneously snapped outward and bent down over the starboard side. (PHOTO COURTESY OF WOODS HOLE OCEANOGRAPHIC INSTITUTION)

their way to help him; but he couldn't have done it if he'd been working anywhere except Woods Hole.

And the Navy seemed happy. They understood that the same robot that could locate and photograph the *Titanic* could also reach lost Soviet submarines. And if *Argo* would soon be mapping the East Pacific Rise for the scientists, she could also map features that might become undersea hiding places for enemy missile launchers or interfere with sonar efforts to "see" them.

All well and fine, but

—"hope you survive the *Titanic*"—

Why this urge to run away? To go into hiding? It was against him. For years Bob had fought the snobbish attitudes of scientists who viewed themselves as members of an elite priesthood. They saw communicating with the public as going outside the clubhouse, as violating the law. "We don't need a Carl Sagan or a Jacques Cousteau in this department" was the common outcry. "Nor do we need Bob Ballard's picture in *OMNI* and *National Geographic* magazines."

"Well, that's a bunch of crap," Bob had said. "And that's because America inherited its scientific institutions from Europe. And in Europe it was a club. Daddy or the estate sponsored Junior to go to the university. Science, back in the days of Victorian England, was a primitive undertaking by wealthy generalists. And the masses? Why would anyone want to even talk to them? What good would that do?

"And that arrogance was passed on to the new continent. Yet science in America today is a ward of the state. Science is paid for by the sweat of a coal miner through his taxes. And it's our obligation, our requirement to tell the people what the hell we're doing with their money."

He tried to tell them, after the *Knorr* docked, after smiles before the cameras and a cheerful reunion with his wife and his two boys. He stood before a bouquet of microphones and said, "This summer's joint expedition by the United States and France was a highly technical undertaking involving the finest technology of these two countries. Jean-Louis Michael, my co-chief scientist on both the *Le Suroit* and the *Knorr*...is a quiet and gentle man who came to embody the mind of the *Royal Mail Steamer Titanic*. The *Titanic* itself lies in 13,000 feet of water on a gently sloping alpinelike country-side overlooking a small canyon below. The bow faces north and the ship sits upright on the bottom…There is no light at this depth…"

…Bob's voice began to crack—

"—It is quiet and peaceful and a fitting place for this greatest of sea tragedies to rest. May it forever remain that way and may God bless these now-found souls."

The audience went wild. Everyone seemed to be going *Titanic* crazy. They wanted to hear more…more…all of it. They wanted him to tell it long, and again. It didn't matter if he was beginning to repeat himself. It's pervasive, Bob judged. People don't know they've got it. That's what was so interesting about what was happening around him. People didn't know they were going to react with the level of excitement they were now displaying. It was inside them all along. It was titanic. It was Pavlovian. And it was too big for Bob Ballard.

In the first place, he'd never expected the damned thing to hit him emotionally. But once it hit him, his response to the media was going to be unpredictable.

A year later, September and October and most of November would be a haze in Bob's memory. He wouldn't know what happened to them.

Actually, he was hiding during those months, ducking low and planning his next expedition. The media caught only the rarest glimpses of him. He surfaced briefly in San Diego, giving a three-minute television interview to John Ritter for the opening celebration of Epcot Center's Living Seas pavilion—which had his imprint all over it, for he was one of its designers. Then, in December, he vanished. He climbed aboard the *Melville* and ran away to the middle of the Pacific, taking his father and a small group of engineers and scientists with him. Three more months would pass before he started "feeling human again."

~ ~ ~

Bob Ballard recalled, as we plodded over the East Pacific Rise, "that by September 5, by that fourth day after we found the *Titanic*'s grave, the world's reaction to what we had done caught up with me, and caught me by surprise. Camera crews jumped aboard helicopters and flew all the way out into the Atlantic just to get a picture of the *Knorr*. Reporters were calling on the ship's radio, continually, day and night. I expected the public to be fascinated with the *Titanic*; but I never thought they'd go crazy about it.

"I never thought *I'd* go crazy over it. And sometimes I think I did go a little crazy. Finding the ship, I did not expect it to hit me in such a tragic sense. I did not expect to feel the disaster to the level I felt it. I was in tears. I must have looked like a real crybaby. I just—I was really depressed. And, believe me, I never expected that. I expected it to be the exact opposite. Instead, I wanted to run away from the *Titanic*. I wanted it out of my life. I didn't want to see a soul, to talk to a soul about the *Titanic*. I just…I haven't told these things to anyone outside my family. I still don't want to talk about it, for some odd reason—very painful. I can't explain it. I just—I…can…remember the reactions. One of the ones that was most surprising—sort of like looking at yourself in a mirror or something, or looking at yourself and seeing yourself and being amazed by what you see. I am amazed at what I saw, after it was all done, on that last day, floating above the wreck. It happened very quickly. I'd just been getting an incredible number of phone calls on the ship-to-shore. I couldn't respond to a small percentage of them, but I was trying to be fair and talk to all the networks, but I was also trying to do my job. I was fatigued. I was tired. All hell was breaking loose. I had to get the final lowering. *Argo*, at that time, only had her 200,000-ASA TV cameras. The images sent up through the tether were videotaped. Hours and hours of videotape. But the resolution had degraded through 2½ miles of tether, and the pictures were, after all, only black and white. We wanted clear, color shots. And the color cameras and strobe lights were on *Argo*'s predecessor, *Angus*. All of our color pictures of the *Titanic* were taken by *Angus* in the last hour.

"I slept under the table on the floor of the lab as they prepared for the final lowering, and then I crawled out from under the table, dragging myself to the flier's station and draping myself over Tom Dettweiler's shoulder as we made that run. Tom looked down and noticed my pajamas hanging out the bottom of my jumpsuit.

"'Haven't you been to bed since we found it?' he asked.

"'No,' I said.

"It was probably the most dangerous thing we've ever done: to make that final lowering and get those beautiful pictures. I have never taken a pill in my life, but I was tempted to take a Valium during this period. If we tangled the robot in the wreck's masts or rigging, the *Knorr*, in effect, would have been anchored to the *Titanic*. And during all that we were getting badgered by the outside world and we're not done. We're in the heat of this battle and…can you imagine a battle during World War II and a reporter coming into General Patton's tent and asking, 'Well, how does it feel?'— and you want to pull out a gun and shoot the guy…the Germans are coming over the wall…the *Titanic* is sweeping up ahead, seen only as a giant flyswatter in *Angus*'s sonar…you're dead on your feet and you have to go up four flights of stairs to get to the radio room. It's like walking up a four-story building a hundred times a day.

"And I can remember, we had finished the lowering. We didn't know what was on the film. We were hauling up stakes and getting ready to leave, and I was on the radio with Tom Brokaw, who I respect from afar. I watch him like most Americans do. I haven't talked to him since. I'm curious, too. I wonder what he thought. He was talking to me as we were leaving the site and all of a sudden I looked up—I was looking out one of the portholes and it had become overcast outside and it just—I—an incredible sorrow hit me and I was talking with him and I started—*I was breaking up on the phone*. I was holding myself, keeping it back, holding the tears, and he sensed it and he was probing very nicely, very gently about it, but he recognized that I was having a heck of a time. And I cut off. I hung up.

"We were leaving the area and I sort of hadn't said goodbye. It was sort of like running out of someplace, jumping into the car and getting whisked away and then saying, 'But I never got to say goodbye.' Sort of like the last time you got to see your grandfather. That feeling of remorse for having improperly bid adieu. I got all choked up and I couldn't talk. I had to get back to the fantail and make my peace."

Tom Dettweiler always looked forward to reuniting with his family at the end of every cruise, but *Argo-Titanic* was different: "We arrived in Woods Hole and it was a big media event—even by the standards of my *Calypso* experiences. And our families were all there to come aboard. And my parents had come to visit from Indiana. And I saw my wife and kids and my parents for the first time.

"Normally you're very happy to see them. But my wife says I was just not there—and I wasn't. She was happy to see me, but it wasn't as it had been after the other cruises. All my thoughts were back where we had come from. I kept going back to the *Titanic*—to Andrews and Hemming and Murdoch—and my wife wondered if I'd really come home at all.

"Fortunately we had *Argo*-Rise to prepare for. We landed in Woods Hole on September 9 and almost immediately we had to pull all our equipment off *Knorr* and ship it out to *Melville* on the west coast. That was very good for us, because we couldn't dwell on the *Titanic* for too long. If we hadn't had *Argo*-Rise, I think it would have taken us longer to get back to normal. As it was, my wife, who always gets depressed when I go off on a cruise, jokingly told Bob and other members of the *Argo*-Rise team to take me away. 'Take him,' she said. 'Take him far away into the ocean. You can have him. Just bring him back normal.'"

As Tom prepared to be taken away, a peculiar story emerged. He was talking with Bob Ballard's wife, Marge, about the immediate public reaction to the discovery of the *Titanic*—which the *Knorr* crew had missed, while exploring the *Titanic*.

"What was it like?" he asked.

"Well, I was really bothered. The phone was ringing all the time. Reporters wanted to talk to me. And the one thing I haven't told

Bob yet is that his father was on TV being interviewed and the reporter asked, 'And what do you think about your son finding the *Titanic?*'

"And Chet said, 'I think it's pretty amazing, considering that he could never find his toys when he was a kid.'"

Two days later, Tom's parents called from Indiana and told him the same story. They'd seen the interview on television. It was the first thing he mentioned, the next time he saw Chet.

"You know," Tom began, "Marge is still kind of afraid to tell Bob what you said about him being unable to find his toys."

"Well, at least it only got local coverage."

"No, Chet. My parents saw it in Indiana. It was broadcast all across the nation."

"Ohhh no-ooo..."

That was a father's reaction.

Weeks later, on the East Pacific Rise, Tom was considering a wife's reaction. I hope this next homecoming is a little more like past homecomings, he thought. We'll be glad to see each other. We'll be thinking more of doing things together, and with the kids. I won't be replaying the *Titanic* anymore, over and over in my head ...I hope.

Far above a Pacific spreading center, nearly four months after he first saw the *Titanic,* Bob Ballard understood that little had changed since the day he hung up on Tom Brokaw:

"I still feel—I don't know if it was a sense of guilt that I hadn't been sensitive enough—about the tragedy. I just didn't expect it to affect me the way it affected me. I actually withdrew from the media, in an unpredictable fashion. I'd already done television specials on the hydrothermal vents and the strange creatures we saw down there. I'd been on the *Today Show* and the *Tonight Show*—on all those sorts of things. But now I have a revulsion to it, for some reason. I came back from the Grand Banks and I refused to appear on any of those shows. I couldn't sit there and talk about...*it.* And that was an interesting reaction. I would never have predicted that that's how I would have reacted. I'd expected that I would have gravitated toward the publicity instead of getting on my horse and running as fast as I could away from it. I basically went into seclusion. And I'm still there. I haven't recovered from finding the *Titanic*. Going on this cruise was as much therapy as it was going on a voyage of discovery. I came out here to get away from the *Titanic*.

"There I was: a professional in pursuit of a goal. It was very difficult technically, very challenging technically, and pursued professionally—and the human that experienced it was not as tough as that professional. The professional could accomplish the feat. The human was a casualty of it.

"I've always bounced back from the difficult times in my life. I'm just not bouncing back this time. I'm just watching to see if I'm going to get off the mat on this one. In a way, I guess it's similar to what we hear about the astronauts—what they experience in space. Each of them has reacted differently, but many of them have been profoundly affected. I don't know if this is the same thing. I don't know. I've never had anything in my life affect me like this, and I'm sort of curious: what am I going to be like in a year, when the *Titanic* is finally out of my life?

"*Will it ever be out of my life?*

"I don't know. My mother said it very clearly to me, because she is very proud of my accomplishments, as any mother would be, and has followed them very closely. She, more than anyone, knew that I'd done a few things to be proud of before I went after the *Titanic,* and she said she's afraid, now, that that's all anyone is going to know about me. That's what I'm going to be pegged for, for the rest of my life: finding the *Titanic*.

"It's sort of like I just married someone—and is this something I want to be married to? It seemed nice at the time—you know, she was cute, she was nice and all that sort of thing—but now I'm married to her and wondering if I made a mistake. And I can't just walk away from this one. She won't let me."

22

Phaeton Rising

EXCERPT FROM A CONVERSATION WITH ROBERT BALLARD
Research Vessel: *Melville*
Expedition: *Argo*-Rise
Date: Thursday, December 20, 1985
Time: 10:00 A.M.
Place: Somewhere over the East Pacific Rise

ROBERT BALLARD: You're very confident in space technology, aren't you?

CHARLES PELLEGRINO: Well, space can be risky business, but I do hope to fly on a Space Shuttle one day, and I know the people who build and maintain those machines. And I know they give it their very best, just like the people who watch after *Alvin*. The thing is, after you've touched *Argo*—which literally went down and shook hands with the *Titanic*—after you've looked at the pictures, you certainly wouldn't climb into a Space Shuttle and say, "Gee, Charlie, you're one hundred percent safe."

BALLARD: I think there's a parallel with NASA and the people who built the *Titanic,* and I think you can see it. It's probably a recurring theme. When we conquer a new field of technology, we become overconfident.

PELLEGRINO: I have no illusions. I watched the *Challenger*'s wings being built at Grumman. I watched her grow up frame by frame, and two years ago I watched her fly. It was that night launch. A mist had come up and they almost cancelled the mission. And when she went, the mist reflected all the light and noise back at us, magnified it. It made you feel humble, and yet, at the same time, it made you feel great, because that tornado of light was man-made and so full of potential, and five people were riding on top of it. And the next morning we had a meeting. A man named Joel Taft came in and he brought up the same subject you just did. He knew I intended to go into space one day, and he told me to get my head out of the clouds. He told me that one of the solid rocket boosters had burned through its casing even as I watched *Challenger* fly up. If it had happened a half minute earlier, before the booster was detached, it could have burned through the external fuel tank and blasted the ship to pieces. And then he warned me that there were people walking around the Kennedy Space Center—even astronauts—who seemed to think Space Shuttle launches were like a bus run. He explained that the shuttle was an experimental vehicle and that it would always be so. It would simply show us our potential and our limitations: Yes, we can carry cargo up and down…Yes, we can reuse a spaceship…Yes, we can step outside the ship and build things, and repair satellites…but not until the next generation of shuttles, the runway-launched scramjets, would spaceflight become routine. He said it is only a matter of time before we have an accident. There're always accidents in test flight. It's expected. You have accidents and you find out where you made mistakes. Then you make it as safe as you can and move ahead. Joel Taft thinks our record of successes has deluded some people into thinking spaceflight is already routine.

BALLARD: You see? Overconfidence. Arrogance. Sooner or later it's bound to happen.

PELLEGRINO: What? A *Titanic* in space?

BALLARD: Exactly.

PELLEGRINO: Sure, sometime in the next ten or twenty years, it's bound to happen.

BALLARD: That's precisely the kind of arrogance I'm talking about. Sooner than you think, Charlie. A lot sooner than you think.

EXCERPT FROM A KENNEDY SPACE CENTER TRANSMISSION
Date: Tuesday, January 28, 1986

Houston, we have roll program...Roger, roll *Challenger*...Three engines running normally. Three good fuel cells. Three good APUs. Velocity 2257 feet per second. Altitude 4.3 nautical miles. Downrange distance three nautical miles...*Challenger,* go with throttle up...*Roger, go with throttle up*...*uh-oh—crackle*—One minute fifteen seconds. Velocity 2900 feet per second. Altitude 9 nautical miles. Downrange distance seven nautical miles...Flight controllers are looking very carefully at the situation. Obviously a major malfunction. We have no downlink...

EXCERPT FROM THE JOEL MARTIN SHOW
Date: Friday, February 14, 1986
Place: Viacom Studios, Long Island, New York

JOEL MARTIN: Charles Pellegrino loves technology. Absolutely loves it. You've got a background as a paleontologist, an astronomer, a marine biologist, a spacecraft designer—a man for all sciences. Now, perhaps we look at the space program a little differently because of what happened two weeks ago—

January 28, 1986: the *Challenger* explodes, it disintegrates. The way it hit you, Charles, emotionally, must have been devastating.

CHARLES PELLEGRINO: Well, first off, the disaster has not changed my mind about space. In fact, I'd accept an assignment on the shuttle tomorrow if the offer were given. I guess I felt what everyone else felt. I can't say I've ever felt more helpless in my life about anything, just seeing something that was spectacular and yet, at the same time, horrifying and unbelievable. And you wanted to deny it and you couldn't do anything about what was happening before your eyes. For the first time, I think I could understand what people must have felt sitting in those lifeboats and watching the *Titanic* go down.

She disappeared into the sea at 2:20 A.M. on Monday, April 15, 1912.

To those who are old enough to have witnessed, from its beginning, this most incredible century the world has ever known, the *Titanic* was, more than any other event, a portent of things to come. She was not the cause of what followed. She was a symbol...a lesson in uncertainty...a lesson the world must never forget.

No one—at least no one in charge—had anticipated anything worse than penetration by another ship at the junction of two watertight compartments. She would easily have floated with two compartments full, so they labeled her unsinkable, and the unsinkable ship went down the first time it sailed.

When he last saw her, on that cold April night, wireless operator Harold Bride pondered the sixth ice warning that had come some three-and-a-half hours earlier.

"Shut up," Phillips had told the caller. "We're busy here."

Smugly confident in the greatest engineering achievement of their day, Phillips and Bride never forwarded that final warning to Captain Smith. Bride would never be so confident in anything again. Before the *Titanic* disappeared, people truly believed that technology could conquer all. After the *Titanic* disappeared, there followed the technological nightmares of two world wars.

By the time she reappeared, seventy-three years later, the belief that great machines could not die had set in again. Within five months of her discovery, an engineer would protest that ice storms in southern Florida—as strange as the bitter cold that had swept into the Gulf Stream and doomed the *Titanic*—made the Space Shuttle unsafe.

"What do you want us to do?" he was told. "Delay the launch till *April?*"

And so, on January 28, 1986, ice warnings were once again ignored. No one—at least no one in charge—imagined that it could all go so clearly wrong.

So clearly wrong…

…so clear as all of history's surprises are, when viewed with 20/20 hindsight. On that cold January morning, a machine Harold Bride could never have imagined hurled itself against the far sky. Inside, the most highly evolved electronic brains in the world—five of them—sensed the flow of air over the wings, determined direction and speed, and knew their exact height from the ground. They could predict the consequences of any action, and decided the appropriate actions at lightning speed, by committee voting. Even without a human crew, *Challenger* was capable of coming down from space and making a perfect runway landing.

Fifty-eight seconds into flight, the computers sensed a loss of thrust on one side—a loss that, left unaccounted for, would have caused *Challenger* to pinwheel broadside into supersonic wind. The computers responded so fast that the right wing flap had already moved and the main engines had already swiveled to compensate for the differential thrust before pilots Michael Smith and Francis Scobee could even begin to notice that a problem existed. But the maneuver had put the ship slightly off course, and the computers turned next to correcting the problem, to pointing the *Challenger* in precisely the right direction as a bright spot appeared below her and expanded with terrifying speed from a place the computers had no control over. Even in that expanding hell, she swiveled her left engine, trying to get the trajectory right. There is something almost humorous in that final, useless gesture—but don't laugh. She was only doing her best.

Twice in one century, Man's proudest machines had crumbled under his feet and disappeared into the Atlantic—quenching all illusions of safety.

In retrospect, we know what went wrong, and it is easy to point accusing fingers. But cruise ships might still be plying the oceans today, with mathematical discrepancies between passengers and seats on lifeboats, if not for the *Titanic* disaster.

Strange, how events can come unstuck in time and wrap around themselves. And strange, too, to think that Bob Ballard might have drowned on the *Orca* if not for the Coast Guard, and all-night radio vigils, and other safety measures instigated by the loss of the *Titanic*. By dying, the *Titanic* saved him, so he could one day go to the *Titanic*.*

Titanic…Challenger…"It's part of our vocabulary," Bob had said…a titanic undertaking…a titanic disaster…

Within minutes of the *Challenger* explosion, even as an observer at the Kennedy Space Center cried out, "Oh, God! Don't let happen what I think just happened!" the Pentagon was on the phone to Woods Hole.

Tom Dettweiler remembers: "The *Argo*-Rise expedition had ended on December 28, and we had scheduled the robot to be moved off the *Melville* when we docked in Mexico. *Argo* was supposed to sit in the storage yard for a week and then be put on a cargo ship and sent to Los Angeles. But like everything that happens in Mexico, it didn't happen. And *Argo* sat there, and sat there, and then the *Challenger* accident occurred.

---

*For quantum mechanics enthusiasts only: We can imagine two universal histories. Either Bob Ballard lived because the *Titanic* had instigated new safety regulations. Or Bob Ballard died on the *Orca* in 1959 because the regulations did not exist, because the *Titanic* did not sink in 1912. Can this mean that, if we choose a universal history in which Bob Ballard had died on the *Orca* in 1959, that the *Titanic* could not have sunk in 1912? Can the future define the past?

"We were called by the Pentagon and put on alert. They wanted *Argo* made ready for the *Challenger* search, and we immediately got on the phone to find out where our equipment was. It was in fact still sitting in Mexico, so we got our agents in California working on it. Within hours *Argo* was on a ship headed for Los Angeles. Trucks were waiting when the ship arrived, and our containers were the first to be unloaded. They put two drivers in each truck and they immediately took off and drove nonstop all the way across the country.

"Normally, bringing truckloads in from Mexico is a major customs problem. This time, the customs people put the cargo under bond and placed seals on the trucks. A customs agent met us at the Woods Hole parking lot when the trucks arrived. Essentially all he did was open the doors—which we were doing anyway—poked his head inside and said, 'You guys got work to do. Go do it.'

"And within days of being put on alert, we were ready to go—yet when we first got the call we didn't even know where our equipment was. The thing was, after it got here, we didn't quite know where it was going. The Navy wanted *Argo*'s cameras—the ones that filmed the *Titanic* and the East Pacific Rise. They have an ASA of two hundred thousand, which means they can practically see in the dark. They didn't want *Argo,* they just wanted her eyes, to be grafted onto their mini nuclear sub, the *NR-1.* I told the commander of the *NR-1* that I couldn't give him *Argo*'s cameras because I had a commitment to get *Argo* ready for the search. He told me I had to do it, and I said, 'Well, you can't tell me I have to do it unless you can also tell me that I don't have to be ready to respond with *Argo.*'

"He made a few quick phone calls around Washington and came back and said, 'No, I can't tell you that.'"

As it turned out, the cameras went to *NR-1,* whose crew quickly learned that, sooner or later, *Argo* must be called to *Challenger*'s grave. The entire area had to be mapped, because old rocket parts that had been lying on the bottom for twenty years were hard to distinguish from *Challenger* debris. The *NR-1* searchers wasted a great deal of time investigating false targets. It was a bone-chilling thought, but maps had to be made, by *Argo,* so that when it happened in the future, searchers could tell *Challenger* wreckage from new wreckage.

And it would happen again. No bridge was ever built that did not cost lives. What was unbelievable was that a shuttle accident had seemed unbelievable. Even after you'd seen it, lying in pieces on the bottom, it was still unbelievable. The loss of the *Titanic* could not have been very different.

*Titanic…Challenger…*Tom Dettweiler pondered the similarities as he waited on call for the *Challenger* search…as he learned everything he could about the Space Shuttle, as he read about NASA's reemergence from the *Apollo 1* disaster. What troubled him most was the ifs that had piled up against *Titanic* and *Challenger*…if they'd seen the berg sooner…if they'd seen the flame sooner…if the watertight bulkheads had been one deck higher…if the insulation had been one-inch thicker…if there had been enough lifeboats …if the escape boosters had not been eliminated to save money… if they'd heeded the warnings of ice…if the ice conditions had been normal (none at all). And he considered ten thousand missiles, tucked away in underground chambers, waiting to fly out against the world. Ten thousand artificial suns igniting in the biosphere. And it became too painfully clear that, to cause all of them to fly out, the ifs need only pile up against one of them.

Tom thought these things as he read an epitaph to *Apollo 1*:

How do you predict which ifs will get you in the end? You don't, because you can't see them. They're hiding down there, in the circuitry, in oxygen tanks, in an overlooked comma that should have gone into the bit error comparator, in innumerable flaws of design and logic that would squeak through undetected.

They could draw some comfort from the "fact" that they'd dredged up every possibility and subjected it to their engineers' intuition, to the scrutiny of computer simulation, even to physical tests. But none of these tools could provide a guarantee against questions unasked—and the nightmares that lurked beneath them, waiting to hatch out.

waiting to hatch out.

waiting to hatch out.

waiting to—

23

Hatch Out

EXCERPT FROM THE LOG OF CHARLES PELLEGRINO
Research Vessel: *Atlantis II*
Expedition: Dr. Aller's *Alvin*/Panama Basin/Peeper Project
Date: Monday, November 24, 1986
Time: 4:00 A.M.
Place: 5°N, 83°W, with 2.5 miles of water below, and the Galapagos
         Islands almost within shouting distançe

NASA's public relations department seems to be making some tentative strides toward recovery. Well, and why not? In a year or so the Space Shuttle should be flying again. There are people who thought they could stop us after the *Challenger* accident. Fat chance. To stop ascents to space would have been as foolish as shutting down the shipping lanes in the aftermath of the *Titanic* disaster. And so the crew of the Space Shuttle *Atlantis*—second on the roster of new flights—is at Woods Hole today. They're being marched before TV cameras, no doubt, and being asked a lot of difficult questions.

The Space Shuttle *Atlantis* is named after the Woods Hole research vessel *Atlantis,* and it was hoped that we would be there to greet the astronauts. It would have been a memorable experience, but there are six times as many scientists requesting dive time on *Alvin* as there is available dive time. She's booked full for the next two years. And since this is *Alvin*'s garage, we had to be elsewhere.

This afternoon, as a satellite passed overhead, Captain Baker sent a message to the port office at Woods Hole.

PLEASE PASS TO VISITING ASTRONAUTS:

THE OFFICERS AND CREW OF THE RESEARCH VESSEL "ATLANTIS II" WELCOME YOU TO WOODS HOLE. WE ARE SORRY NOT TO BE THERE SO YOU COULD VISIT WITH US AND SEE OUR SHIP. THE VERY BEST OF LUCK IN ALL YOUR FUTURE VOYAGES.

SINCERELY
ALL HANDS HERE

Challenger...Titanic...Atlantis II...

Last summer the *Atlantis II* went to the *Titanic*. In that short phrase, in that simple fact, lies enough irony to keep historians amused for a very long time.

But there is more. There are forty of us aboard the *Atlantis II*. I learned during our first boat drill that our lifeboat holds twenty-five. The lifeboat is reserved for the crew. The scientists are obliged to crawl into rubber suits (if there is time), jump overboard, and hope that depth-charge canisters mounted on the deck will release inflatable rubber rafts as the ship sinks. If anything has the power to give scientists a perspective on their real worth, it is a boat drill aboard the *Atlantis II*.

But there is more. I've had the curious pleasure of being told by a crewman that it could never come to putting on a wetsuit and jumping overboard. "Haven't you noticed that you have to walk up and down stairs or ladders to get anywhere on this ship?" he said. "That's because of the unique arrangement of the *Atlantis II*'s watertight bulkheads. Unless we capsize, like the *Melville* almost did in a storm, this ship is unsinkable."

The unsinkable ship. That's an interesting thing to be thinking about, if ever you find yourself standing without a lifeboat on the deck of a ship that just came back from the *Titanic*'s grave and is named after a mythical continent that we remember only because it *did* sink.

24

Mission to Destiny

July 12, 1986

Captain Baker gave his navigator a fictitious target some 800 miles due east of Woods Hole. He was sending the *Atlantis II* on the proper heading, but the distance he gave would have taken his ship right over the top of the *Titanic* and far beyond it. Bob Ballard had told the captain that he didn't want anyone except Tom Dettweiler and the other members of his scientific party to know the location of the wreck.

Keeping the *Titanic*'s exact latitude and longitude secret was the least of Baker's worries.

"It's that guy from England," said a messenger from the radio room. "He claims to have a helicopter."

Baker grinned. They hadn't even arrived, and already it was turning into a circus. The media were pressing in from all directions, trying to grab every possible scrap of information while the expedition was still a hot, breaking story.

What to do with all the photographs, videotapes, and verbal descriptions of the things they were about to see? In the months that had just passed, the institution and the Navy had decided that all photos and information would go to Woods Hole—encoded. There, they would dispense the news. Theoretically, everyone would have equal access to the story. No one would be able to grab an exclusive. Preventing this was becoming the captain's biggest headache, next to what he was going to do about Bob Ballard. Or what he was going to do about the Navy, which had sent an escort ship and bumped scientists from the expedition by putting three officers and a public relations man aboard the *Atlantis II*. Or what to do about the BBC representatives, who managed to bump a few more scientists. Or what to do about their boss. The "guy from England" was determined—absolutely determined—to come aboard. His excuse was that he owned the TV camera and the company that was producing the documentary and he wanted to be certain that his men were doing a good job. Presently he was said to be flying out in a helicopter and was willing to pay $90,000. Captain Baker decided that the man was an out-and-out newshound in search of a scoop. He kept changing his plans. First he was going to fly out, tour the ship, and go. Then he was going to come and stay and ride the ship in. And it just went on and on.

"Listen," Baker radioed back, "I've spoken with Dr. Steel, the director of Woods Hole Oceanographic Institution, and he tells me that you signed a contract with us as to what is supposed to happen and what is not supposed to happen. Flying out here in a helicopter is simply not supposed to happen."

"I'm coming out and I'm coming aboard the ship."

"No, you can't come because I don't have room enough for you. You'll have to get your information from the institution, like everyone else."

"But I have a right—"

"*I* have a right to refuse you permission. You'll never get aboard my ship. I can assure you of that—*one hundred percent*."

There. That ought to keep him back, thought Baker. I imagine he'll continue to protest, but he'll never—

Now, the captain looked at his watch and saw that the *Atlantis II* was about to overshoot its target. It was almost 9:30 P.M. when he walked onto the bridge and said, "Okay. Stop here."

The precision depth sonar showed the water to be just a tad shallower than the level recorded for the *Titanic* in 1985. Successive pings revealed a slope toward a familiar canyon. Baker ordered a course change.

At that moment, one member of Navstar's constellation of global positioning satellites was coasting 10,900 miles overhead. Using positioning pulses from the satellites, the exact locations of the *Atlantis II* and *Alvin* could be determined within a few tens of meters on a map of the world. This would be accomplished by laying down a net of three sonar transmitters on the sea floor. Each transmitter became the corner of a triangle ten miles on a side, with the *Titanic* lying somewhere in the middle of the triangle. You fixed your position on the Earth by first fixing the positions of the three beacons, and you did this by letting the ship's computer determine its distance from the satellite—measured as the travel time of radio waves flying back and forth between ship and space and satellite at the speed of light. The computer then collated this information with signals from the triangle's three corners, and the rest was all a matter of simple triangulation mathematics—high school stuff.

Baker was a cautious man. Knowing he was in the vicinity of the wreck, the first obvious move would be to go chasing after the target with the ship's echo sounder. He could have found it in minutes. He might also have found it in hours, or days. After much thought, he had decided that when he knew he was near the *Titanic,* he would turn the global positioning computer over to Ballard's lab and have them immediately lay out a navigation net, rather than go after the *Titanic* straightaway. In keeping with Bob Ballard's desire that the wreck's location remain secret, only the scientific party would know exactly where the sonar transmitters were put down.

This decision quickened the mounting friction between Bob Ballard and the *Alvin* pilots. Even before they sailed out of Woods Hole, Bob had struck a sour note by telling reporters that the mission saddened him because *Alvin* would be piggybacking a robot to the *Titanic,* a robot whose descendants would ultimately put *Alvin* out of business. "*Alvin* is doomed," he said.

Alvin mechanic David Sanders felt as if Ballard had just shot his team right down. The mission was turning out to be all Bob Ballard and his faithful robot sidekick "*JJ*." Basically, *Alvin* is nothing, David thought. That's how Bob sees it. Yet if it wasn't for all of us on the *Alvin* crew busting our butts putting in new motors and rebuilding the sub during the months before the expedition, Ballard wouldn't be here today. David remembered working until late at night mounting *Argo*'s 200,000-ASA cameras on *Alvin*'s face, tearing out battery packs to make room for equipment and just crashing on the ship night after night at Woods Hole. His house was in Woods Hole, but he never got a chance to go home. He was too busy setting up for *him;* and—right, "*Alvin* is doomed."

And the sonar transmitters belonged to the *Alvin* crew, but they weren't allowed to put down their own transmitters—all in the name of "strict security." That's what stuck in every pilot's mind: strict security. They weren't allowed to talk to their families on the ship-to-shore without a Navy information officer or the captain or *both* of them and Bob standing by. They weren't allowed to take photographs or keep diaries without their becoming the property of Woods Hole and the Navy.

Security…it wasn't as if we were tangling with another Russian submarine, thought *Alvin* pilot John Salzig.* This was the *Titanic*. This information was supposed to be public domain. But I'm not allowed to mention the wreck to my parents for fear that they'll talk to a reporter and give someone an exclusive story. I'm allowed to take Bob and his people two-and-a-half miles down to the bottom of the ocean and have their lives, but I can't have one 36-exposure roll of film, or put my own transmitters overboard.†

---

*The *Alvin* crew has a story that puts *The Hunt for Red October* in the Little Leagues; but you'll never hear of it—at least not in this book.

†Bob Ballard's main concern was that a certain wealthy oil man, who planned to retrieve artifacts from the *Titanic* and hoped eventually to raise it, would love nothing more in the world than to know its exact location. Anyone who knew where the beacons were automatically knew where the *Titanic* was, and though it probably would not take long to find, and fire, the engineer or pilot who provided such information, he might not care a great deal, for his financial needs would probably be taken care of well into the next century. Hence, the fewer people who knew, the better. The temptation to talk was too big—as demonstrated by the fact that the oil man was willing to pay $6000 for a single thread of carpet from the *Titanic* (part of a larger piece that someone had grabbed as a souvenir, and then fashioned into a slipcover for a piano stool). As for raising the *Titanic,* the fact that it lies broken in

John felt as if they didn't trust him to do the job properly, even though he'd deployed the beacons dozens of times before. He was preparing *Alvin* for the next day's launch when word came to him that someone on Bob's team had thrown one of the transmitters overboard without tethering it to its recovery system. It will be lying down there gathering dust for the next thousand centuries, "but that's okay," said one of the pilots. "We can even the score. Just kick one of Bob's cameras overboard the next time he has his back turned."

By 2:00 A.M. the navigation net was down and a new global positioning satellite was rising on the horizon. Once he knew the positions of the transmitters—and he was one of only a handful of people who knew exactly where they were—it was easy for Captain Baker to pinpoint the latitude and longitude recorded for the *Titanic* during the 1985 expedition. Directly he drove the *Atlantis II* through the center of the net, with the naval escort *Ortolon* tagging behind. Fifteen minutes later both ships were hovering over the wreck. Baker could distinguish the bow on his echo sounder. It was that easy. You could find it with a common tuna boat's sonar, if you knew where to look. For that reason he knew it would be unwise to reveal the *Atlantis II*'s location. Salvors had already been talking about bringing up artifacts. They planned to lower plows at the ends of long cables, dragging the bottom in search of teacups embossed with the White Star insignia. Last year's reconnaissance had revealed whole fields strewn with china. It must have spilled out of the kitchens when the stern broke off. Hopeful salvors would probably break a hundred teacups for every one they recovered, and if they recovered a dozen....Hoping to prevent it, Baker and Ballard

---

pieces makes the job easier. A ship capable of hauling large portions of wrecked (Soviet) submarines from depths of three miles already exists (currently in "mothballs") and could be adapted to the task. However (ethical considerations aside), the pieces would have to be put immediately into giant tanks of cold, fresh water, and then pumped full of electricity for about two years, to prevent the metal from crumbling into red dust. Only then could restoration begin. The price tag for total restoration: $3 billion (give or take a few hundred million dollars). No government can justify such an expense; but an eccentric billionaire with an urge to turn the *Titanic* into his private yacht needs no justification except the urge, although the story might end with someone equally mad arranging for some nasty leaks on the starboard side the first time it sails.

had decided that all published accounts of the *Titanic*'s position would be fictitious—off by twenty miles or more. That far off, salvors will have a hard time finding the wreck. The captain was determined to try anything short of murder to keep the secret, though he'd known men he would have killed with fewer qualms than letting the *Titanic* get raped.

"What's going on?" asked a passing ship. "What are all the lights about? Over."

Baker had expected to have run-ins with people trying to find the location of the *Titanic* by finding the *Atlantis II*. But this query was from a transient, a cruise ship following its normal course to Europe.

"Do you read me? What are all the lights about? Over."

"We're doing some oceanographic research," said Baker. "Over."

"Sounds interesting. Are you the *Calypso*? Over."

Baker had no intention of revealing his ship's name. Too many people had heard it on the news. Simply utter *Atlantis II* and the caller would guess immediately what kind of oceanographic research was being done, if he hadn't guessed already. Surely he knew that his cruise ship was passing near 41°46′N, 50°14′W, and anyone who sailed on salt water knew what those coordinates meant. Telling him what ship he was seeing might give him an even clearer fix.

"Who are you?" the caller pressed.

To Captain Baker's relief, his support ship came up. "This is the United States naval vessel *Ortolon,* and we're undergoing some experimental investigations here. Over."

That cured the caller's push for more information. The exchange would be repeated nightly, for the *Titanic* rested beneath one of the Atlantic's major shipping lanes. Each time, the *Ortolon* broke in and shut the transients up; and none of them ever learned that they were talking to the *Atlantis II*.

July 13, 1986

On the first dive, Bob Ballard brought with him the *Atlantis II*'s toughest and most experienced *Alvin* pilots: Ralph Hollis and Dudley Foster. They would go down for reconnaissance. Judging from the previous year's pictures, the *Titanic* appeared to be in pristine condition. Even the deckwood seemed to be intact. Yet, for all anyone knew, the pictures might be lying. She might be so badly corroded inside that her steel plates were merely a house of cards. Even with an underwater weight of only two hundred pounds, *Alvin* might collapse the deck and be pulled below. Of course, if the crew ever got into that kind of trouble, *Alvin* could open up like a clamshell and eject the sphere to the surface. But a good pilot didn't get into a situation like that.

Bob recalled a curious parallel as he considered the house of cards scenario. It was almost identical to one of the more hair-raising theories about the surface of the moon. Neil Armstrong and Buzz Aldrin had been warned that lunar dust might be so deep and so loosely packed that it would act like quicksand. It seemed that getting sucked below the surface was a vision reserved exclusively for men contemplating landing in a strange place for the first time.

So the first dive would be a search for traps in waiting. Perhaps there would even be time for a very gentle landing. The two chief pilots also planned to judge the difficulty of potential landing sites against the skill levels of their junior pilots. And, of course, they'd give *Jason Junior* its first pressure test. "*JJ*" was a roving eyeball attached to *Alvin* by an umbilical cord. It was little more than a video camera enclosed in a crystalline sphere with propellers. You flew it from inside the submarine, like a remote-controlled toy. It was a mere parody of the stereo-eyed, multilimbed *Jason* that Bob hoped to eventually bring into existence; but it was, as such, an ancestor of what could be. It was an early, telepresent species.

Yet even if telepresence had already reached the stage where you could put on a helmet and be convinced you were there without leaving your living room, Bob Ballard understood that only by putting himself there could he truly feel the *Titanic*'s presence. No, he thought, Buzz Aldrin would never have pissed his pants, cried out, "Magnificent desolation!" and then suffered a nervous breakdown if he'd simply looked at the moon through a helmet. And Bob Ballard would never have wept and hung up on Tom Brokaw had he not been standing where fifteen hundred people died moaning and bleeding under the stars. No...you can buy a lifelike copy of a Gauguin or a Van Gogh, but only the original can touch your spirit and bring you to tears.

Bob Ballard was determined to see the *Titanic* with his own eyes, and *Alvin* gave him the opportunity. Tom Dettweiler and the others remaining aboard the *Atlantis II* would have to settle for the pictures and descriptions Bob would bring back. They did not have the luxury of telepresence provided by *Argo* the year before. They had to work with *Argo's* ancestor *Angus* rather than *Argo* itself, because *Argo* required a larger scientific party. Ten people were needed to support *Alvin*, so automatically they'd cut the scientific party by ten. Add to this *JJ's* support team. And add to this the Navy officers and TV crews, and there simply wasn't enough space left aboard the *Atlantis II* to take a large support group for *Argo*.

Angus was simpler—merely 35-mm cameras and strobe lights towed on a sled, with *Argo's* down-scanning sonar mounted on front, looking forward, so they could get an indication of anything big sweeping up ahead and haul the sled up on its cable before it became just another hole in the *Titanic*.

For Tom Dettweiler the lack of telepresence removed some of the excitement he'd felt the year before. In the *Argo* control room, bathed in red light, staring at sonar displays and being surrounded by TV screens, he eventually came to feel as if he were part of the system, as if the robot's eyes were actual extensions of his eyes and that he was down there seeing what *Argo* was seeing. Telepresence had been a very real factor. He'd felt much closer to the *Titanic* then. Over there, directly ahead, was where Frederick Fleet first saw the iceberg. And down there, to the right, was where Thomas Andrews ushered Miss Sloan into the last lifeboat.

Angus could give no live coverage. You brought up film on the sled, developed it, and looked at it after the fact. But it was not merely the lack of telepresence that quenched much of the excitement for Tom. It was also the fact that he'd had a whole year to take in the shock of the *Titanic's* first sighting, to sort it out in his head and adapt to it. He was finally feeling human again: able to spend time at home with his wife, to play games with his children. And most of the time he did not think of the ghost under the Grand Banks...most of the time.

Bob, too, seemed different. Tom noticed not the slightest sign of depression in him. He wouldn't have expected that, to look at him last year. A year ago, Tom would have worried about Bob going to the ship directly; but it was clear today that sitting on the actual decks of the *Titanic* would pale by comparison to the emotional impact of those first pictures.

No one really understood why this was so. Tom guessed that after studying videotape footage and photographs for a year, even the extreme things could become routine. She was simply a part of their everyday lives now, so Bob was merely excited and intense as he climbed into the submarine on the morning of July 13, 1986. There would be no hanging up on TV anchormen this time. Bob looked as happy as a clam.

The happiest clam in the world.

It's always cramped inside *Alvin*. The crew compartment is a titanium bubble seven feet across. Most of the equipment is piled near the ceiling on the port and starboard sides. Only the pilot, seated in the middle of the sphere, has room enough to stand. The two passengers sit or crouch at the port and starboard view ports, under the equipment racks.

On this particular mission there was barely room enough to move your feet. There was the remote control box for *JJ*, plus the extra TV monitors needed for a robot's-eye view of the promenade deck and Grand Stairway. Videocassette recorders surrounded you completely. There was no room to do anything except crouch low and look out the window, or pop videotapes into recorders every twenty minutes. If you got tired of crouching and wanted to squirm into a cross-legged, sitting position, you cradled boxes of videotapes in your lap.

"We had ten pounds of shit in a five pound bag." That's how one *Alvin* pilot characterized it.

"Contact in two-and-a-half hours," said Ralph Hollis as he pumped the air out of *Alvin*'s flotation tanks and let gravity yank them down. In seconds the sub was ninety feet under. Its white fiberglass shell was still visible from the surface—a beautiful turquoise splotch on the water. It deepened to sapphire blue and was gone.

As he watched Atlantic dawn in reverse, Bob became acutely aware of all the chance turns his life had taken to put him in this place at this time...the *Orca*...Ho...growing up in a meeting house for engineers...being assigned by the Navy to Woods Hole...a professor who decided he wasn't scientist material—Oh, yes; he almost lost this moment, then. He almost gave up and ran away to a career in accounting. Yet here he was, living in one of those special moments when something was happening, something important. He was an eyewitness to history—no, more: he was a participant in history. Sinking toward the *Titanic* through outer darkness, the *Alvin* and her three occupants seemed to be the focus of the world, as *Apollo 11* and her crew once were on another July morning seventeen years ago. But the comparison was wrong.

As far as the public was concerned, the men who went to the moon were as important as their destination. Few people really cared what the moon looked like when the Apollo astronauts got there, or what scientists might learn from its rocks. The man on the street cared only that Neil Armstrong and Buzz Aldrin were going to leave their bootprints on the Sea of Tranquility. They were heroes even before they flew. And seventeen years later, people still remembered their names. That tomb at the feet of the Grand Banks was all that the public cared to see or hear about today. They wanted to know what it looked like up close. Was it really in museum condition after all those years? Was the Marconi shack still there, and was a crewman's skeleton inside it? Ask the man on the street who Ralph Hollis was, or Dudley Foster, or Bob Ballard,* and he'd give you a

---

*Although Bob Ballard did come into the public eye after his 1986 expedition, few people knew him up to that point. He had, after all, been living in seclusion during the year following the *Titanic*'s discovery. If you missed him on John Ritter's Epcot interview (broadcast on NBC in January 1986), or on *Good Morning, America* (where he talked briefly about the *Argo*-Rise expedition on January 4, 1986), or in the *Omni* interviews (published in the July 1986 issue, which hit the stands in June), chances are you never heard of him before July 1986.

blank stare. Their names were unimportant. Their destination was all that mattered.

The bottom drifted slowly up toward *Alvin*. Seen from below, the ocean seemed as deep as space itself. The World Trade Center twin towers would have to be stacked on top of each other ten times to reach from the *Titanic* to the *Atlantis II*. The *Titanic* was still nine "twin towers" away when Ralph Hollis discovered that the sonar had begun to act flaky. With no long-range vision of its own, the *Alvin* would have to locate the wreck by using instructions called down on the mother ship's acoustic telephone. Navigators aboard *Atlantis II* would guide the pilots by charting the position of the sub's signal relative to the positions of the three transmitters deployed earlier on the sea floor.

Eight twin towers from the bottom, Ralph Hollis saw another problem developing on his monitors.

"Okay, boys," he said. "We've got trouble with one of the battery packs."

"How bad?" Bob asked. "Do we have to go back up?"

"We've had an undervolt. Okay, stand by. I'm looking at it."

The monitors showed salt water leaking into a battery tank. The batteries themselves were immersed in oil. Oil did not conduct electricity, but salt did, and salt was definitely ungood. They were going to run out of power more quickly than they'd anticipated. Hollis knew that an undervolt was something to be concerned about, but it was not life-threatening. They still had a backup battery tank for the motors and floodlamps, and enough life-support power in the sphere itself to sustain them for seventy-two hours. If they were on the bottom and both battery tanks were lost and they had to make an emergency ascent, they'd arrive on the surface two-and-a-half hours later with sixty-nine hours of life support to spare.

"What's your diagnosis?" asked Foster.

"I say watch it closely and continue down. But we're going to have to cut the trip short."

"How short?" Bob asked.

"We'll only have time to go down and spot it, get a fix, and start up again."

Alvin sank down and down and down. Two hours passed. Steel plates dropped away and Woods Hole's inner spaceship slowed to a hover. Hollis kicked on the floodlamps and pumped the motors. A gently rolling countryside of deep-ocean mud drifted forty feet below. It looked like a field of fresh-fallen snow, but it was different from the fields Bob had seen before. It was criss-crossed with the etchings of crabs and worms. It seemed as if there was more wildlife than one normally sees at this depth. And there was wind. It had transformed the landscape, piled the mud up in dunes and ripples. A stiff, half-knot current was blowing from the south, carrying with it minute particles lifted from the bottom—a dust storm in inner space. It wasn't natural: a wind down here. The sea floor is normally as silent and changeless as the mountains of the moon.

And the sea continued to gnaw at the battery pack. And the wind taxed *Alvin*'s power reserves severely, for the voice from *Atlantis II* said the *Titanic* was due south, and Ralph Hollis was forced to drive against that infernal storm. Warning alarms came on and had to be cleared. The undervolt was getting serious, and Hollis began to think about returning to the surface.

Outside, something strange had begun a crazy garden. They looked like Venus's-flytraps, but they were not plants and they stood more than a foot tall and were translucent. And their teeth looked like long sabers made of glass. The deep range was strictly alien. Two silver shapes were lying on the bottom. They were two feet wide and they resembled maple tree polynoses grown out of control. They were clearly metallic and they might have been taken for fragments of the *Titanic*…until they flapped their wings and disappeared into the night.

"Biology shit," said Bob. If it wasn't volcanic or *Titanic,* it could be ignored, as far as he was concerned. More than once he'd seen creatures totally unknown to science hauled up from the bottom and felt mild irritation at the fact that there were no biologists or formaldehyde on board. When they discovered giant clams and tube worms residing near hydrothermal vents, the ship had to be scavenged for rum and vodka—the only preservatives on hand. And so followed one of the driest cruises in maritime history.

Something really ugly skittered away from *Alvin*. It looked vaguely like the monster from that Sigourney Weaver film.

Rule: always leave the cat at home, Bob mused.

An excited voice called down from above: "*Alvin*, *Titanic* should bear fifty yards to the east."

As Hollis turned east, the bottom began to slope up along his starboard side. He was straddling the edge of a plateau. It stretched north and south for many miles. At first glimpse, with *Alvin*'s lamps illuminating only forty feet of it, Bob thought he was looking at a mound of mud pushed up by the *Titanic*'s impact on the bottom. But the mound was peppered with craters blasted out by falling boulders. The boulders had been stripped off North America by glaciers and deposited here by melting icebergs. They dated back undoubtedly as far as Egypt's Isis cults and the building of the pyramids, possibly as far back as the Stone Age.

Any excitement Hollis might have felt about closing in for the first sighting of the *Titanic* was broken by a rapid-fire barrage of warnings from *Alvin*'s alarms. The two pilots were still clearing alarms and watching cabin displays when Hollis looked out his forward view port and...*and there it was*—a dark and steadily growing shape directly ahead. Already it dominated the mound—as much as could be seen of it—and in seconds it was not merely a shape, but had become a wall extending as far as human eyes could see. It was a wall of steel. In places its surface was still shiny, but mostly it was a dull, drab gray, with rust breaking out all over and streaming down its sides. Hollis saw what appeared to be wrinkles in the hull, vertical cracks that started somewhere below the sediment, thrust beyond *Alvin*'s hemisphere of light, and became shadows whose tops could not be seen.

"I-see it!" Hollis announced. "And I think I see what the iceberg did. I think I see the tear."

"Let me see," Bob said. He saw only sediment outside his down-looking, starboard view port.

Hollis needed a few seconds to get the submarine stable so it wouldn't drift off. The current was fighting him at every turn. There was no time to sightsee or think about where he was. At all costs, he must not let the *Titanic* overwhelm him. That way lay lapses of attention, carelessness, and perhaps even death. Only Bob, his passenger, could afford the luxury of awe. The pilot had to extend his mind throughout the body of the sub, and include everything that was happening outside. Seventy thousand tons of water were trying to get in at him. It was a pressure sufficient to crush Styrofoam coffee cups almost out of existence, and the junior pilots liked to create conversation pieces by wiring Styrofoam objects outside. Coffee cups smaller than shot glasses; that was the meaning of six thousand pounds per square inch. If the fluid wind blowing across the plateau picked up or shifted and crashed *Alvin* against the wall with sufficient force to produce even a hairline fracture in the sphere, the narrow stream of water entering the compartment would be so powerful that a man waving a hand across it would have his fingers sliced off.

No, Hollis had no desire to become just another permanent fixture on the *Titanic*. He got *Alvin* stable in the wind. There was a loud whirr of propellers and a barely perceptible jar as he landed under the starboard bow.

Now Hollis squirmed to one side to give Bob enough time to take a quick look out the forward view port and try to determine what part of the ship they were at. Warning lights flashed menacingly on the instrument panel. One battery pack was flooded with seawater and undoubtedly finished for the rest of the expedition, perhaps forever. The other pack was running low on power.

"Better make it quick," Hollis said. "I've got to pull the plug."

Bob had studied the deck plans, he'd been studying photos and videotapes for nearly a year until he thought he knew her…882.5 feet long…displacement 66,000 tons…the numbers rolled easily off the tongue, but there was one thing no videotape or photograph or deck plan could possibly convey—and that was the size of her.

She was bigger than he'd expected her to be. He had to remind himself that the thing was almost as large as an aircraft carrier, that the broken off forward half alone dwarfed the *Atlantis II*.

And he could see only a tiny piece of it. Human eyes simply weren't sensitive enough. The 200,000-ASA cameras borrowed from

Argo could see ten times farther, to distant steel plates illuminated only faintly by *Alvin*'s lamps. Bob glanced at the camera monitor and saw no end to the wall of steel. And directly ahead, only a few feet away, were the cracks. Steel plates had buckled and sprung. Rivets were popped. On the other side of the wall lay the bulkhead between the fourth and fifth watertight compartments.

A picture began forming in Bob's mind. For years people had been talking about a gash dug in the ship's side by the spur of ice. Now he saw rivets popping and inch-thick plates of steel bending out of shape to let water in between suddenly mismatched seams. Instead of a gash he now imagined a three-hundred-foot-long series of leaks. The picture was only half true, for it was derived from the wrong evidence.

Identical cracks were waiting to be found on the exact opposite side of the ship, where the iceberg never made contact. The damage outside the forward view port occurred nearly three hours after the collision with the iceberg, during those first seconds of contact with the bottom.

The *Titanic*'s bow nosed into the side of the plateau at slightly more than thirty degrees, burying its head almost up to the anchors. She was dropping almost vertically, then, and the sediment of the plateau held her head as if it were embedded in glue, while inertia kept everything aft—the superstructure of the captain's bridge and the uncountable tons of water falling in behind the descending wreck—pushing full force toward the bottom. She must have been traveling near forty miles per hour, and the physics behind the destruction that followed is as simple as breaking a stick over your knee, as simple as your ribs continuing forward into the steering wheel after you have stopped your car against a brick wall at forty miles per hour. The *Titanic* snapped like an old stick. The foredeck is still slanted down thirty degrees, while the captain's bridge, located just aft of the bulkhead separating the fourth and fifth watertight compartments, is level with the bottom.

Inertia broke her ribs, buckled her sides like an accordian. That's what Bob Ballard was looking at: the *Titanic*'s broken ribs.

For long seconds, he stood dumbstruck by the giant that had

come out of the dark and now filled his world. For a moment—just for a moment—that sense of depression began to well up inside of him again. And then Hollis motioned him back to his post at the starboard view port. More important things were afoot. The current was dragging *Alvin* north, and the remaining battery tank was draining fast.

Now, after only two minutes, it was time to leave. Hollis started the motors and began pulling clear of the hull. There was a slight jolt as steel ballast dropped away, and the sub started its one mile-per-hour ascent.

For human eyes, there was nothing but black outside. Bob turned to the TV monitor and began manipulating the controls. The *Titanic* was moving away as fast as he could swivel the outside cameras. He supposed he got a clear view of the portholes for perhaps a half second, and that half second would haunt him for the rest of his life. Straining to snatch up details of the receding *Titanic*, the portholes struck him as resembling the eyeless sockets of a skull.

25

An Unnatural Calm

"Bob Ballard is blessed." says *Alvin* pilot Paul Tibbetts. "After seeing the *Titanic* for only two minutes, it looked as if the entire expedition might be over—and it should have been over. Under normal conditions there was no way we should have been able to fix *Alvin* and send her back down. She came up with one of her main battery tanks flooded with water. It had to be rebuilt and put back in. This is very intricate work. It could only be done in port, on steady ground. The closest port was St. John's, Newfoundland. It was about a day-and-a-half steaming each way.

"But the strangest thing happened. The Atlantic suddenly got very calm. It was—there were no waves at all. We'd never seen the North Atlantic so quiet. I'm telling you, I doubt anyone has seen it so quiet—not since...the night the *Titanic* went down.

"The *Atlantis II* was as steady as a dock on the shore—which was what we needed to do the work. Any other day and it would have been 3-foot waves—minimum. And there would have been no way possible. We're working with a battery tank that weighs twenty-six hundred pounds out of the water. It's an involved process. It takes half a day to take the tank out. You've got people sticking their arms around it and under it as you ease it out the bottom of the submarine. And then it would have taken us two or three more days to rebuild it, if it could be rebuilt. The battery pack was a real mess; but wouldn't you know it—we were doubly blessed.

"We happened to have an extra battery because during *Alvin*'s 1985 overhaul someone slipped a decimal point. We were originally going to put three battery packs in, instead of the two *Alvin* was now carrying, but all the new equipment made her so heavy that we didn't have sufficient flotation to carry all the battery tanks. We were six hundred pounds too heavy, so the short-term solution was to go with only two battery tanks, which cut down our ability to drive along the bottom at full speed. As a result we ended up with a "spare" battery tank—which should have been in the sub the whole time, but it wasn't, so we happened to have a spare.

"We were scheduled for twelve dives on the *Titanic* II expedition, and we ended up with eleven. And the reason we lost only one dive is because Ballard is charmed. He definitely is.

"The Atlantic just cleared up for him; parted the waves for Bob."

~~~~~~~~~~

26

The Ghost under the Grand Banks

> They never built another one like her; she marked the end of an age—an age of wealth and elegance which was swept away only two years later, by the first of the world wars. Oh, they built faster and bigger, but no ship ever again matched the luxury of the R.M.S. *Titanic*. It broke too many hearts when she was lost.
>
> —*Arthur C. Clarke*

"Contact in one minute," said Hollis.

Forward...ten feet, down two and a half, kicking up some red dust...

Alvin's propellers sent a rusty powder swirling. Mingled with it were needles of pulpy matter. The deckwood was disintegrating as they descended toward it. Most of it appeared to have been eaten away, and what remained looked like pieces of sponge bored through and through by worms.

In about thirty seconds, thought Hollis, we'll know if she's a deck of cards. No one really believed the ship had deteriorated into a stack of steel plates, standing up and waiting to collapse as soon as it was touched. If that were the case, the half-knot current—which did not belong here—should have collapsed her long ago. Even so, Hollis would land with caution, and be ready to lift off and run for it if he had to.

Four forward...drifting right...

The forecastle below him, from which Hemming had realized the *Titanic*'s fate, was slanted down thirty degrees. Hemming had never mentioned the foredeck being so out of line with the rest of the ship. No iceberg did this. Something happened on the way to the bottom, Hollis guessed. But there was no time to figure it out.

Drifting right...

Foster watched the monitors. Ballard watched the swirls of pulp. Hollis slowed the motors and made contact. Nothing happened. Absolutely nothing. He slowed them further, and still nothing happened.

Okay, engine stopped...*descent engine override off...the Alvin has landed.*

"Oooh! It's like landing on the moon!" said Bob. And he did feel a kinship with the crew of *Eagle*. Not since Armstrong and Aldrin first looked out the window and saw the Plain of Tranquility had men known a feeling such as this. Here, near the feet of the broken foremast, on the forecastle roof, the reality of scientific achievement had once again caught up with the fiction.

Outside the view ports, the reddish-orange cloud of powder and needles that had surrounded the sub was blowing away over the port side, unveiling glittering brass capstan heads, spool-like rollers, and twin bits for securing mooring lines. Bob looked down and saw that his interpretation of last year's pictures had been wrong. What had looked like lines of teak planking lying intact on the deck were in fact little more than hollows where the planks had been. The caulking between the planks was still standing, still raised. The filled seams standing up were a mere fossil image of the planks themselves, which had become the shriveled, spongy pulp that blew apart under *Alvin's* propellers. Thousands of little white calcium tubes were strewn among the pulp. They were the lifeless shells of wood-boring mollusks or worms. Normally these animals are confined to the very lowest levels of a shipwreck. Tom Dettweiler had said that in wrecks he'd seen in other parts of the world, the wood borers never extended more than a few feet above the mud line. They shouldn't have been able to migrate this far up. How did they—?

The wind! Bob guessed. The wind must have carried their larvae up here.

Then, a thought: *If they got to the top deck...?*

Bob began to sweat. There flashed through his horrified mind a fast-forward movie of a worm that lived in small numbers on the bottom, managing to survive by feeding on whatever died or fell out of the sky, by living in an environment so difficult that other organisms simply didn't bother—or couldn't. By happy circumstance, these creatures were able to digest wood—though it normally did not come into their world—and one morning in 1912 food fell out of heaven. Wherever the wind circulated through the ship, it carried their larvae...to the top deck, to the gymnasium and the Grand Stairway...in a few short years their numbers must have surged into the millions...into the billions.

And now their dead shells littered the foredeck. They probably diminished in numbers as the wood disappeared, starved to death during a famine of their own creation.

Well, God damn them! Bob thought. What would the Grand Stairway look like after the larvae-laced wind blew through it? Was there even a rotten remnant of the delicately ornate woodwork of the first-class dining saloon?

Hollis tapped Bob on the shoulder and pointed. "Over there, to your left, they look like stalactites."

Bob hadn't noticed. He'd been too preoccupied with nightmares about the wood, and hopes that there might be sealed off sections of the ship, compartments full of anoxic water, places that the wind and the worms never got to. Unfortunately, those sections would also be sealed off to exploration by the robot *JJ*.

Stalactites. Yes. Hollis was right. There were stalactites on the *Titanic*. They looked just like the formations he'd seen hanging from the roofs of caves. But these stalactites weren't created by limestone drippings, they were made by iron flowing down the sides of capstans and rollers and—how did that happen?

"Rustsicles!" Bob said. "Rust icicles. As the iron dissolves, it recrystalizes into stalactites."

"Sure. I'm reading more oxygen in the water than you normally find at this depth," said Foster. "The iron must be slowly oxidizing."

"Yes," said Bob. "The current and the oxygen have finished her.

There can't be many places like this on the ocean floor. The *Titanic* was unlucky to the very last. If she'd fallen almost anywhere else she'd probably be in perfect condition right now. She couldn't even sink in the right place."

Oxygen had very little to do with the deterioration of the *Titanic's* iron, and the three explorers should have guessed as much from the brass capstan heads—which displayed no sign of wear and tear, or oxidation. Their polished appearance in the previous year's photos had led Bob to believe that all the *Titanic's* metal was in a similar condition. In his present disappointment he dismissed the clean brass as the result of scouring by the current (though nearly seventy-five years of scouring would also have removed the manufacturer's delicately engraved numbers from the metal, and the numbers were completely unmarred), or to some kind of electron exchange taking place between the brass and the iron (though brass, copper, and silver fixtures would be found lying on the bottom completely out of contact with iron, and still they would be just as shiny). Evidently, salt water at high pressure was squeezing into the spaces between microcrystals in the iron to create undersea stalactites. Perhaps iron-oxidizing bacteria also played a role. Why brass and tin and other easily corroded metals were immune to this effect and failed even to tarnish remains one of the *Titanic's* unsolved mysteries; for if you threw a brass tool into one of New England's marshes, it would be ruined after only a few weeks in salt water. More than seventy years had passed aboard the *Titanic,* yet every brass lamp the *Alvin* crew would see over the next few days, every silver goblet, every copper pot, would look absolutely new.

Hollis lifted off. Flying into the wind, he swept *Alvin* into a graceful bank, as if it were a helicopter, and headed aft. From an altitude of twelve yards, Bob looked out his view port and saw only darkness below. He turned to the TV monitor. *Argo's* deep-penetrating cameras showed the crow's nest passing beneath his feet. It was still attached to the foremast, which lay broken across the bridge.

The sub circled the bridge and turned down along the liner's port side, passing beneath the davit for Collapsible D—Mary Sloan's boat, the last boat down. A wooden block still dangled from the davit head. The worms had been unable to climb out on the davit and the wood appeared to be in perfect condition.

Hollis paid close attention to the steel cables he found hanging over the side. They were big; three inches in diameter—stays for the foremast and smokestacks, probably. The pilots judged that they were more like solid objects than something they should worry about getting tangled in.

Alvin glided up to the promenade deck, hovered there for a few moments, then flashed her strobe lights. Stalactites were hanging everywhere. Many of the windows still had glass in them. Bob remembered looking in one window and seeing nothing but black. Cold and cheerless, not the slightest glimmer of light was reflected back from inside. He looked in another window and its inner surface was covered with stalactites, but the outside was clean. The window frames were brass, and they, of course, looked new.

From the promenade deck, Hollis flew *Alvin* over the bridge, and then parked on it, with the bronze post of Captain Edward J. Smith's wheel standing just a few feet outside his forward view port. The wheel house had been a wooden enclosure. By now, no one was surprised that the roof and walls were gone. The worms would surely have gotten to them.

But the pictures coming in from *Argo*'s TV cameras hinted that the wood might not have been there when the worms arrived. The starboard wing bridge looked as if a mighty fist had struck out from the wheel house and exploded it from the inside. The damage had been seen in the 1985 pictures and attributed, then, to the first smokestack falling across the starboard side. But a smokestack crashing down upon the roof of the wing bridge would simply have crushed it flat, not peeled it open from the inside while, at the same time, leaving the lamppost on top of the roof untouched. And the smokestack never came anywhere near the port side, yet the port wing bridge was peeled open in a manner identical to the starboard wing bridge. In the center of the bridge and on both sides, all the sheet metal bulkheads forward of the wheel had been wrenched apart and bulldozed toward the bow.

Aft of the wheel, the steel roof seemed to have caved in on the officers' quarters. But it wasn't merely a matter of the roof falling in. The walls were pushed out, as though a mighty explosion had taken place directly overhead, and the center of the impact was in the center of the ship.

Alvin was sitting in the footprint of a downblast. A funnel of water had fallen in behind the forty mile-per-hour void created by the descending *Titanic*. The *Titanic* eventually stopped, but the water did not. It pounded down with the force of a tidal wave, punching in the roof of the Grand Stairway, bending out the walls, then traveling on to shatter the stairway's highest decks.

The bridge burst apart like a ripe grape.

Farther aft—much farther aft—the stern had been cut loose by a grisly incision. Whole stacks of rooms lay bare at the tail end of the liner's forward half. Without the rest of the ship to support them, the exposed decks collapsed under the push of water, forming a wedge that deflected the downblast into the sediment, where it dug out an immense blow hole behind the four-hundred-foot-long bow section.

Narrow portions of the *Titanic* drew a smaller volume of water behind them and survived relatively unscathed. Most of the railing around the forecastle deck was still intact, except on the broad sections aft where it had been pushed out, as if by a terrific wind emanating from the center of the ship. The rails surrounding the bridge and the officers' quarters, directly in the line of fire from blown-out walls, had been stripped off the boat deck, along with the davits to boat number 4, and deposited as a spray of debris over the port side.

Downblast and broken ribs....It was difficult to believe that most of the damage surrounding *Alvin* was due to the power of inertia, and that such destruction had taken place in barely more than the space of a hiccup, seventy-four years ago.

Up to this point, Ralph Hollis did not have time for reflection, but he was parked on solid ground, and he was hungry, so he broke for lunch. That's when he could take pause, look out the window, and think about where on the planet he was. It was a pretty wild idea: eating peanut butter sandwiches on the decks of the *Titanic*, and he supposed the only thing that could ruin this moment would be the specter of the *Atlantis II* coming down and settling beside the liner.

From the forward view port, Hollis looked out across the floor of the bridge toward a horizon that was only forty feet away. It was mostly orange and red out there, and the colors faded with the distance to black and white. The only light was the light you brought with you, and *Alvin*'s lamps seemed to cast ten shadows for every object they illuminated. At forty feet it was all dark shapes. Beyond that it was simply dark. Up close, the colors were vivid: a little bit of blue and green and yellow mixed in with the orange. And over there: a white crinoid standing up—flowerlike and ghostly. Hollis could distinguish traces of green around the edges of the bronze steering post where poor officer Murdoch had made one of history's most spectacular wrong turns. Some minor oxidation of the bronze must have taken place after all, but the gears looked as if they would still turn, and he had no doubt that the post could be polished up to look brand new. He thought of William Carter's Renault town car, out there under the forecastle, about six stories down. It was all bronze fixtures. Like the post, one would have a hard time believing that it had been lying since 1912 on the floor of the Atlantic.

Hollis guessed that he saw the *Titanic* differently than the others. If you can imagine a ghost ship, he thought. If you can imagine the *Flying Dutchman*—or the artists' renderings of it, with the moon shining through the rigging and moss hanging down from its masts...just a vague outline...the paintings instill in you a real sense of mystery, a feeling of ghostliness. That was the impression he was getting from the *Titanic*. It was something out of a ghost story. As he thought about it, he understood that if he'd approached an artist before he came here, and asked her to let her imagination fly far and wild, so she could paint a picture of the *Titanic* lying on the bottom as a ghost ship, it would have come out just the way it looks—and oh it looks exactly like a ghost, with stalactites hanging down everywhere, like *Flying Dutchman* moss. When you go up to a window and you look in the window and it's dark inside

—*there's mystery in there*—

You can't see it, but you *know*. You know the ship is still full of mystery.

27

JJ and the Pit

They glided down from the bridge, down past a stalactite-encrusted placard that warned in bold brass letters:

THIS DOOR FOR USE
OF CREW ONLY

The submersible skimmed low over the starboard side. The wash from its motors tugged at a spongy mass of dark red deckwood, riffled a crinoid's feathers, pulled loose a tiny white crab and cast it overboard. There was a moment's hesitation, and then it landed beside the ruins of the gymnasium.

Near this spot the first lifeboat was lowered away, thought Bob Ballard. At moments like this he could feel their presence: Murdoch and Bride and the Astors. Across the deck, through the large gymnasium windows, he could see that all the wood paneling which had lined the bulkheads was gone. *JJ,* the roving eyeball, was too fat to fit through the windows, so it hovered outside, sweeping a probing flashlight beam through the room. Very little was recognizable. Something inside glittered like three silver rods. Electrical wires and stalactites were hanging down from the ceiling. Stalagmites had formed on the floor. Among them Bob could distinguish the posts of T. W. McCawley's mechanical horses and camels, and an iron net meant to keep ladies' ankle-length skirts from getting tangled in the gears. Whatever machines had stood on top of the posts were gone. The ship went down vertically, so the furniture and exercise equipment probably broke away and went to the forward wall. On the way to the bottom she must have gone through such angles that all the loose furnishings were tossed around inside. Lumpy shapes were piled up in a corner—remnants, possibly, of the horses and camels and rowing machines. The orange powder covered them and softened their outlines.

In his mind's eye, Bob saw the gymnasium clean and new and well-lighted. Over there, at the far wall, J. J. Astor had sat on a bench at about 12:30 A.M., cutting open a lifejacket to show his wife what was inside. Bob could almost see their faces and hear the band playing cheery ragtime. Because he'd read so much about those final hours, he was reliving them as he sat on the decks inside the titanium shell of *Alvin*. Behind him, women and children were being loaded into boat number seven. Harold Bride stood here. Murdoch was there. Little knots of curious, confused passengers stood by and watched. Almost without exception, they were wealthy, famous, immaculate. In the darkness below, the gates to the boat deck were probably still locked against Irish farmers and their families. Slim as their chances were, they had a far greater probability of reaching the lifeboats than the Italian kitchen staff. Owing to British suspicion and animosity toward Italy, they were ushered to their quarters on E Deck aft and locked in. It was one of the strangest nights the Atlantic had ever seen: twenty people and a dog crowded into a lifeboat built for sixty-five.

Bob had read that the ship listed more and more toward the coal-heavy port side as the night wore on, and she sat now, on the bed of the ocean, still with a slight list to port. Near the end, Charles Lightoller, who had a deep, powerful voice, shouted, "Everyone on the starboard side to straighten her up!" As passengers and crew crossed over, the farmers, miners, dressmakers, and their families found openings to the top and surged up from below. Many of them were already wringing wet. Soon the boat deck was so full that people stood shoulder to shoulder jostling each other. Soon afterward the stern swung slowly into the air, and while some were pitched into the water, the majority clung to the rails or piled up against walls transformed suddenly into floors. In this position they were taken down with the ship, to pop back up to the surface long moments later and fill the air with that heart-rending sound.

The disaster was all around him. Bob couldn't hear the people, he just felt them. He remembered Mrs. Straus refusing to enter a lifeboat without her husband. "We have been living together for many years," she said. "Where you go, I go." He remembered Benjamin Guggenheim standing in his best evening clothes, asking a lifeboat-bound passenger to tell his wife that he'd gone down like a gentleman.

He remembered the Astors in the gymnasium. And the gymnasium itself...strange...strange to think that he was poking fingers of light into a room that hadn't been seen since the liner sank.

Very slowly, *Alvin* lifted straight up from the boat deck, then drifted leisurely across the sky, roughly following the spine of the *Titanic* over a bouquet of jagged steel surrounding a hole where the number two smokestack had been.

The current washing over the Grand Stairway was a serious hazard. The staircase itself was a deep pit. The pilots had no intention of getting blown inside, stuck under a ledge, and stuck forever.

Fortunately, shipbuilder Thomas Andrews had provided a solution. An iron lip ran around the edge of the pit, where the foundations of a crystal ceiling in the shape of a Tiffany lamp had once stood. If *Alvin* parked in front of it, the current would push her up against the foot-high ridge and hold her in place like a ship driven against a shoal by wind and waves. There was still some concern about tipping over into the pit, but Andrews had unknowingly provided even for this contingency. A pipe emerged through the roof of the Marconi shack. *Alvin* landed there, let the wind drive her against the lip, and grabbed onto the pipe with her robot arm.

Two-and-a-half miles above, an off-duty crew member had popped a cassette of George Pal's 1953 film *The War of the Worlds* into the video deck at the after end of *Atlantis II*'s galley; but apparently something more important had caught his attention, and the film ran on and on, on and on, unwatched. In the cellar of a ruined farmhouse, Gene Barry and Anne Robinson were being menaced by a robot eye at the end of a tether. Dispatched from a Martian vessel hovering outside, it had come in through an opening in the roof.

Bob Ballard guided *JJ* down into the hole. A TV screen showed him what the robot saw at the end of its tether. The reception room was a more beautiful version of Lurey Caverns—more beautiful in having been shaped by manmade lines, and having rows of crystal chandeliers dangling among the stalactites. It was very easy to get disoriented very quickly. Stalactites were hanging down. Stalagmites were sticking up. The robot whirled onto its back, and continued whirling, and through its eye Bob could not tell up from down, for stalagmites looked just like stalactites. Every time the tether touched one of the iron oxide needles it crumbled into orange powder—which was promptly sprayed all over the place by the churn of *JJ*'s propellers.

Damnation! Bob thought. We need robots that can avoid obstacles automatically. And determine up from down. And we need them untethered.

The TV screen showed a swirl of dust clearing away. *JJ* was two decks down, yet the only trace of the stairway seemed to be the tall columns that once supported it. A crinoid growing on the wall testified that the deep wind brought enough oxygen into the shaft to sustain life. By now it was no surprise that all the wood of the stairway had vanished, that a billion calcium tubes lay in its place.

Surely there were chambers within the ship unreachable by wind and worms, places where oak panels and horsehair sofas were still intact, where cheeses were still edible. Most of the portholes they'd seen were closed and still had glass in them. The flooded rooms on the other side—especially the ones buried under the plateau—might be the undersea equivalent of refrigerators. Surely such places must exist, but Bob would never see them. He was more held back by the tether than he cared to admit.

Glancing out a view port, Bob could see a faint glow along the far wall of the pit. The ghostly flicker of light from the decks below illuminated shapes that were dark and vague and strange. A deckhouse stood opposite that mighty space. Tall and faint, its door appeared to have been thrown unpropitiously open. He turned away from the view port, turned back to *JJ*'s control box while his pilot and copilot peered into the shimmering pool of light, while all about them the *Titanic* lay in state in her orange shroud.

28

Rendezvous

In keeping with their decree of equal access to all the networks, Captain Baker and Bob Ballard imposed a policy of strict security aboard *Atlantis II*. For Baker, censoring everyone's conversation on the ship-to-shore radio was one of his hardest tasks, because any time one of his crew made a call, of any nature, he or the Navy information officer had to be present. Bob, too, fell under the security regulations. He was permitted to talk to the networks on the satellite link, provided he outlined beforehand what he intended to say and stuck to it.

Every day, while Ballard and the pilots were on the bottom, requests for interviews would come in from TV stations, newspapers, and periodicals. Bob was allowed to talk to them in the evening, and Baker was there to make sure that all the interviews went off equally, that the information was always the same.

The media alone kept the captain hopping. But he had more important concerns, such as launching and recovering the submarine and dealing with the dirty-white mist that kept creeping in—and not on little cat's feet, either! It blotted out the whole world beyond a radius of three-hundred feet and seemed to materialize every afternoon, just as *Alvin* headed for home. It was difficult enough recovering the sub in clear weather. When she surfaced in fog, the *Atlantis II* could easily determine *Alvin*'s direction from its radio calls, but knowing her distance was another matter. The sail, the part of the submarine that stands out of the water, is fiberglass—so it doesn't show up on radar. To avoid running over the sub, the *Atlantis II* would stay still, send a rubber launch out to find *Alvin,* attach a rope to her, and haul her to the ship.

At night they reviewed videotapes brought up from the bed of the Atlantic. Captain Baker found the debris field behind the severed bow section particularly interesting. Something like a child's skull was lying on the bottom. "It scared the hell out of me," said Baker, "but it turned out to be only a doll's porcelain head."

Even some of the organic furnishings seemed to be intact. If it wasn't made of iron, or if wood borers didn't like the taste of it, it might just as well have been sitting in ice these past seventy-four years. There were redwood beams, portions of stairways…a strewn-field of gleaming copperware from the kitchens…leather suitcases …a shoe, a shirt, and a sock…a dinner jacket…a bottle of champagne with the cork and wrapping still in place…a silver seltzer water dispenser in working order…and then, the ship itself.

The broad windows of the stern's upper decks drifted across the TV screen, barely distinguishable in a large heap of metal that had pounded down amid boilers just a few hundred feet north of the fantail. The windows were glassless and horribly deformed. They were all that remained of the French café and

…(*There!*)

There, near the crushed palm veranda, on the port side of the missing fourth smokestack, was where stateroom A-36 had been. If breakup and downblast hadn't sent them scattering in pieces, then surely bacteria and scavenging organisms must have devoured the piles of deck plans and notes spread across Thomas Andrews' desk. One of those notes had been Frederick Fleet's request for binoculars.

Bob Ballard's stateroom was piled high with photocopies and blueprints. It contained every book and article worth looking at that had anything to do with the building and history of the *Titanic*. When he looked in an open window, Bob knew exactly what should be on the other side. Margaret Tobin Brown's cabin was all orange. Bedsprings and broken shapes were piled up in the corners. The colorful millionairess from Denver had attempted to take command of a lifeboat away from a crewman who refused to return to the scene of the sinking in search of survivors. Years later, astronaut Gus Grissom put in a formal request that his space capsule be named after "the unsinkable Molly Brown."* A brass doorknob still shone in her room. The posts of her bed were still bolted to the floor.

No one looked inside the Marconi shack. Officially, Bob Ballard was concerned about getting *JJ* in and out of the two rooms without snaring the tether—and the doorway was too narrow for easy maneuvering. Unofficially, Bob wondered if the bones of the man Harold Bride had killed were lying somewhere in the shadows of the telegraph room. He just wasn't ready to creep in there. He hadn't built up enough nerve.

The pictures of the bridge made Captain Baker shake his head. It was said that Captain Edward J. Smith went down with his ship. Good career move, thought Baker. After ignoring ice warnings and steaming full speed ahead into the field, they'd have crucified him in the courts. It was hindsight, of course, but Baker would never have done to any vessel what the men in charge of the *Titanic* did to her that night. He'd always been taught: you take care of the vessel, and the vessel will take care of you.

Near the end of the first week, three minutes of footage were excerpted from thirty hours of videotape and made available to the networks. The *Atlantis II* had no capability for transmitting TV pictures via satellite. Someone would have to physically come out to the middle of the ocean to pick up the released film. It was agreed

*Gus Grissom's request was denied; but the story did not end there. Even as Bob Ballard and his team probed the *Titanic*, the Smithsonian Institution was formulating a request that *Argo/Jason*, when it was completed, be used to recover Gus Grissom's *Mercury* capsule—which sank in three miles of water.

that a helicopter would meet the Naval support ship *Ortolon* outside the transponder net. The *Atlantis II* would also sail away from the *Titanic,* keeping the location secret.

The helicopter came out from St. John's, Newfoundland. The networks dubbed it their pool chopper, because it was hired through pooled money and the film was for everyone. For three minutes of videotape and a dozen color slides, the media paid $45,000—and that only covered the flight between St. John's and the *Ortolon.* They then had to get the film to New York, London, and the world.

29

Double Encounter

"As we travel throughout the ship, there's a lot of beautiful artifacts and, it's tempting, but we've made a promise to ourselves not to take anything. We've seen beautiful silver plates. They're still there.

"Also, one of the expansion seams is split open and we could look inside the bow and see a wood-burning stove.

"There's a very strong current—at least one-half knot, which makes maneuvering very difficult. There are days when *JJ* simply cannot work in the current, so we do not deploy it. We just have to wait. The currents seem to follow a three-day cycle, sort of like tides. Every third day there is almost no current at all.

"The severed stern section is about a third of a mile away from the bow. Between the bow and the stern is a field strewn with debris that fell out after the ship broke open. Yesterday was an easy day because the currents weren't so bad and it was easy to negotiate through the debris field except for the stern section of the ship. That was a little dicey. The stern is hardly recognizable. It is just a tremendous twisted pile of wreckage that is very difficult to maneuver in because it is so irregular and overhanging. Still, we inspected a large part of it, almost the size of a city block, it seems, and radiating out around it is a tremendous series of artifacts. It is actually like going to a museum, there are just thousands and thousands of items that were laid all over the bottom.

"We found reciprocating engines and three of the big boilers laying near the stern. An unbroken coffee cup rested on one of them. It must have fluttered down like a leaf and settled on the boiler, which had come crashing down.

"The most striking feature of the stern is how badly beaten up it appears to be. It landed propeller-end first, and the propellers are buried deep in the sediments. Near the break, it looks as if it had been hit by a giant explosion. The sheet metal of the upper decks is peeled back like the skin of an orange. You look at a wall with a porthole in it and there is ribbing from the inner surface of the bulkhead next to the porthole and you realize that you're looking *out* the porthole, that the bulkhead has been turned inside out. And yet many parts of the stern are recognizable. One of the cranes is still sitting in place. It's spooky. You really felt it when you were there, the sheer carnage. It looked violent and destructive. The bow is majestic. It still has some nobility. But the stern—it's mostly chaos. Yet it was amazing to see a big twisted steel bulkhead, then next to it a teacup still unbroken. To see gentleness next to massive destruction. And it was strangely peaceful and restful, that silent ship resting there slowly dissolving in the ocean."

The broadcast ended with a close-up showing a copy of the bronze plaque Bob Ballard had pushed near the lip of the Grand Stairway, using *Alvin*'s robot arm. It read:

> IN RECOGNITION OF THE SCIENTIFIC EFFORT
> OF THE AMERICAN AND FRENCH EXPLORERS
> WHO FOUND THE R.M.S. *TITANIC*; BE IT
> RESOLVED THAT ANY WHO MAY COME
> HEREAFTER LEAVE UNDISTURBED THIS SHIP
> AND HER CONTENTS AS A MEMORIAL TO
> DEEPWATER EXPLORATION

In a hundred million homes, people watched the three minutes of videotape footage. Though the pictures were repeated as often as a half dozen times on any given news program, Bob Ballard's narrative added a dimension no film could possibly convey, for the narrator had been there. He had actually sat on the decks of the *Titanic*. He had looked out his window and seen the demolished stern with his own eyes. In a dozen countries a million viewers drew their breath in astonishment. Among them, watching from London, was Eva Hart.

She was utterly fascinated, and she had nothing but applause for Dr. Ballard; but the news commentator had referred to him as being on the *Titanic*.

On the *Titanic*? thought Miss Hart. *On* the *Titanic*? He was only near the *Titanic*. *I* was *on* the *Titanic*!

In 1912, seven-year-old Eva Hart was headed for Winnipeg, Canada, where her father, a master builder, planned to start a new business and a new life. She did not complete the journey until 1980, sixty-eight years after leaving the dock at Southampton. Walking the streets of Winnipeg, the houses about her stood tall and dim and strange. This is where I would have lived, she thought. She was looking at a life that had never been.

Eva's mother didn't sleep very well the night before the *Titanic* sank. "Not only that night," she recalls. "My mother didn't go to sleep in that boat at all. She sat up every night and slept in the day-time. She had a terrible premonition. She didn't know—a premonition of what. She had a premonition of danger. Thank God she was sitting up, otherwise I shouldn't be here now.

"She made up her mind that she would rest in the daytime, while my father was awake, and my father said, 'What will people think?' and she said she didn't care what people thought."

If not for a coal strike, the Harts wouldn't have been there at all. Mr. Hart had planned to sail on the *Philadelphia*, but the strike left a number of North Atlantic vessels short of fuel. The *Titanic* needed 650 tons of coal per day to keep her pushing forward at twenty-two knots. With coal reserves limited, the White Star Line cancelled the sailings of its other New York–bound ships and transferred their coal and passengers to the *Titanic*. White Star also bought coal and passengers from competing liners, including the *Philadelphia*, whose departure had been put on "indefinite hold."

Mr. Hart thought it was a lucky break. Though it meant paying more, second-class passage aboard the *Titanic* was better than first class on other ships. When he mentioned the change to his wife, a fearful expression passed across her face and she asked, "Isn't that the ship they say is unsinkable?"

He put an arm around her and said, "Not that they *say* is unsinkable, my dear, but *is* unsinkable."

Now Mrs. Hart knew why she was frightened. It was flying in the face of God. Already it was beginning to look like a real-life reenactment of Morgan Robertson's tale of an "unsinkable" ship named *Titan* that went down the first time it sailed.

"We had no difficulty getting a lifeboat," Eva remembers, "because my mother had been sitting up and woke my father the moment she felt the impact. It came to her as a very small bump. The first thing I knew was when my father picked me up and carried me onto the deck. My mother had him come with her straightaway to the lifeboats, and he went with very bad grace, thinking there was nothing to make a fuss about. When they did launch the boats much later, I remember my father coming back from talking to one of the officers. He said it was just a precaution. 'You'll be back aboard for breakfast,' he said.

"My mother knew better.

"The last time I saw my father he was leaning over the rail watching our boat being lowered. I remember him calling out, 'Be a good girl. Stay with Mummy. Hold her hand.' And I started to wail."

Eva Hart left the *Titanic* in boat number fourteen. A boy not much older than her was found hiding under a seat as officers got ready to lower away. One of them drew a revolver on the child, telling him he was old enough to be a man, that the boat was for women and children only. The boy started to cry and the officer threatened to blow his brains out if he did not get back on the ship. Mrs. Hart and the other women in number fourteen were sobbing. A little girl pleaded, "Oh, Mr. Man, please don't shoot!"

As the lifeboat lowered away—with five of its sixty-five seats empty—Eva Hart saw the boy curled up and crying near a coil of rope on the *Titanic*'s deck. She never did see him again.

At about 1:35 A.M., ropes were unhooked and number fourteen struck out. Portholes still glowed below the surface. Pretty, thought Eva. From five feet under, in a room that was still unflooded, a man was peering out into the ocean. Adjacent portholes illuminated the white bottom of a lifeboat. Looking up, he watched it cast away.

The boat departed on the port side, below stateroom A-36 and the fourth smokestack. That portion of the stern is so badly torn up that it is anyone's guess where number fourteen's davits are.

A writer of fiction might have depicted a survivor's response to the *Titanic* photos as horribly traumatic. But reality is often more surprising than fiction. Miss Hart did not mind looking at videotapes of the deck upon which her father had stood and watched her leave, and then waited for the end. "I think the footage is absolutely wonderful," she says. "I think Dr. Ballard has done a wonderful job there. I don't feel the same about people who want to go down and bring things up. I feel very different about that. But I do tremendously applaud Dr. Ballard. I think he is wonderful, as are the pictures. I like seeing the *Titanic* at rest like this. It's fitting.

"I remember seeing it from the lifeboat…sinking. And I can't bear to look at pictures of that—pictures of the sinking ship, such as in the movies that have been made of it. Well, there's only one movie worthwhile, isn't there? *A Night to Remember*. What I saw in the lifeboat that night—the *Titanic*'s final moments—looked very much as they appear in that movie. Yes. They did indeed. Something I will certainly never forget. I just can't watch that scene in the movie. Even though it's only a model, I can't bear to look at the model. Even though Dr. Ballard's pictures are the real thing, they don't affect me in the slightest. I don't connect them with the *Titanic*. I am just full of absolute admiration that such technology exists, that such a wonderful thing can be done. But it doesn't churn me up, from the point of view of being the *Titanic*, at all. It's only that scene in the movie, and photographs of the actual ship in its entirety, at the dock in Southampton or on its way out to sea, that horrify me. What we saw on the floor of the ocean was only bits and pieces. The lights from the submarine only show you a little bit of it.*

"As for the night itself...what I felt...My God! I can tell you exactly what happened the night of that disaster and you can put it in your book in one word: *terror*."

The *Atlantis II* news release contained one particularly clear five-second sequence, shot with the 200,000-ASA camera. It showed the point of the *Titanic*'s bow from above. Visibility was more than a hundred feet, and the sequence did churn Eva Hart up a little bit. *Titanic* survivors Marjorie Newell Robb (who was twenty-three years old in 1912) and Ruth Blanchard (who was also in her twenties) agree with Eva Hart in their response to the *Titanic* photos.

30

Trace Fossils?

> What I remember about that night—what I will remember as
> long as I live—is the people crying out to each other as the stern
> began to plunge down. I heard people crying, "I love you."
>
> —*Charles Lightoller*

At first, no one understood what the shoes could mean. The explorers had become accustomed to seeing articles of clothing scattered on the bottom...a shirt here...a jacket there...and over there a slipper. These were automatically regarded as items that had fallen out of drawers and closets when the ship broke in half, and not as places where bodies had been.

They had seen no skulls or tibiae associated with the clothing, and they hadn't expected to, for only a handful of people were believed to have been trapped inside and to have truly gone down with the ship. The rest floated off the top deck, most of them in life jackets, and froze to death.

"No...no bodies there," Bob had said. So the little cluster of shoes near the demolished stern was ignored as an irrelevant oddity. Bob shrugged at them, photographed them, and then asked his pilots to drive on toward the boiler field.

Six months would pass before anyone noticed that the shoes had been deposited on the bottom in matching pairs.

Plunging down two-and-a-half miles in the flooded *Titanic*— what could be more horrifying? The only comforting thought is that it was quicker than freezing to death. Two minutes, perhaps, waiting for the severed stern to glide under, and then several seconds of rapidly building water pressure. At a depth equivalent to the *Titanic*'s length, eardrums and lungs would have imploded. By then, no one within the ship could possibly have been alive.

The pressures two-and-a-half miles down are such that large Styrofoam beer coolers will shrink smaller than beer cans and will not float up from the bottom. Similarly, if there were bodies lying near the stern on the morning of April 15, 1912, they should not have floated up.

But, no...no bodies there. There are no skeletal remains among the shoes. The shoes must have fallen out of staterooms in shoeboxes, and then the cardboard decayed, leaving behind only the pairs of leather shoes.

But, no...the shoes are, without exception, spaced almost eighteen inches apart, with the toes of each pair appearing to point in the same direction, as they would if they'd been attached to feet. If they came from shoeboxes, they should be packed side by side, literally right next to each other, not eighteen inches apart.

But, no...no bodies there. Some microorganism—something—would have had to eat the bones yet leave the shoes behind. And teeth, though they decay so easily during life, are the last things to disappear after death. They can endure dozens of centuries. There should be teeth among the shoes, if not whole skeletons.

But, no...a shoelace has survived. It is pulled snug, as if around a foot, and it is tied in a bow.

We are left to ponder unsolved puzzles: what eats teeth and bone —calcium, phosphorus, and sulfur—yet leaves leather and cloth intact? If the shoes do indeed represent places where bodies were coughed out of the fallen stern, why, then, if a shoelace has survived, are no shirts or jackets associated directly with the shoes?

(*I can tell you exactly what happened the night of that disaster and you can put it in your book in one word*)

Can this be true? Are shoes round the stern the *Titanic*'s version of Hiroshima's shadow people?

(*...in one word*)

What can be more chilling?

(*...terror*)

31

Graveyard Shift

No astronomer viewing the very first *Voyager* photos of the new worlds circling Jupiter and Saturn could have been happier than Tom Dettweiler was every time a new roll of *Angus* film was developed. He could not know the excitement of sitting on the *Titanic*'s boat deck and looking through the gymnasium windows. There was not even the secondhand thrill of telepresence, it was true, yet he was, in his own way, exploring parts of the wreck that no one else had seen before, not even Bob Ballard.

One of Tom's jobs was to find new objects for Bob to go look at. There was part of a wooden stairway lying in the debris field. Only a tiny fraction of it appeared to have been nibbled by worms. He saw hundreds of wine bottles with their corks intact, and leather suitcases, and carpet bags. Judging from the dissolving iron and the worm-eaten decks, he wouldn't have expected carpet bags to come through. Tom wondered if deep-buried sections of the bow—its head was immersed all the way up to the anchors—might be unreachable by worms and fish. If compartments of dead, stagnant water existed. If boilers and motors did not tear loose from their beds and plunge through the bow with bulkhead-ventilating force, some of the woodwork might look as if it had been underwater only since last month.

A pattern was emerging. If the *Titanic*'s organic furnishings were inaccessible to worms, as in the case of wooden blocks at the ends of davit heads, or if they were unappetizing to scavenging organisms, as were patent leather shoes and carpet bags, they remained unharmed. Had she gone down in shallower water, little more than an outer shell of inch-thick steel would remain today. She'd look very much like her sister ship, the *Britannic,* which was built after the *Titanic* disaster, with a double-hulled bottom extending up the sides. The walls that divided her watertight compartments were raised above E Deck. In theory the *Britannic* could float with the first six watertight compartments flooded, rendering her "unsinkable" by the damage that had doomed the *Titanic.* In practice she struck something on the starboard side, opening the first seven watertight compartments to the sea. Adding irony to irony, some of the *Titanic*'s lifeboats, brought to New York aboard the *Carpathia* and returned to the White Star Line, appear to have been fitted to the *Britannic* as she was being built. As the lifeboats cast off, the captain tried desperately to drive the *Britannic* toward land and beach her; but the bow dipped under in four hundred feet of water. The propellers climbed slowly out of the sea. They were still churning— churning fiercely—and the lifeboats were drawn into them and chopped up and strewn about. The *Britannic* went down vertically, like her sister; yet, unlike the *Titanic,* there is almost nothing left of her. Sixty years after she sank, Captain Jacques Cousteau visited the liner. There is not even a spongy, worm-eaten trace of her teak planking. The sheet-metal bulkheads of her superstructure have disintegrated. It is difficult to tell where the *Britannic*'s Grand Stairway used to be. There are no gleaming brass fixtures. No copper pots lying on the bottom in pristine condition. No leather. No carpet bags. Nothing except a corroded skeleton of a ship whose bronze is indistinguishable from its iron.

The preservative qualities of the deep Atlantic are not very much unlike the cold bottom waters of the Great Lakes. In both places, the temperature remains forever near freezing. A chief difference is that the stagnant waters of the lake bed do not support scavengers.

During his voyages on the *Calypso,* Tom had explored an ill-fated liner on the floor of Lake Ontario. Iron had begun to rust, but carpets and furniture were merely waterlogged. Lengths of rope were coiled over teakwood decks. The men in the engine room looked as if they had drowned yesterday; but they'd been there since 1925. Tom could still read startled surprise on their faces.

And if that was not cause for astonishment, two nineteenth-century wrecks lay with their wooden masts still standing not many miles away. The wood itself was in a condition similar to worm-protected blocks dangling at the ends of the *Titanic*'s davits. A slow bacterial assault had softened the features of an oaken figurehead. A sailor's bones lay scattered at its feet. A porthole's tin collar had dulled only slightly, and looked as if it could be polished up to look absolutely new; but iron cannons, cutlasses, boarding axes, and anchors had begun to sprout stalactites.

Looking for interesting objects was not Tom's main job. Carpet bags, safes, and wooden stairs were identified only as a by-product of the *Angus* team's mapping mission. They guided the camera sled over the full length and width of the bow, flashing strobe lights and producing an array of pictures from which a photomosaic map could be assembled. Since *Angus* did not carry air-breathing passengers, it could stay down far longer than *Alvin,* whose bottom time was generally less than four hours per day. By the end of the expedition, more than fifty thousand *Angus* photos would provide complete, down-looking coverage of the bow and stern, and a crisscross map of the strewnfield between them.

EXCERPT FROM TOM DETTWEILER'S POST-EXPEDITION REPORT TO CHARLES PELLEGRINO
Date: September 1, 1986

Dear Charles,

How good it is to be home and with the family again. Every bone still aches from long shifts with the camera sled, and I'm glad to report that the *Titanic* does not haunt me the way she did last year, after the first contact.

I know you are anxious to see the completed strewnfield map, and no doubt my earlier reports have raised a raft of questions.

Now, where do I begin? Of course you're familiar with life on the night shift from your *Argo*-Rise adventure. It was pretty much the same with *Titanic II*, except that we did not have *Argo* with us. We worked instead with the more primitive *Angus,* which we sent down every night. *Angus* was always exciting because you're flying fairly blind on a long length of wire. You only have the sonar indicator of where things are and that's very crude. Plus you have your global positioning satellite navigation, which is only precise to tens of meters. So it was really a requirement that you have a picture of the ship in your mind—and that picture was what you flew the sled by. Once you made contact with the *Titanic,* you knew where you were relative to the terrain of the ship. Sometimes you could close your eyes and fly the sled based on the picture in your mind. It's an incredible experience—it's fun. But you really didn't know what was going on until you brought the sled up and started processing the pictures. It would be midafternoon and *Alvin* would already be down there before we saw the photos. Then, based on the pictures we took with *Angus* the night before, we would call down and give them interesting things to go look at. If we saw something interesting, we knew where it was on our ever-enlarging map, based upon the time the photograph was taken—which was recorded on each frame of film. We'd go back into our navigation records and find exactly where we were in the transponder triangle at that time.

So, we'd analyze our photographs during the day. We'd see what sections of the debris field or the ship itself were missing in our coverage, plan the next night's *Angus* dive, pass on the interesting coordinates to the *Alvin* group—and that's how the *Alvin* people would plan their dives.

The *Angus* team was sort of invisible during the expedition.

We worked the sled at night, after *Alvin* surfaced and the rest of the ship was asleep.

We wouldn't put *Angus* down on the tether while *Alvin* was down there, during the day, because even if the probability of a collision was maybe one chance in a million, we didn't want to take that chance. *Alvin* will allow other equipment in the water column while she's down, as long as they're widely separated. We can, for example, put an off-load package down as long as *Alvin*'s crew knows where it is falling and can avoid it, or we can release packages from the bottom, as long as they are not in the same vertical column.

Under these guidelines it was possible to have *Alvin* down at the *Titanic*'s bow, and *Angus* a third of a mile away at the stern; but we didn't want to do that. If you're doing an operation where you're throwing a remote package overboard and letting it drop to the bottom, that's one thing. *Angus* is quite something else. To lower it or raise it on the tether takes almost two hours. Had a problem developed with the submarine, we'd have had a two-hour delay before we could respond to the submarine's needs—unless we cut *Angus* loose, and we didn't want to put ourselves in that position, so it was best not to have *Angus* and *Alvin* operating at the same time. As soon as the sub came up, in the late afternoon, we made preparations to put *Angus* in the water. And then we hauled *Angus* back on deck about the same time the *Alvin* group was making preparations to go down.

Some days, though, we had a delay. *Alvin* would come up, and then we had to do a garbage run before sending *Angus* down. The *Alvin* group does a garbage run because they operate in the same area for long periods of time, and that requires putting swimmers in the water to assist the sub and perform rescue in case of emergency. So, if they dumped garbage in the same area all the time they would attract a population of sharks, which would just hang around waiting for food every day and be a danger to the swimmers. In order to dump garbage, the ship had to go out a minimum of five miles from the site we were working. Usually they did a garbage run every other night, which delayed us with *Angus*—two hours to run, dump, and come back. It was frustrating. We had a large area to map and an amount of time that was pretty limited to begin with.

We had things we wanted to look for. We wanted to find smokestacks. We didn't. They started falling off at the surface and probably tumbled and fluttered away to distant places. We wanted to find the propellers, and all we know now is that the propellers are most likely buried with the stern section. The stern is driven very deep into the mud. We saw the top of its rudder sticking out, and that rudder was six stories tall.

There are several safes down there. We saw one safe in particular that had a big bronze handle on it and they went over with *Alvin*'s mechanical arm and pulled the handle and the brass gears turned perfectly, as if it was still on the ship, not like it was on the bottom of the ocean for almost seventy-five years. Of course, its iron sides were streaming stalactites and the safe looked a little battered from having rattled through the broken ship. The handle was bent and the door seemed out of line with its frame, or welded shut by dissolving iron. We never did learn what was inside.

For decades there has been talk of treasure in the *Titanic*'s safes; but this is only talk. About twenty minutes after the *Titanic* struck the berg, passenger Lawrence Beesley was walking up the stairs of the second-class entrance near boat number fourteen, near what would ultimately become the tear in the stern—from which the safes must have fallen. He passed the Purser's window on F Deck and noticed a light burning inside. He heard the clang of a safe door closing, followed by the hasty retreat of footsteps along the corridor leading to first class. There was little doubt in Beesley's mind that what he'd heard was a Purser clearing valuables from the second-class safes and heading forward to the first-class safes. Other passengers remember the Chief Purser passing up and down the boat deck pulling watches and jewelry out of a mail bag and returning them to their owners during the hours before the ship went down. Lawrence Beesley had left an envelope in the Purser's Office, but it was never returned to him. It contained only some money and some papers and it is probably still in the safe.* Water has undoubtedly leaked in, but if the safe is well sealed, as it appears to be, you might still be able to read the papers inside—especially since they tended to make paper out of rag in those days. They'd be of great historic value, and collector's value; and they'd probably command a higher price than jewels.

The stern section was always tough. It was scary to look at our *Angus* photos the next day, because we'd see how close we'd come to major pieces of wreckage. Being such a tangled mess, our sonar didn't respond to it the same way it responded to an intact piece like the bow. So, sometimes we didn't get a very clear indication that we were close to something.

The extreme portion of the stern, the poop deck, is fairly intact. Not very far forward, the deck is actually ripped up and peeled back, and forward of that, the sides of the ship are just layed out and the decks between them have been punched down.

---

*Charles Pellegrino comments: Lawrence Beesley's envelope contained paper money for his trip to America. The envelope was sealed, with his name written across the flap. It was handed to a purser in return for a card reading:

WHITE STAR LINE R.M.S. *TITANIC.* 208.
THIS LABEL MUST BE GIVEN UP
WHEN THE ARTICLE IS RETURNED.
THE PROPERTY WILL BE DEPOSITED IN THE PURSER'S SAFE.
THE COMPANY WILL NOT BE LIABLE
TO PASSENGERS FOR LOSS OF MONEY, JEWELS,
OR ORNAMENTS, BY THEFT OR OTHERWISE, NOT SO DEPOSITED.

The same safe should also have contained a similar envelope deposited by Eva Hart's father, Benjamin, along with his "FORM FOR NONRESIDENTS OF THE UNITED STATES. STEAMSHIP *TITANIC:* No 31444, D." During the summer of 1987, a French expedition returned to the *Titanic* and recovered the safe. It was opened at sea and was found to be empty—as Lawrence Beesley had said it would be. Not far from the safe was found a leather satchel belonging to Mr. and Mrs. R. L. Beckwith (two first-class passengers who departed in boat number five at 12:55 A.M.). It contained a pair of glasses in a leather case, American bank notes, gold chains, a pocket watch, an initialed silver jewelry box, a set of 18-karat stick pins, several gem-studded rings, a gold pendant inscribed with "May This Be Your Lucky Star," a bracelet with the name AMY spelled out in diamonds, and a bag of silver and gold British coins. On October 28, 1987, the safe was opened on global television. The satchel, too, was opened. Interestingly, it no longer contained the bag of coins. Via the miracle of television, the bag had transmigrated to the empty safe (in a plastic box).

The current added a new dimension of excitement to the expedition. *Alvin* had to avoid the open end of the stern, because it could actually be carried into the wreck and it might have been difficult to get out. The current was so strong that it was able to steer *Angus,* which is a sixty-five hundred pound sled. Shoes and things somehow appeared to stay in place on the bottom, but *Angus* was like a sail at the end of a rope—something like a kite. We'd be pulling along with a lot of momentum, set perfectly on course, and suddenly it would be steered away from the hull by the current—which had a habit of disappearing suddenly, every third day or so. On those days the submarine would rush in and try to do all the difficult areas, for example, the stern.

This situation with the currents is something we discovered only when we were down there. We didn't notice it in 1985. It wasn't something we could prepare for in advance, so it took a few days to scope this out, and plan our dive schedule around it. As for why it happens, there are a lot of major currents in the Grand Banks area. We were dealing with the very edge of the Gulf Stream. We were also dealing with the Labrador Current. They may be shearing each other, creating underwater tornadoes and driving oxygen-rich water to the bottom. The area has always been known for its good fishing. While driving water down, the currents must also be upwelling nutrients from somewhere far below.

While we were at the site, we ended up taking a sample from the *Titanic* by accident. We were cruising along, flashing *Angus*'s strobes, and we really didn't know anything unusual had occurred until we brought the sled up. As it approached the surface, we looked over the side of the ship and noticed that there was a piece of cable hanging off the sled. We brought *Angus* alongside and held it against the side of *Atlantis II*. I got Bob and told him we had brought something up—which we had not intended to do. The plan was not to recover anything. So we went out on the fantail and had a look. It was about ten feet long. It was hung up around the bridle and it did appear in some of the pictures we developed later, so it was long enough to hang down in front of

Angus's cameras. It was a piece of iron cable that had rusted. When we pulled it off the *Titanic,* we had knocked off the outer layers of rust and all we had was the center core of iron remaining. It was black and sort of slimy looking.

We decided on the spot that anything we did raise from the *Titanic* was going to go back over the side. It was never even brought on board. We just climbed on top of *Angus* and immediately pitched it over the side into the water. All we had left was the black slime on our hands. People wanted to shake our hands, perhaps to collect some of the slime—souvenirs—you never know.*

As far as I know, there were no pictures taken of the event. We did not take any *official* pictures, that's for sure.

Regards,
Tom Dettweiler

---

*The collection of souvenirs seems to be a most irresistible human drive. Despite Bob Ballard's efforts to prevent such activity, someone wiped a hand on his shirt and, right under Bob's nose, collected one: the world's first *Titanic*-slimed T-shirt.

~~~~~~~~~~~~~~~~~~

32

Verdict on the Gash

> And as the smart ship grew,
> In stature, grace and hue,
> In shadowy silent distance grew the Iceberg too.
>
> —"The Convergence of the Twain" *by Thomas Hardy*

**EXCERPT FROM ROBERT BALLARD'S *TITANIC* II
EXPEDITION REPORT**
To: Shelley Lauzon, Public Information Officer, Woods Hole
        Oceanographic Institution
Date: Tuesday, July 22, 1986

We ran along the entire length of the hull along the waterline, along the sediment line—looking for a gash—and could see absolutely no evidence of a gash. So the question is, were we deep enough to see the gash? I know up in the bow, the very bow portion, [we'd never see it] because the ship is buried so deep [in the side of the plateau]. But as we got further aft around the Bridge line and aft of the Bridge [beyond the vertical cracks where the *Titanic's* ribs had broken], we were below the water line on the hull of the ship. We could see the water intakes, we could see the copper-painted hull, so we were definitely below the water line and down where the gash should be from the Bridge on and we didn't see any [gash]. In fact, we were all the way down near the end at the stabilizing fins on the hull part that helps with the anti-roll. So we haven't seen any suggestion of the gash, but we have seen several places where the hull is buckled in and plates were sprung—the rivets were sprung. Whether that was caused by the iceberg encounter or whether that was caused by the ship's encounter with the bottom, we'll just have to sit down with a lot of people and look at it.

EXCERPT FROM A CONVERSATION WITH CHIEF *ALVIN* PILOT
RALPH HOLLIS
Research Vessel: *Atlantis II*
Expedition: Dr. Aller's *Alvin*/Panama Basin/Peeper Project
Date: Monday, November 24, 1986
Place: Somewhere over the Panama Basin, with 2.5 miles of water below

As for the gash, it does seem, from what I saw, to be mainly separation at the seams between bent plates, and not necessarily a gash in the steel. In the part we were looking at, aft of the bridge, the steel is just bent in. But we did see three little holes in one of the plates. I think the ice had to do that. You don't punch holes in the side of a ship by falling down against soft sediment. That's the only damage we saw that we can be pretty sure was done by the iceberg, but the total surface area of those three holes couldn't have been anymore than a few square inches.

EXCERPT FROM A CONVERSATION WITH *ALVIN* PILOT
PAUL TIBBETTS
Research Vessel: *Atlantis II*
Expedition: Dr. Aller's *Alvin*/Panama Basin/Peeper Project
Date: Tuesday, November 25, 1986
Place: Within sight of Punta Ramos, Costa Rica

I saw a hole where the gash should have been. It couldn't have been any more than four inches in diameter.

Tradition has it that the damage done to the *Titanic* was a two-hundred-and-fifty foot gash. Woods Hole's "Operation *Titanic*" logo depicts a broad, jagged tear in the inch-thick steel of the hull—the same thickness of steel laid over workers' ditches on Manhattan's streets and driven over daily by cars and trucks. The traditional gash is high enough for a man to step through without stooping, and gives the appearance that the *Titanic* was slashed open by a mighty sword.

Had the liner received such a wound, an unquenchable tumult would have poured instantly through the chasm, leaving barely enough time to pray, and certainly no time for Captain Smith and Thomas Andrews to learn the nature of her injuries, for within three minutes water should have slopped over the bulkhead between the fifth and sixth watertight compartments. Two minutes later the sea would be lapping at the base of the bridge, having swallowed the forecastle.

At the British inquiry into the loss of the *Titanic,* naval architect Edward Wilding, who knew the ship as well as Thomas Andrews had known her, testified that, based upon what portions of the *Titanic* had been flooded by 11:50 on the night of April 14, some four thousand cubic feet of water must have spilled into her during the first ten minutes. This measured up to an opening whose total surface area was twelve square feet. A two-hundred-and-fifty foot gash with a surface area of twelve square feet could only be three-quarters of an inch high. No metal sword known, much less a sword of ice, could make a continuous, three-quarter-inch-wide incision through inch-thick steel without dulling or breaking. Working from scraps of paper, Wilding concluded from simple mathematics and logic what future explorers, equipped with satellites and submarines, would need the ship in front of them to understand: there was no gash. The hull was merely bent in. Seams had split and leaked, and a series of stabs and punches from boulders of ice breaking off and getting smashed between the berg and the ship had opened up holes in the steel.

Through twelve square feet, 24,000 cubic feet of water entered the *Titanic* during the first hour, flooding the first five compartments until they dipped underwater and overflowed into the sixth compartment. When the sixth was full, it spilled over into the seventh, and so on. Once the anchors slipped below the surface, at about 1:10 A.M., the holes through which their chains ran opened up an additional twelve square feet to the sea. The pace of her sinking doubled. By 1:40 the forward well deck was awash. This added hundreds of feet more...air vents...cargo hold doors...windows. ...Forty minutes later she was gone.

It did not have to end that way. Had Thomas Andrews thought of opening the doors separating the watertight compartments, the *Titanic* would have sank on an even keel, with only twelve square feet open to the sea all night long. Another plus for this strategy is that the most powerful pumps were located in the engine rooms aft (where, as it turned out, they were never used). She should still have been floating by the time the rescue ship *Carpathia* arrived.

It probably doesn't matter. The idea would have seemed crazy at first glance: opening the flood doors on a sinking ship. If Andrews had thought of it (and we'll never know that he did not), he would have had a lonely time waiting for someone to listen to him, and they'd probably have shot him if he tried to do it himself. You can't hold them at fault for this, any more than you can hold Murdoch at fault for trying to avoid hitting the iceberg. Few people understand that the craziest idea is sometimes the most sane idea. The best shot Murdoch had was to crash his ship directly into the iceberg and break open only the first three watertight compartments. The liner could have been towed home and patched up, then, and history would have remembered Harriet Quimby, and forgot the *Titanic*, instead of the other way around.

33

~~~~~~

Voice from the Past

July 24, 1986

There was a surprising amount of glass left in the large square windows of the promenade deck. Three times they'd tried to send *JJ* into rooms and three times *JJ* was bumped back by glass so clean that it wasn't until the robot tilted in different directions and showed its reflection in the monitor that the explorers realized how much glass had survived.

Rows of plate-glass windows amid all this destruction. Bob wondered. There were a lot of contradictions down here.

Finally, after gliding through falling stalactites, tangling *JJ*'s tether and then maneuvering feverishly to untangle it, they found an open door. But Bob never got a peek inside, for his pilot ordered the robot out. It was time to haul up stakes and head for home, if they were going to surface in daylight.

And so they left. Having penetrated less than twelve feet into the promenade deck, and twenty feet into the reception room in the open pit of the Grand Stairway, they left. They'd barely scratched the surface. The *Titanic* was still a ship full of questions. Only one thing seemed truly certain to Bob Ballard as the weights dropped off and the boat deck shrank away below him, as the floodlamps winked out and she was once again left in darkness and alone— only one thing: there was no going back.

Although he and his crew had not openly made a decision never to return, they all knew inwardly that when this cruise was over, the *Titanic* was over.

It was time to move on to something else.

So this was going to be it, most likely—at least for Woods Hole.

When he arrived on the deck of the *Atlantis II,* people would notice a change in Bob. There was a new attitude and facial expression. He was no longer the gung ho—"Let's go do it!"—jump-out-of-the-submarine-and-be-excited-about-the-video Bob Ballard that everyone had known throughout the expedition. He became much more subdued and seemed very far away.

When Bob glimpsed the *Titanic* for the last time—a misty shape on the 200,000-ASA monitor—he understood that the dream of a lifetime had been made real, had become the adventure of a lifetime, and was now over. He was a member of that lucky handful of people on this Earth who had managed to spend an entire life exploring—who had held onto that childlike sense of wonder by always finding new astonishments. But there was sadness in him now. Somehow a part of the child in him seemed to have been lost down there in the gymnasium and the pit, and on the sloping deck of the forecastle. Whatever discoveries lay ahead in the Mediterranean and the Pacific, he knew that nothing would ever be so new or astonishing or so full of mystery, ever again.

A man leaning against a rail. That is how it ended: with a man standing alone in the shadows of *Atlantis II*'s starboard side, overlooking the *Titanic*'s grave.

He found the air sticky and close, the water dead calm, as he pulled a gold wedding band out of his shirt pocket and turned it back and forth between thumb and forefinger. It belonged to a friend who had worn it for nine short years, thinking he had all the time in the world

—Blurp!—

and he should have known better. Only *Voyager* spacecraft live forever.

The man pulled out a second gold ring. A more ornate one with a little brown stone in the middle. Raised letters proclaimed: EAST ROCKAWAY HIGH SCHOOL. CLASS OF 1975.

It had belonged to his friend's wife. Memories must have built up around it. Uncountable memories. They were stuck in time, now—like flies in amber.

With all the reverence of a burial at sea

—Blurp!—

he sent the ring hurrying for the bottom. It tumbled down and down and down, throwing the last rays of the setting sun back at him. For many seconds it remained visible. In an hour it would reach the *Titanic*.

During the seventy-four years that had just passed, silver and brass did not even tarnish down there. Gold should last almost forever. Eventually, the same convective spasms that have created the East Pacific Rise and sent whole continents adrift will carry the *Titanic*, like a parcel on a conveyor belt, westward to the edge of North America. She will complete her maiden voyage, about 250 million years after leaving the dock at Southampton, England.

By then the *Titanic* will be an iron oxide stain sandwiched between layers of sedimentary rock on the verge of reentering the Earth at one of the deep-sea trenches. The rings should still be there, long after the pyramids and the *Titanic* and the love of a man for his bride have ceased to be even a memory.

34

Introducing
Edith Russell's Pig

EXCERPT FROM THE DIARY OF CHARLES PELLEGRINO
Date: Wednesday, January 28, 1987
Place: Magen's Bay, St. Thomas

Odd coincidence continues to surround the *Titanic*.

Coincidence... that is how I eventually found myself in an underground vault, face to face with Edith Russell's pig: through a chance encounter with the author of *A Night to Remember*—which was very much like that famous meeting of the *Titanic* and the iceberg. I'd just purchased a copy of *The Night Lives On,* Walter Lord's update on the book that became the movie Eva Hart finds so difficult to sit through. I stepped out of a bookstore onto Lexington Avenue, leafing through photographs and captions and bits of text as I walked, and only half paying attention to where I was walking. Of all the millions of people crowding Manhattan's sidewalks, the odds of bumping into a familiar face were exceedingly low—much less the probability of bumping into the author of the book that was so distracting me that bumping into *someone* became a certainty.

I brushed by on the starboard side (of course!), uttered a quick apology, and then recognized the face from the picture on the dust jacket—but, no, that was silly. It couldn't be him...but it couldn't hurt to ask.

"Are you Walter Lord?" I asked.

"Yes, I am," was the reply.

He noticed the book I was carrying, and that led naturally to a curbside conference about the *Titanic*...and Bob Ballard...and downblast...and ultimately to a new friendship and an introduction to one of the *Titanic's* most unusual artifacts.

The artifact is a little toy pig, about the size of a kitten and covered with white fur. It was given to Edith Russell, a fashion correspondent for *Women's Wear,* by her mother. In the aftermath of an automobile accident and numerous other near-fatal calamities, Edith's mother gave the pig to her as a mascot, having heard that the pig was a symbol of good luck in France. "Keep it with you always," her mother had said. And she promised to do so.

Years later, and in a way her mother could never have anticipated, the pig saved Edith Russell's life. To hold it in your hand, you can almost *feel* history, almost know the irony.

On the morning of April 15, 1912, as she climbed onto the deck of the *Carpathia,* Edith wondered how she'd ended up on the *Titanic* in the first place. She had originally booked passage on the *George Washington,* which was to have left on April 7, but when she learned that this wonderful new boat was leaving on April 10, and that the three-day delay would permit her to cover the Paris Fashions at the Easter Sunday races, yet arrive in New York on the same day as the *George Washington,* she was overjoyed.

Yet her joy soured as she sat with the Astors in Cherbourg, aboard a huge tender designed to ferry passengers and luggage to the ship. "The tender had been especially constructed for the *Titanic,* and her sister *Olympic,*" recalled Edith in a diary entry dated April 11, 1934. "I have a very strong recollection of a most unusual occurrence—As we approached the ship, although the sea was perfectly calm, the tender began rocking in the most violent and inconceivable manner, throwing the passengers completely off their feet. I remember turning to a sailor and remarking, 'Well a boat that will produce this uncanny upheaval, in this kind of calm sea, is dangerous. I wish I were not going.' I have often wondered since, perhaps foolishly, if the powerful draught of the *Titanic,* creating such an upheaval in a calm sea, did not possibly have that same effect on the iceberg, attracting same with a sort of magnetic force under water—*even as she steered nearly free.* We drew alongside the *Titanic,* the tender pounding against her sides with such force that I thought she would break in half. The gang-plank was held down by ten men on either side, as it shook and swayed and pulled in every direction. I was the last one to leave the tender, hating the idea of crossing that gang-plank, and no sooner had I boarded the ship, then I went below to find out if there wasn't a possibility of locating my luggage, as I wished to turn back. I told Nicolas Martin, General Manager of the White Star Line, of my fears. He said, 'All *right!* Take another boat; but your luggage must remain!' I was taking with me not only my own wardrobe, but many orders executed for business firms and private clients—some $3,000 worth. When I asked him if I could apply for insurance on the luggage he answered, '*Ridiculous.* This boat is unsinkable.'

"As this was my first trip to America in many years, and all my most precious belongings were in my trunks, I laughingly answered, 'My luggage is worth more to me than I am, so I better remain with it,' and then stood aside and watched crowds of cooks, bakers and stewards carrying huge wooden boxes aboard. I asked a steward what they were, and was told that they contained tinned vegetables and provisions of all sorts for the trip over and return. He added, 'We have a pretty good crowd going over, but it is nothing compared to what we shall have coming back, as I understand we are booked full.' The process of transferring food supplies took fully two hours."

Edith's first-class stateroom was located on the promenade deck, almost directly below the bridge, immediately to the right and just in front of the first smokestack. The steel ceilings and walls on the deck above protected stateroom A-11 from the full force of the down-blast. Her room is still intact. Her luggage, too, might have survived nearby. Stewards had carried it up from somewhere below and placed it in a vacant cabin opposite A-11.

On that first night, en route from Cherbourg to Queenstown, Edith was amazed at the size of the dining room. This was not a ship. It seemed to her more like a floating city, and it made her uneasy. She was not a superstitious woman, or given to following her instincts, but the memory of a recent trip to Biskra, Africa, kept creeping up on her. An Arab man had been scratching something in the sand. He held up his hands in apparent amazement and said, "Madame will be in a very grave accident at sea." She naturally discredited the warning. Fortunetellers were always making such predictions—especially to people who were obviously from foreign lands and therefore traveled by sea. Still…during the three months that had just passed, she'd felt an impending sense of calamity.

No matter, she decided, as the ship approached Queenstown. Common sense must prevail. *I shall continue on to New York.*

Her uneasiness about the maiden voyage can be read in a letter she wrote to her secretary in Paris. It was scrawled on *Titanic* stationery and posted in Queenstown:

My dear Mr Shaw:

This is the most wonderful boat you can think of. In length it would reach from the corner of the Rue de la Paix to about the Rue de Rivoli. Everything imaginable: swimming pool, Turkish bath, gymnasium, squash courts, cafes, tea gardens, smoking rooms, a lounge bigger than the Grand Hotel Lounge; huge drawing rooms, and bed rooms larger than in the average Paris Hotel. It is a monster, and I can't say I like it, as I feel as if I were in a big hotel, instead of on a cozy ship; everyone is so stiff and formal. There are hundreds of help, bell boys, stewards, stewardesses and lifts. To say that it is wonderful, is unquestionable, but not the cozy ship-board feeling of former years. We are now off Queenstown. I just hate to leave Paris and will be jolly glad to get back again. Am going to take my very much needed rest on this trip, but I cannot get over my feeling of depression and premonition of trouble. How I wish it were over!

Yours sincerely,
Edith

On Sunday, April 14, Edith Russell awoke to a brilliant day, but the air outside had turned icy cold. Her steward explained that the cold was due to the proximity of ice fields. Edith decided that her bed was the warmest place around, so she stayed there until late afternoon. Then, venturing out onto the promenade, she encountered a little knot of men gathered at the starboard side. Their attention was fixed on the water being churned up by the blades of the propellers. The foam was a glittering white carpet, stretching from stern to horizon. As the sun set, the foam began to glow scarlet. The *Titanic*'s side glowed, too—blood bright.

Edith was in her room, starting to undress for the night, when the shock came. It seemed more powerful to her than to Thomas Andrews, whose room was nearly two blocks aft on the port side. It came to her as a slight jar, then a second one quickly following— a little stronger and seemingly a little closer, as if someone were drawing a giant finger along the side of the ship. The third jar came as a bang, violent enough to make her cling to her bedpost. Directly under her feet, the steel bulkhead separating the fourth and fifth watertight compartments had cracked open. Through her stateroom window, Edith saw a large white shape gliding by. She slipped into a fur coat, banged on a friend's door, shouting, "Come along, let's see what's happened!" and ran onto the deck. Five other people were already there. One of them called out, "That's an iceberg!"

Edith, joined now by her friend and several others in various stages of dress, saw it drifting about one hundred yards astern. For a time it stood out against the night, higher than the boat deck and ghostly white in the backscatter of the *Titanic*'s lamps. Then it slowly faded with the increasing distance between it and the lights, diminished to a black outline against the starlit horizon.

"Frankly," recalled Edith Russell in her 1934 diary, "I was thrilled. I had always wanted to see an iceberg, from the time of my geographical school days.

"Looking down toward the forecastle, across the well deck, we noticed a number of sailors walking. We heard a crunching sound. I remember remarking that they were walking on a ground of ice. We ran to the forward part of the deck, picking up bits of ice scattered about. Someone suggested a snowball fight. Nobody had any thought of fear or danger. A perfectly calm sea and a brilliant starry night reassured us. The only hideous feature was the intense cold, which I can describe by saying that if you were to go inside your frigidaire, or hold your hand over a solid block of ice, you would get an idea of the temperature. We walked about the deck and I questioned several officers. They said that we had struck an iceberg, but there was absolutely no need to worry. The best thing for us to do would be to go back to bed, so at 12:30 I decided to do so, had started to undress, and had nearly retired when a strange man came to my door, saying that an order had been given out that all passengers were to put on life belts. I questioned, 'What for?' and he replied, 'That's an order.' I do not ever remember seeing this man again. He was lost.

"Quickly slipping on a dress, seizing anything that came to hand, I put on a long fur coat and rushed out into the lounge, wearing only slippers on my feet. But before doing so, I did a most extraordinary thing, when I regard it in calmer moments: I took everything I had in the room in the way of jewelry and dresses, and threw them into my trunks, shutting the trunks and locking them, and closing my stateroom windows and shutters."

Up to this time, a trio of shady figures, known in politer circles as "the *Titanic*'s cardsharps," had been gleefully arranging high-stakes games and fleecing every target in sight. This was an easy thing to do, given the friendly climate of shipboard life and scores of wealthy, thrill-seeking passengers. Poor, calamity-prone Edith Russell, who already had a car crash, a flood, and a fire to her credit, was sooner or later bound to run up against the swindlers. Presently, the ugly tilt of the smoking room floor had interrupted an otherwise profitable voyage. They hauled up stakes and went to the starboard side.

Passenger Lawrence Beesley was standing on the boat deck, on the starboard side, when a rumor began circulating: men were to be taken off on the port side. He never did learn how the rumor started, but its effect was spectacular. One minute there were more than forty men standing with Mr. Beesley. A minute later they had crowded over to the port side, leaving the starboard side almost deserted. It was 12:40 A.M. Beesley had remained on the starboard side. He did not understand why. Three other men stayed with him; not for any reason that he was consciously aware.

Officer Murdoch was in charge of lifeboats on the starboard side. His policy was women and children first, but men when there were no women. Since few women seemed willing to come forth and enter the lifeboats, and the only alternative was to send boats down half empty, Murdoch began calling for men. Mr. Beesley and the three cardsharps encountered very little competition for available seats. Most of the men, after all, had gone over to the port side. Beesley eventually got away in boat number thirteen. By then the cardsharps were long gone, having taken quick advantage of a rumor that was, little doubt, of their own creation.

Meanwhile, having searched her room in vain for a life jacket, Edith Russell gave up and started off toward the Grand Stairway. She stopped at the open door of a friend's room. The friend had just purchased a beautiful bulldog puppy in France. It was whining and crying. Edith picked it up, kissed it, and tucked it under the bed covers. The friend stood by as she patted the dog's head. When it was calm, they closed the door—very gently—and went to the stairs, where Edith met her bedroom steward, Wareham. He was fully dressed in an overcoat and derby hat.

"Wareham, do you think there is any danger?" asked Edith. "Or is it simply the rule that all passengers should put on life belts?"

"It is a rule of the board of trade that all passengers must put on life belts, and that women and children are put aboard the lifeboats. Now, I do not think that the boat can sink. In all probabilities we shall tow her to Halifax."

"If you have any idea of going to Halifax, here are my trunk keys, and you better clear my trunks at the customs."

"Well, if I were you, I would kiss the trunks goodbye."

Edith paused, as if stung. "Wareham," she said, "do you think the boat is going to sink?"

"No one thinks anything, we hope."

Edith began thinking of the good luck pig her mother had given her

—*keep it with you always*—

"Wareham?"

—*keep it with you*—

"Don't you think it would be a good idea to fetch my mascot?"

"Certainly. Where is it?"

"I left it on the dressing table."

"I'll be right back!"

When Wareham returned with the pig, Edith wrapped it in a warm blanket. The people gathering about the stairway smiled at her. Few of them seemed to sense danger, though the stairway and corridors were decidedly aslant. "I hope we get out of this all right," Wareham said softly. "I have a wife and five kiddies at home."

He then hurried away, and Edith never did see him again. The next day, his body would be picked up by the *Mackay-Bennett,* and eventually buried in Halifax.

An order was given out: "Women on this deck kindly go to boat deck. Women only." Edith headed up the Grand Stairway to boat number four on the port side. But no one could get in. Officer Lightoller had lowered the boat level with the promenade, one deck below. He reasoned that there was less chance of people falling overboard if they climbed out the promenade windows. As lines of men suddenly crowded over from the starboard side, Lightoller ordered Edith and the other women whence they came—back down to the promenade deck. There, they discovered that the portion of the promenade directly below number four's davits was closed in with broad glass windows. While someone was called to get the windows open, another order came down: "Women will go back again to the boat deck."

Confused and tired, Edith hissed, "Go to hell," went to the lounge, and sank peacefully into an arm chair. Five gentlemen were seated nearby.

"I understand they have already launched lifeboats," said one of the men."

"Surely there is no danger," said Edith.

"No, but the English are a great people for rules and regulations. They are the greatest sticklers for that sort of thing. They very likely will take the women and children off, and return them for breakfast. But, danger? Ha! We're on the *Titanic,* for crying out loud."

"Well, if it's a question of rules and regulations, I am not going out on the deck, or getting in a lifeboat and freezing to death."

Again the order was issued: "All women immediately go to the boat deck!" Something in the tone of the sailor's voice prompted her to move. As she ascended the stairs she encountered a parade of bakers carrying loaves of bread. They reminded her of a carnival procession at Nice.

"A young man threw a life belt over my shoulders," says Edith's diary. "It was untied, just hanging loosely. I had searched my room for one, but was too unnerved to find it. If I would have had to put the life belt to practical use, it would have been of no avail, as the thing was just flung on, not even tied. I then went out on the boat deck and stood with Mr. Bruce Ismay, the Managing Director of the White Star Line. I remember him with a white night shirt, open at the neck, no hat, and a pair of trousers. He cried out, 'What are you doing on this boat? I thought all women had already left. If there are any women around, come over here at once!'

"Mr. Ismay pushed me swiftly down the narrow staircase which led down from the boat deck to the promenade deck aft, on the starboard side. When I got to the promenade, there was a narrow cleared passage made by the sailors, through which I was passed to boat number eleven. Two burly sailors caught hold of me and attempted to throw me head first into the lifeboat. But when I saw how far below the water was, I must say I was terrified. My feet seemed rigid and my slippers dropped off. I screamed, 'Don't push me! You frighten me!' And they answered, 'If you don't want to go, then stay.'

"I spent fully five minutes looking around for my slippers, and came back again to gaze over the side at the lifeboat, which was completely filled up with people—one of the last boats remaining on the starboard side, and one of the few that did not go over half empty. One of the sailors grabbed my toy pig mascot from under my arm, thinking it was a baby wrapped in a blanket and, throwing it into the lifeboat said, 'Well, at least we will save your baby.' I felt that I had to follow my mascot, as my mother had told me never to be without it, and I turned helplessly to a man who stood beside me.

"He said, 'Madam, if you will put one foot on my knee, and your arm around my neck, I will lift you to the rail, and from there you can jump into the lifeboat with less danger, and you will be less frightened.'

"The queerest part of this is that this gentleman was the one to whom I had remarked on the tender that a boat capable of creating an upheaval in a calm sea was dangerous.

"Jumping from a boat rail in those days of hobble skirt fashions of 1912 was pretty difficult. The gentleman helped me, immediately following; both of us falling into the bottom of the lifeboat. I remember groping about, hunting for my little pig, which I eventually found with its little forelegs broken.

"It was 1:25 A.M. The boat was slowly lowered, in utter silence, with the exception of hoarse cries of, 'Shove her off! We shall be sucked in.' The lifeboat was heavily laden and tipped over to one side. The ropes were cut loose with knives. As we struck out, we looked up from the water. The *Titanic* seemed the biggest thing in the whole world. All was calm and still, the reflection of the lights on the water, passengers leaning over the rails, strains of music filling the air: Nothing to indicate the coming horror."

By 2:05 the last boat had been launched. Edith kept her eyes fixed on the *Titanic*'s bow light, which shone bright green over the crow's nest. It seemed to be dipping nearer and nearer the water's edge. "She can't hold out much longer," someone remarked.

At 2:15 the green light vanished. Slowly, gracefully, the ship stood on end, looking to Edith Russell like a skyscraper, fully lighted up.

At 2:17 the lights went out, and there came to Edith a sound like a thick detonation under water. Then a second. Then a third.

A shout carried across the water—hundreds of voices calling out as if from a single throat. The men in number eleven asked the women to cheer, saying, "Those cheers that you hear mean they have all gotten into the lifeboats and have been saved." And the women did cheer, believing that the shriek in the night was one of thanksgiving. Not until she approached the *Carpathia*, and saw the flag at half mast, would Edith realize that there had been loss of life. It is easy to laugh at her for not knowing the extent of the tragedy, until one considers that the *Titanic* was equivalent to an office block stretching from 38th Street to 42nd Street. It was very easy to lose touch, for the view from the boat deck that night was almost identical to the view from *Alvin* seventy-four years later. Beyond a radius of forty feet, you saw practically nothing. Beyond a radius of forty feet, you knew nothing.

So Edith worried only about the intensely cold air as she sat in a leaky lifeboat on the morning of April 15, 1912. Some of the passengers were very seasick, and the seven babies were perpetually crying.

One of Edith's favorite features of her toy pig was that it was also a music box. When she wound its tail it played *La Maxixe*. She used it to amuse the two Hoffman boys, whose surname was not really Hoffman and whose father had been in the process of abducting them to America when the *Titanic* made its acquaintance with the iceberg. Edith let the boys crank the tail, until their little hands grew tired. Then she cranked it for them, until it broke.

"After we boarded the *Carpathia*," Edith recalled, "little groups collected wondering which of their loved ones had been saved. The few rooms were given up to the *Titanic* passengers, but most of us were glad to sleep on the dining room tables where blankets had been placed. One thing was startling in its peculiarity. On Monday night, April 15, two of the brightest flashes of lightning I have ever seen seemed to rip the sky, followed by two thunderclaps that shook the boat. We survivors rushed onto the deck wondering if we had escaped from one death for perhaps a worse. We found, however, that it was the beginning of a storm, and we were fogbound."

Edith Russell was a fashion correspondent and, once aboard the *Carpathia*, began moving among the passengers, doing what journalists normally do. She became an information-gathering machine. She collected business cards and addresses, and eagerly made acquaintances. Unfortunately, she made acquaintances with the *Titanic's* cardsharps, who were also collecting business cards and addresses, but for entirely different reasons. From their vantage point, the voyage to New York couldn't have turned out luckier if they'd planned it this way: crowded together with so many targets—widows, most of them; distraught and frightened…and wealthy. Bogus real estate deals and racetrack schemes sprang immediately to life.

One of the targets remembered a young woman, who said she was Edith Russell of Far Rockaway. He gave her his card, and was later approached by a man who seemed to be accompanying her—a cardsharp with a wire-tapping game in mind.

The story eventually surfaced in the *New York Sun* and, not surprisingly, Edith Russell was in the middle of it. A June 26, 1912, front-page headline announced:

SWINDLERS AT WORK IN
TITANIC LIFEBOATS
ONE OF THEM A WOMAN

And so began some famous first words in the history of American libel—which ended, typically, with some not-so-famous last words tucked somewhere between the real estate pages and the automobile ads:

A CORRECTION: Miss Russell Wrongly Named in Article Regarding Sharpers…The article was sent to THE SUN by its Newark correspondent after its publication in Newark and was printed by THE SUN in good faith as a matter of current news. It gives us pleasure to state after careful inquiry that Miss Russell's name should not have been mentioned in connection with the article in any way, and any unfavorable inference as to her which might be drawn from the article was an unfortunate error. THE SUN regrets that Miss Russell and her many friends have been subjected to any embarrassment or annoyance in the matter and gladly disclaims any imputation upon her conduct or character.

Having survived the *Titanic* and *The Sun,* Edith Russell decided that she could survive just about anything. By the autumn of 1912, the British and the Germans were saying many dangerous things to each other, and Edith's interests began turning away from fashion reporting toward more serious concerns.

When World War I broke out, she was living with soldiers on the front lines. There, in the trenches, she became the world's first woman war correspondent.

By the time she died, she'd witnessed a Second World War, jet aircraft, the birth of *Alvin,* landings on the moon, and Project FAMOUS. She also added a few more calamities to her credit, including car accidents, fires, floods, tornadoes, and at least one more shipwreck. Boarding an airplane, she decided, would be daring God. So she went everywhere by steamship or car and, at the age of ninety-eight, was able to say she'd had every disaster except a plane crash, a husband, and bubonic plague.

35

What Mrs. Abbott Saw from the Stern

Of the approximately fifteen hundred people who stayed aboard the *Titanic* till the very end, only forty were ever rescued by lifeboats (nearly thirty of these survivors ended up standing with Charles Lightoller on the keel of Collapsible B). One of the forty was Rosa Abbott, the only woman to actually go down with the *Titanic* and live to tell about it. In addition to this curious distinction, her story sheds light on the mystery of how some 163 women and children failed to get away as lifeboats were being lowered from the ship half empty in the tackles.

Historian Walter Lord had puzzled over this mystery for many years, and only found answers in 1988, totally by chance. He was seeking a 1912 volume of the *Philadelphia Evening Bulletin,* wanting to verify some minor point. By mistake he obtained a copy of the *Providence Evening Bulletin,* opened it up, and stumbled across an obscure interview. Mrs. Abbott's account of escape from the *Titanic* answered many questions, but Lord saw immediately that the answers had been staring him in the face for a very long time. The White Star Line's list of passengers notes, among third-class British subjects embarked at Southampton, Rosa Abbott (saved), Eugene Abbott (lost) and Rossmore Abbott (lost).

Eugene and Rossmore were Rosa's two sons, aged nine and fifteen. A seamstress by profession, she had been married to an American prizefighter and sports promoter who apparently viewed his wife as just another sparring partner. During the summer of 1911, Rosa left him, taking the two boys home with her to England, where she began her own business. Eight months later, her business was showing signs of success, but her sons had been born and raised "Yanks," and were adapting poorly to the more rigid British lifestyle. By February 1912, Eugene and Rossmore were extremely homesick. Weighing her roles as entrepreneur and parent in the balance, entrepreneur came up short and Rosa Abbott decided to go back to America, for the sake of her boys.

The Abbotts occupied a third-class stateroom on the ship's stern. Located more than three blocks aft of the gash, the impact communicated through the walls as a faint shudder at 11:40 on the night of April 14. They slept through it. Shortly after midnight, a steward banged on the door and told them to put on life jackets. Rosa and her sons waited with scores of other passengers at the foot of the third-class stairway on E Deck, waited in vain for help from above. As the floor began tilting noticeably toward the bow, Rosa took her sons by their hands and struck out on her own toward the top deck.

On that night, any boy over age eight was considered old enough to be a man, and a boy's life could depend on which side of the boat deck his mother went to. To First Officer Murdoch, who was in charge of the starboard side, the order "women and children first" meant women first, but men when there were no women. At 12:50 A.M. he sent Mr. and Mrs. Richard L. Beckwith and four of their friends away on boat number five, with twenty-four of its sixty-five seats still empty.* Fifteen minutes later, Murdoch cast number one

---

*Mr. Beckwith almost missed the boat. He wanted to go back to his stateroom, several hundred feet aft, to retrieve a leather satchel of money and jewels. "There's no time for that," Murdoch insisted. "You must get in at once." At 2:18 A.M., the ship broke in half, spilling the contents of the Beckwith's first-class stateroom. Seventy-five years later, a French expedition recovered the leather satchel from the *Titanic* debris field. Though waterlogged and in need of a cleaning, both the satchel and its contents were found exactly as Richard Beckwith had left them, on that first night. Miraculously, bank notes are still readable.

off with seven members of the ship's crew and five passengers, none of them children and only two of them women.

On the port side, Second Officer Lightoller interpreted "women and children first" as meaning women and children only. The Abbotts emerged onto the port side. Members of the crew kept them from passing through a guarded gate on the after well deck because in the eyes of the White Star Line the boys were "men." An officer told Rosa that she could go to the boats, but refused to let the boys walk with her through the barrier. She, in turn, refused to leave her children. There was no reason for Mrs. Abbott to suspect that the rules were any different on the starboard side, not that the difference would have mattered. The well deck was filling with third-class passengers, and the gates to first class and the boat deck were locked and guarded on both the port and starboard sides. Fifty-eight percent of women and children in third class would soon be lost, compared against six percent of those in first class. On the *Titanic,* male crew members and first-class businessmen, even a first-class dog, had a greater chance of survival than third-class children.

By 2:10 A.M. the bow had sagged into the ocean. Rosa put an arm around each of the boys and clasped them to her. Overhead, men from steerage were clambering up a cargo crane, crawling out on its boom in an attempt to reach the boat deck. The lights burned with a reddish glow. As the stern swung up, passengers discovered to their horror that they could no longer stand. Rosa Abbott heard—more felt than heard—popping and cracking iron. Then the electric lights snapped out, and a hundred crashes and groans carried up from below, as if all the boilers and turbines were breaking loose and rumbling down through the ship. What she had in fact heard was the *Titanic* tearing itself in half, and suddenly the after part was no longer plunging down. It actually seemed to be floating back and righting itself. The floor was horizontal again. Stairs were no longer impossible to ascend. High on the flagstaff, a kerosene lantern still burned. In its dim glow, Rosa saw hundreds of shadows swarming onto the deck. And then the *Titanic*—what was left of her—tipped onto her port side and began to plunge. Suddenly Rosa was in a swirl of ropes, deck chairs, broken planks, and flailing bodies. Twenty-eight-degree water kicked the air out of her lungs, and though she held the boys in a death grip, they were yanked out of her arms, as if by a giant. Something unseen tugged at her feet. Twice it pulled her down, and twice a maelstrom of ascending timbers buoyed her to the surface, battering her nearly to death. People were all around her. They almost tore her clothes away struggling in the water. A man tried to climb over her back and pressed her under. Rosa swallowed some water, but she managed to wiggle away from him. For ten minutes she paddled aimlessly in the mid-Atlantic, calling her children, suspecting that they were already dead, and expecting nothing but death for herself.

A hand saved her; someone grabbed her by the shoulder, and two men pulled her into a half-flooded boat, Collapsible A. Like the upturned Collapsible B, A had never been launched. It simply floated off as the bow glided down. Like B, it was badly damaged. No one could raise the canvas sides up, so A's gunwales remained almost flush with the ocean surface. Water kept spilling in. Within minutes more than two dozen swimmers had gathered around the boat. By the time passenger Olaus Abelseth came aside, none of the men standing inside were willing to assist him. "Don't capsize the boat!" one of them shouted. So he hung on for a minute before climbing in.

Slowly, the boat drifted away from the *Titanic*'s grave, with thirty standing or slumping inside. The smart ones stood up, continually moving their arms to keep warm. By 3:00 A.M., swimmers and calls for help came only at infrequent intervals. By 3:30 they stopped coming altogether and the cold Atlantic became as empty and silent as the deeps of space.

One by one they froze to death and were lowered over the side, all but fourteen survivors, including Rosa Abbott. They tried to keep their minds off the biting cold by singing, until they were rescued by number fourteen, Eva Hart's boat, at 6:00 A.M.

Rosa had suffered several broken ribs. She had in fact been battered so severely by *Titanic* debris that she did not stir from the *Carpathia*'s infirmary during the trip to New York. Upon arrival at Pier 54, she was driven immediately to St. Vincent's Hospital, still in critical condition. By the time she began to recover, two weeks later, nine-year-old Eugene Abbott had been pulled out of the Atlantic and buried in Halifax. When they found him, he was still wearing the suit and two overcoats his mother had put on him, before striking out in search of lifeboats, only to find the way barred.

36

Over the Panama Basin: A View from the Pilot's Seat

EXCERPT FROM A CONVERSATION WITH MEMBERS OF
THE *ALVIN* CREW
Research Vessel: *Atlantis II*
Expedition: Dr. Aller's *Alvin*/Panama Basin/Peeper Project
Date: Monday, November 24, 1986
Time: 11:30 P.M.
Place: Somewhere over the Panama Basin, with 2.5 miles of water below

PAUL TIBBETTS: Let's get this straight right now. Diving on the *Titanic* was no great experience. It was a job, and we did it to the best we could. It happened to be a pretty glamorous job at the time, but I think a lot of the people who didn't go down had a lot more to say than those of us who did.

JOHN SALZIG: It sure seems like it.

TIBBETTS: Yeah, it does. A lot's being made of it, and I really don't quite see why. You know, you go down there, you do your job, and you come up and you move on to the next dive site.

CHARLES PELLEGRINO: But you're so close to it. Maybe too close to—

TIBBETTS: Well, not close to the *Titanic*—

PELLEGRINO: —close to the project. When it becomes everyday life, it's hard to—

TIBBETTS:: Well, that's where I am! I don't know how you feel about it. But to me—it was kind of neat. I enjoyed telling my friends and family about it.

SALZIG: Well, it *was* a unique dive site. And for me, as a very new pilot, it was a challenge because on earlier dives I had climbed around on things that were pretty much rock piles— scarps and lava pillows and the calderas of dead volcanoes. This was different. There's manmade objects down there. And this hull! Going to the stern section in the debris field—this hull that extended as far as I could see in any direction. And that's what gave me the sense of awe: the massiveness of it. I never got that feeling landing on top of a volcano. You expect volcanoes to be big. You're used to gliding along the bottom and seeing piles of rocks stretching on for miles and miles. You don't expect to go down there and find the whole world filled with manmade objects. It never really happens. A volcano is thousands of times bigger than the *Titanic;* but it was the *Titanic* that made me feel insignificant.

TIBBETTS: It could have been the *Nippon Maru,* or some freighter that went down in some obscure storm. The impact would have been the same for me.

SALZIG: What really got me, what I'm trying to say, is that it's such a massive piece of manmade equipment—sitting there, at that depth. I'm not used to that on a dive site. I mean—sure, I'm in awe when I see a caldera stretching up beyond *Alvin*'s lamps, but this was a giant artifact. Not a cliff of rock, but a cliff of steel. And it had portholes in it. Somehow the word awesome just didn't seem big enough. And it was twisted all out of shape, the stern. There was shrapnel all around the place, pipes sticking up. It was destruction.

TIBBETTS: I'm more in awe of an intersection in Manhattan, where over the last seventy years fifteen hundred people have died, probably. You know, it's a tragedy that all those people died at the intersection. Well, great. I saw the intersection. Let's move on. Everyone seems weird when I tell them this. Everyone seems to want me to tell a big adventure story, but I don't have it.

PELLEGRINO: That's not so weird. I hear pretty much the same thing from the people who went to the moon, and from the people who built the ships that put them there. Basically, as one guy put it, "From where we worked, if you stopped and you thought about it as a moonship and became awed by what you were building, then you could make mistakes—you don't want people around who are overwhelmed by what they are building and where it is going."

SALZIG: Yes, you lose your concentration.

PELLEGRINO: Yeah. You have to just make it part of your everyday life—at least while you're there. Let the awe seep in by hindsight, weeks later, if at all. I'm sure even the *Titanic* survivors were not immediately awed about having survived the *Titanic*. Hell! One of them actually climbed into a lifeboat and slept through the whole thing.

TIBBETTS: Well, in terms of being awed in the presence of the *Titanic,* or thinking about the people who died there, and the iceberg—to be honest with you, I spent more time thinking about what the oxygen content was inside the sphere, what my battery voltages were and—how many peanut butter sandwiches do I have left to eat? Did I eat my share yet? I spent more time thinking about things like that.

SALZIG: Is the videotape ready to run out? Am I getting too close to that sheet of steel?

TIBBETTS: Is that a ground? What's that noise I just heard?

SALZIG: Ballard was the sightseer. We're the bus drivers. And I'll tell you something: by the time it was all over—what with the BBC people and so on—I was so burned out hearing *Titanic, JJ,* and Bob Ballard that I didn't want to hear anything about that trio for a month and a half. I went on vacation just after that, and it was ridiculous. Friends and relatives kept saying, "Oh, you were on the *Titanic*." I couldn't get away from it.

TIBBETTS: I had friends grab me by the shoulder and run me up to the bartender and say, "Hey! Get this guy a drink. He was down on the *Titanic*." And I'd say, "Come on. *Come on.*"

SALZIG: And, really. It knocks the wind out of their sails, but—

TIBBETTS: "How was it?" they ask. "It was all right."

SALZIG: What can you say?

TIBBETTS: I didn't get caught in any wires. I brought them back alive.

SALZIG: Didn't die at the bottom of the ocean.

TIBBETTS: And we got some good video to boot.

SALZIG: I gotta admit: to me it was a real suspenseful time, driving along through the debris field and finding all these strange things. I remember seeing buttercups spread around in a small area. They must have fallen in a wooden container, and the wood was eaten. It is pretty neat to be driving along at the bottom of the ocean, down two-and-a-half miles, and there's things like teacups, wine bottles, spitoons, a silver punch bowl—shiny as if it was just put down there. You're not used to seeing them down at the bottom of the ocean. We're driving along and it was almost as if it was staged: suddenly Ballard yelled out, "I see a box!" And then, "Holy shit! It's a safe! Stop!" And we settled down on the bottom. And we approached it and at first he didn't even want to touch the thing. He just wanted to photograph it. Jim and I—Jim was the pilot and I was the copilot—came in close to it and Jim was in control of the manipulator and he convinced Bob: "Let's try and open it." The idea that there might be something—diamonds or jewels or something...*suspense*. But as it turned out, the safe didn't open. The handle did turn. You could rotate the brass handle 360°. We left it there. We left everything there.

TIBBETTS: I must have begged him a hundred times: "Can I pick this teacup up, Bob? Come on, let's just pick it up. Just a little something. You know; we'll get one for each of us and we'll just keep our mouths shut." But he says, "No, no. We can't take anything."

SALZIG: We couldn't take anything. We lifted the safe clear off the ocean floor. It would have been no effort at all to take it, put it on top of *JJ*'s cage, and go up to the surface with it. But Bob didn't want to do that. I offered him fifty bucks and he said no.

TIBBETTS: I said I'd split it with him. I said, "Let's go back and get it. Whatever's inside: half for you and half for me." He didn't go for that, either.

PELLEGRINO: (laughing)

TIBBETTS: Why do you think that's funny? We're trained to go down and take samples. We're trained to go down and pick things up and bring them back for analysis. That's the whole beauty of the submarine. If they just wanted to take pictures they could send a remote camera down. It was like it was a *sin* to go down there and think of picking things up.

PELLEGRINO: Yeah, but then again—

TIBBETTS: Then again, what? You attach some kind of reverence to the *Titanic*?

PELLEGRINO: To leave it as a memorial.

TIBBETTS: Who said that? I didn't say that.

SALZIG: They don't do that with 747s that crash at Dulles Airport.

PELLEGRINO: That's because they have to bury the dead, and clear the runway of wreckage, and above all figure out from the flight recorder what caused the crash, so it won't happen again. There's no comparing that to the *Titanic*. And Bob *couldn't* have brought anything up—not after having Congress draw up a resolution declaring the *Titanic* a memorial.

TIBBETTS: He couldn't say he was wrong? Changed his mind?

PELLEGRINO: But he didn't want Woods Hole setting the precedent. Or at least *he* didn't want to set it. Good on him!

TIBBETTS: I'm going to feel really shitty next year when I hear that someone went out there with a fishing boat and raped the thing.

SALZIG: And made millions when Woods Hole could have. I really think it would have been neat to pull up a few artifacts and set them up in a museum—it would be great funding for the institution: a two-week expedition every year or so, a growing museum collection to fuel public interest in marine archaeology and deep-sea exploration.

TIBBETTS: But, nooo...

RALPH HOLLIS: Well, how many ships have been found after fifty, or a hundred years, or more, and left untouched? None that I know of. They found the *Bounty*'s anchor. They found the *Pandora* and the *Scourge*, and there has never been any question about whether they should bring things up or not—not up till the *Titanic*.

PELLEGRINO: But the *Titanic*...so many stories were told by survivors. Told and retold until they became part of our culture—a symbol for tragedy, blind arrogance, heroism, cowardice, irony—so many things. Maybe you don't want to touch a symbol too intimately. In the very least, you don't want to tread on it.

HOLLIS: Yeah. That could be it. I think if it was done correctly there would be no hard feelings and the world would accept it. But you'd have to do some careful planning. For example, I think the safes probably should be brought up. Not just for an *Andrea Doria*–type TV special, but just to learn. Open the safes and see what's inside. Then build a *Titanic* museum, or put the safes and their contents on display at the Smithsonian Institution.

PELLEGRINO: But there's a guy in Texas who wants to haul up a bunch of plates and sell them for $6000 apiece.

HOLLIS: Yeah. That's hard to accept. That would not be proper. But certainly we have salvors who go out to wrecks and bring stuff up all the time. And people make a living that way. And it's an honest living. They're continuously bringing up boats.

SALZIG: What I'd like to bring up: we saw some silver goblets, some teacups, the green bow light—

TIBBETTS: I saw a Miller Beer can. That probably belongs to Dave Sanders. He's the one who brought the case of Miller on the ship. We found the can up near the bow.

· SALZIG: I saw a few stained glass windows in the debris field. And bed springs. That's such thin metal I would have expected it to rust away by now.

PELLEGRINO: Apparently the process that formed the stalactites doesn't involve a great deal of mass wasting. On the video, the stalactites crumble very easily. They must be mostly empty space. The iron, as it dissolves, must bubble out like Styrofoam.

SALZIG: You know, the sub is twenty-seven feet long. We saw pieces of the *Titanic* forty feet long, stuck in the sediment, I don't know how far, just laying there and just twisted, like the top of it had been cut open. And it's all rusted now, but it's very jagged, as if it exploded. And, in among this twisted wreckage were portholes still intact, still closed with the glass unbroken. It really impressed me, that amid all this exploded steel we had unbroken glass.

TIBBETTS: Yeah. I tried to open a porthole, but ended up breaking it. I went down with two Navy lieutenants on that one.

SALZIG: Well, that's a good story: how you climbed into the sphere—

TIBBETTS: You mean, as a civilian?

SALZIG: —and came out as an officer.

TIBBETTS: Yeah. I went down with two Navy guys in their nuke jumpsuits. Basically, our mission that time was to go down and take pictures. Bob needed some color slides, so we went down and just explored. We probably made five passes around the bow. Now, there was a Navy public relations guy aboard the *Atlantis II*. This was his big day. Two Navy guys were going down on the sub, and he couldn't wait for them to come out of the sphere so he could take pictures. Unfortunately, the two officers brought an extra jumpsuit for me, and I don't look regulation Navy at all.

SALZIG: Your hair is a little too long.

TIBBETTS: And the mustache is not regulation Navy. The sideburns are nonregulation. So, as we climbed out of the sphere with the three jumpsuits on, the PR man almost had to shit right there on the deck: "Oh, I can't use any of this video! Oh, no!"

SALZIG: Because, in his video there's this long-haired civilian who climbs in with two Navy boys and, in the next shot, out pop three Navy guys in their jumpsuits.

TIBBETTS: He was *pissed*. Obviously we don't go in much for this Hollywood-type stuff—"Cut! Take two. You're going to have to climb back in the submarine and do it over." And then, "Hey! Can you do that again? You know, go underwater and turn *Alvin*'s face toward the sun." And we had these two Navy guys who had the dive of a lifetime, and the sum total of their conversation was, "Oh, wow. Holy shit. Oh, fuck, look at this." That's all they said the whole dive. I mean, here's a chance to send people down who can really observe and describe it to the world. Just imagine how Arthur C. Clarke or Walter Cronkite would have responded to it. And we had these guys. There's nothing wrong with them. I mean, they're just normal, red-blooded American guys. But why did *they* go down?

PELLEGRINO: The Navy financed *JJ* and *Argo*.

SALZIG: That explains it, huh?

TIBBETTS: Anyway, the Navy wanted some good action stuff. So I tried to open some portholes, and we raised the *Titanic* once. That was pretty good. There's this big shackle hanging over the very point of the bow. I brought *Alvin* bow to bow with all the cameras running. Then I grabbed the shackle with *Alvin*'s arm and lifted the sub up and down. From the video you can't tell if the sub is stationary and the *Titanic* is being lifted up and down, or if it's the other way around—it depends on your perspective. Basically, it looks like I was wagging the *Titanic*.

SALZIG: So I've got a question: why didn't you bring it up if it was that easy?

TIBBETTS: I was told not to bring anything up. *No souvenirs*. Hey! John, does Charlie know about the *Alvin* motto? The 4-S's?

SALZIG: I don't think so. We ought to inform him.

TIBBETTS: Well, the Coast Guard has their motto, and I'm sure the astronauts have some famous saying. The *Alvin* group has the 4-S's: Safety, Science, Sex, and Souvenirs. In that order: safety first, and then science, and then sex, and then souvenirs.

SALZIG: The 4-S's, you learn.

TIBBETTS: The *Titanic* expedition had only two of the 4-S's: there was a little science, there was no sex, and there were no souvenirs. But there *was* safety.

SALZIG: Everyone—all thirteen people who saw it came back alive: seven pilots, Ballard, Chris von Alt, Ken, Martin, and two Navy guys.

TIBBETTS: What was interesting on that last expedition: Imagine the pictures of the *Titanic*'s bow when it was new, with all the capstans and winches and chains—all that stuff is there and recognizable. It's just covered with a dusting of sediment and rust. And there's broken railings. What you see is almost like lighting up a stage. There's absolutely no backlighting—except with *JJ*. That was the weirdest—I couldn't quite put my finger on what was so weird about having *JJ* around. There was backlighting! *JJ* was new to me in terms of coming toward me with lights glaring—and riding out on its tether, illuminating things more than a hundred feet away in the dark. Normally you can't see beyond forty feet. And you never see shadows pointed toward you.

DAVID SANDERS: Mostly what *JJ* did was dance in front of *Alvin* so the sub and the robot could take pictures of each other, with the *Titanic* as a backdrop. Personally, most of us on the *Alvin* crew didn't like the robot. Bob talks about all the wonderful things he sees happening in the oceans during the next twenty years and it's all robots. He sees no place for manned submersibles.

SALZIG: So there were some hard feelings, on that expedition, between some of us on the *Alvin* crew and Bob Ballard, who seems to want to put us out of business. But we found ourselves confined inside a seven-foot-wide ball, in a hazardous environment, having to work together, and having to work with a robot. And that's all there was to it. We worked.

SANDERS: Sometimes I think Bob must hate *Alvin.* I really don't think he wants anything to do with us.

PELLEGRINO: It's funny. We have the same polarization going on in the exploration of both inner and outer space: do we do it with robots or humans? Why should it be either-or? There are some instances where I'd like to have robots do the work—but you've *got* to have a human presence. Never mind the sheer thrill of knowing that human beings have penetrated into strange, new places—just on a practical level, you need to put human senses there. Robots took thousands of pictures of the *Titanic* in 1985, and it wasn't until we put human eyes down there—

TIBBETTS: Right. For a year, everyone thought the *Titanic* was in *pristine* condition. The wood was in perfect condition on the deck.

SALZIG: We went down there. There's no wood on the deck. It's all fluff and sponge—or it's gone.

SANDERS: It's true that if it weren't for Bob we wouldn't have ever seen the *Titanic.*

TIBBETTS: On the same token, though, we would have been at sea that month anyway, maybe doing some geology. That would have been fun, too.

PELLEGRINO: Well, what it comes down to is that if it weren't for Ballard you wouldn't have seen the *Titanic.* If it weren't for you guys, Ballard wouldn't have seen the *Titanic.*

SANDERS: Exactly.

PELLEGRINO: The only thing I really think Ballard is in error about is *Alvin*'s fate. While we were on the *Melville,* he said a lot of things about robots and telepresence; but he couldn't quite justify why he was so determined to go down personally to the *Titanic* in *Alvin*. I pressed him on this point when we arrived in Mexico: If manned submersibles are less efficient than robots, and more expensive to operate, why not wait until the robots are perfected and let them explore the *Titanic* for you? He finally gave in and said that when adventure—when real adventure is involved, arguments based on logic and efficiency and money go out the window. And there I have to agree with him. I don't care if it's Mars or Europa or the bottom of the Atlantic Ocean. Only a human presence can create a sense of adventure. There will always be a need for manned submersibles, and for manned spacecraft. And, who knows? A new class of rockets, now on the drawing boards, has begun to make manned expeditions to Europa thinkable. It looks like there's a whole new ocean to be explored there. Imagine that: sending *Alvin* into space? A submarine in space? Oceanauts may eventually become astronauts. We'll always be doing that: sending people into new frontiers. It's one of the greatest things about being human and living in these times: the sheer adventure of it all. Only human explorers can truly carry the spirits of stay-at-home observers with them and excite the imagination. Only humans can come back and give you such different views as, "The *Titanic* made me feel insignificant," and "It might just as well have been the *Nippon Maru*." No, *Alvin* will never be out of work. People will keep rebuilding and perfecting her. She will remain state of the art. And when they are ready to explore the Europan sea, there is little doubt in my mind that they will bring *Alvin* with them.

37

Her Name, Titanic

FROM THE DIARY OF CHARLES PELLEGRINO
Date: Monday, February 23, 1987
Place: New York, New York, U.S.A.

"There's a sort of curse that goes along with the ship," said Bob Ballard as we sailed somewhere between the East Pacific Rise and Mexico.

"A curse?" I asked. I was grinning. Ballard has a sharp sense of humor, and I remember waiting for him to have me on, but he turned very serious.

"Yes," he said. "You'd probably like to be remembered for oceans inside a moon of Saturn, or for those damned antimatter rockets you're always talking about; but you won't. No more than I'll be remembered for hydrothermal vents. You've been touched by the *Titanic*, I can tell."

"And?"

"It's there in your eyes when you look at the expedition photos. Sometimes she makes you very sad. She touches something in you, and you've begun to touch back. You better think about that long and hard. Write a book and, before you realize it, you're living with her. Before you realize it, you're married to her. And let me tell you something:

"*There is no divorcing the* Titanic. *Ever.*"

Mrs. Rosa Abbott, the only woman to actually go down with the *Titanic* and live to tell about it, recovered from her injuries in St. Vincent's Hospital in New York City. Her church in Providence, Rhode Island, took over from there, eventually finding her a job as a seamstress. By 1914 she had remarried and moved to Florida. Still childless, she was last known to be living there in 1928. What happened to her beyond that point remains unknown.

Alvin, Woods Hole Oceanographic Institution's "inner spaceship," remains in use, is booked solid for the next three years, and should continue to be rebuilt and upgraded for many decades.

Angus, the first unmanned workhorse of Woods Hole's Deep Submergence Lab, continues to be used despite rumors of obsolescence and retirement. Having proved its worth during the *Titanic* II expedition, the camera sled is now known by the motto: "Takes a lickin' and keeps on clickin'."

Argo, the robot that found the *Titanic,* remains in use and is being continually upgraded.

John Jacob Astor died April 15, 1912. His body was found wrapped in a lifejacket and horribly mangled. He was apparently one of the many swimmers near Lightoller and Bride who was crushed to death when the first smokestack toppled over. His wife survived in boat number four, and received from his will 1.7 million dollars. For her unborn son, Colonel Astor left a trust fund of 3 million dollars, with an additional 5 million dollars when he came of age. In 1919, Madeleine Astor remarried William Dick, an elderly stockholder, and was soon widowed a second time. She next married Enzo Fiermonte, a professional boxer, and in 1937 committed suicide. The lifejacket she wore on the *Titanic* is now on display in the Philadelphia Maritime Museum.

Atlantis II, Woods Hole Oceanographic Institution's support ship for *Alvin,* remains in service.

Captain Reuben Baker continues as captain of the *Atlantic II*.

Bob Ballard continues to infect everyone around him with his enthusiasm for the exploration of inner space. There is, however, at least one instance of infection from the other direction. Bob talks a lot more about outer space than he used to. He even glances, from time to time, toward Europa.

Chet Ballard has retired from Rockwell and occasionally sails on expeditions with his son Bob. His Project Navaho became the precursor to many of NASA's space launchers, including the Redstone and Atlas. Navaho milling techniques and hull structures eventually found their way into the X-15, Apollo, and the Space Shuttle.

The *Titanic*'s band continued to play cherry ragtime music almost to the very end. According to accounts by the most reliable observers, including Harold Bride, and contrary to legend, the band never did play *Nearer My God to Thee* as the ship began to glide down. All band members perished.

William Beebe, the writer and naturalist who became the world's first deep-sea explorer, died in 1962 at the age of eighty-five. The Beebe-Barton bathysphere is on display at New York's Coney Island Seaquarium.

Lawrence Beesley was a school teacher at the time the *Titanic* sank. He continued to teach until retirement, and wrote a 1913 book about his experiences aboard the liner. Beesley remained interested in the *Titanic* and appears to have even become a little obsessed with it throughout life. He died in 1967 at the age of eighty-nine.

Chief Engineer Bell died April 15, 1912.

Ed Bland, who survived the sinking of *Alvin,* continues to work for Woods Hole.

Harold Bride, the *Titanic*'s junior wireless operator, went back to sea. In 1922 he was a wireless operator aboard the *Cross-Channel Ferry,* and was living about seventy miles outside London. That was the year he disappeared, leaving historians speculating for decades about what happened to him. Then, in 1987, Walter Lord learned that a man claiming to be Harold Bride turned up at a hospital in Glasgow in 1956 and died. Bride allegedly vanished deliberately in 1922. Despite the fact that he could have picked his job in the Marconi Company, he hauled up stakes and decided to become a traveling salesman. He left no forward address and covered his tracks so completely that no one knows even what he sold.

"Be assured that Harold S. Bride, who checked in to the hospital in Glascow is THE Harold Bride," writes private detective David O. Norris. "While having dinner with Walter Lord a couple of years ago, and being an amateur radio operator, I asked Lord what had become of Harold Bride. Walter glanced over the top of his glasses and challenged me with, 'You're the private detective, David, you should be the one to find Harold Bride.' It was a wonderful chase, and a pleasant personal victory to have located him after so many years. I was *thrilled* to call Walter with the results."

During his investigation, Norris identified Bride's father and mother as Arthur John Larner Bride and Mary Ann (Rowe) Bride, of 58 Ravensbourne Avenue, Shortlands. The Register of Death of Harold Sidney Bridge, #010625, independently confirms these two people as his deceased parents.

Bride was married to Lucy Johnstone Downie Bride, a Scottish schoolteacher, and was indeed a traveling salesman. His death on April 29, 1956, was due to bronchial carcinoma.

He had three children: Lucy (born March 9, 1921); John (born September 7, 1924); and Jeanette (born September 23, 1929). Daughter Lucy became a State Registered Nurse and at the age of twenty-eight married a Colonial Administrative Officer by the name of William D. Desmond. John earned a degree at Oxford, worked for the British Forestry Commission, and died in a car accident in Nigeria. Jeanette became a schoolteacher, like her mother, and went to work in Ethiopia.

Harold's wife, Lucy, died in 1973, at the age of eighty-three, in Prestwick, Scotland.

"I am told," writes Norris, "that when he returned to England, within a week or two of the *Titanic*'s sinking, Bride's hair had turned white. [Note: John Pellegrino remarks that this does sometimes happen to people in terrifying situations. He witnessed it at least twice during action in World War Two.]

"Harold Bride remained comfortably unknown in Scotland, according to a niece, working his own amateur radio transmitter, tinkering with antennae, and staying up late at night to talk with people all over the world. His callsign is presently unknown, but I'm certain that many old timers could search their logs and discover, 'Harold QTH Ashcliffe Dunning, Perthshire, Scotland.' Little did they know then that they were working one of the most notable wireless operators in history.

"It appears that Bride never spoke of the *Titanic* after the original inquiries into her loss. I am advised that his own nieces and nephews were unaware of his place in history until they found newsclippings in a family Bible he'd left behind. My research indicates that the Marconi Company presented Harold with a gold watch in honor of his dedication in the *Titanic* disaster. The inscription read, IN RECOGNITION OF HAVING DONE HIS DUTY, AND DONE IT BRAVELY. I am very interested in where that watch is now.

"I believe there is no greater monument on Earth to Jack Phillips and Harold Bride than the brass telegraph key now resting in the abandoned wireless shack of the *Titanic*. Like the operators, it is silent now, having done its full duty. And there it shall remain, while over the *Titanic*'s grave, satellite communications undreamed of in 1912, flash around the world."

The *Californian* was close enough to the *Titanic* on the night of April 15, 1912, to have seen her distress rockets. The rockets were ignored, possibly because those in charge feared that if they drove toward the source through mountains of ice in the dark they would end up in the same predicament as the ship that was firing the rockets. Edith Russell has described the *Californian* incident in her diary: "Aboard the *Carpathia*, we stood about waiting for the other lifeboats. By 9 o'clock, 16 had arrived, and we proceeded on. We were surrounded by icy fields, and it was best to go on and not jeopardize the lives of the rest of the passengers. The *Californian*, which stood alongside, was asked to remain about the scene of the wreck and pick up whatever passengers it could. We were under the impression that the *Californian* had saved many lives. However, we afterwards found out that not only did it save no one, but made no effort to do so. The only rescue boat was the *Carpathia*. Captain Stanley Lord of the *Californian* tried until his death in 1962 to clear his name, and never succeeded. The *Californian*, whose command he lost, was torpedoed during World War I and sank.

The *Titanic*'s cardsharps, who were sailing under assumed names, hatched schemes aboard the *Carpathia* that stung some *Titanic* survivors for as much as $30,000 (in 1912 dollars!). One of the cardsharps suffered a broken nose and other humiliations in New York. All of them soon vanished under assumed names. Popular myth has it that one of them eventually resurfaced as a New York City mayor.

The *Carpathia* was torpedoed by a German submarine on July 17, 1918, and sank 170 miles from Bishop's Rock.

The *Challenger*—what was recovered of her—as buried in an abandoned missile silo in early 1987. Several tons of debris still lie scattered on the continental shelf.

Jacques Cousteau continues to explore the world's oceans. He is much maligned by marine scientists, who point out, as a basis for criticism, that he has no advanced degrees in oceanography. Ironically, many of these same critics were inspired by Cousteau as children, and as a result became marine scientists. Tom Dettweiler, who sailed with Cousteau, comments: "Cousteau has never publicly claimed to be a scientist. He claims to be an explorer and that's exactly what he is. When he does science he brings in the experts on whatever subject he's looking at, and he provides the boat, his equipment and his crew as a tool for them to do science. And he includes it in his TV specials. But when the scientific statements are made in the specials, it's by the scientists themselves. He may take their words and paraphrase, or give an elegant overview as part of the theme he's trying to get across in the film, but the statements come from the scientists. You know, a lot of this criticism of Cousteau—that he's not being scientific—is unfair. He has never claimed to be a scientist, but he is. He is a very intense man when he gets turned on to something. He investigates to the minutest detail, and he learns his facts. I think his detractors envy him."

Tom Dettweiler continues to work for Woods Hole's Deep Submergence Laboratory, primarily on the still-evolving *Argo/Jason* system. Future plans for the robots include an expedition to the Mediterranean in search of a lost Roman fleet.

Frederick Fleet, the crow's nest lookout who first sighted the iceberg, survived the sinking of the *Titanic* but was ostracized by Charles Lightoller and other surviving officers after he complained publicly about the denial of his request for binoculars. He nevertheless continued sailing until 1936, when the depression closed down much of the world's shipping. As relations between Great Britain and Germany deteriorated into the birth cries of World War II, Hartland and Wolff found work for him in its shipyards. Upon retirement in 1955, Fleet sold newspapers on streetcorners in Southampton. On January 10, 1965, at the age of seventy-six, he hung himself from a post in his garden.

Dudley Foster continues to work as a WHOI Chief *Alvin* pilot.

Jean Francheteau returned to Paris after the immensely successful *Argo-Rise* expedition. He continues to work as a marine geologist for the Institut de Physique du Globe, University of Paris.

Archie Frost, the engineer who had stayed by Thomas Andrews' side, hoping to one day make him proud, died on April 15, 1912. Evidently, he was planning to immigrate to America at the time of his death, and the *Titanic* was to have been his last voyage with the White Star Line. A friend had invited him to sail across the Atlantic a week earlier on the *Celtic*. The change of plan would have saved Archie Frost, but he decided instead to stay with the *Titanic* and Thomas Andrews. This information has been brought to light by Mary Ann Whitley of the *Indianapolis Star,* who, after the first edition of this book went to press, wrote to say: "When your book came across my desk . . . I flipped through the index, going by my habit to the F's, just to see, but not really expecting to find . . . Frost, Archie—no kidding? This book has something on him? Most of the books I've seen don't even list him on their passenger/victim lists. One, 'The Memorial Edition, Sinking of the *Titanic*,' published in 1912, did list an A. Frost. But all these years I had only my late father's story about how my grandfather, Edward Whitley, almost sailed on the *Titanic* and how his friend "Jack" Frost went down with it.

"As I read that short passage about Archie Frost and Thomas Andrews, I felt chills. For one thing, it confirmed that the old family story was true; for another, it was like touching a piece of my past—a past which so very nearly wasn't . . .

"My dad and his brother had made a tape in 1980 for me and my cousins, talking about their memories of growing up in Belfast and how they came to the U.S. I fast-forwarded to the part about Grandfather's Atlantic crossing and then heard my dad's voice clear as if he were still alive and in the next room: '. . . in the meantime,

Father was working on the *Titanic* (he helped build the turbines) and after it was finished and went on its sea trials, he decided to immigrate to America and booked (one way) passage on the *Titanic* with a fellow called Archie Frost—you can guess that his nickname was Jack Frost. So they got a good cheap passage on account of working on the *Titanic* and along comes another fellow who tries to talk my father into coming with him a week earlier on the *Celtic* and stand there in New York Harbor and watch the *Titanic* come in. So one word led to another and he went to Jack Frost and told him that he was going to sail a week earlier. He did . . . but Jack Frost decided to stay with the *Titanic* . . . and went down with her . . .'

"If my grandfather had stayed with the *Titanic,* my grandmother would have been a widow with two small children. It is doubtful she would have come to the United States on her own. I've wondered many times, who would I be if my dad had never left Ireland? One decision sends out a lot of ripples in time."

Eva Hart was deported back to Europe after arriving on the *Carpathia* in New York. The *Titanic*'s second- and third-class survivors had lost most of their money, their possessions, and their men. With no viable means of support, they were branded "an unacceptable liability" by the U.S. government. Eva grew up to become a British magistrate, and was honored by the queen for her charitable work. She has traveled over much of the world, and lives in London.

Samuel Hemming, the first person to understand that the *Titanic* was sinking, and best known for the phrase, "Plenty of time, sir," testified at both the American and the British inquiries. He continued to work for the White Star Line, but his whereabouts after World War I are unknown.

Ho ran away after Bob Ballard was transferred to Woods Hole.

"Mr. Hoffman" was really Mr. Navratil. He died on April 15, 1912.

"The Hoffman children," Lolo and Momon, became known as "the *Titanic* waifs." Their father had abducted them in Nice, and was heading to America for a new life under an assumed name, in hopes that his former wife would never find him. They were put off on Edith Russell's boat, and played throughout the night with her toy pig. The boys were too young to tell anyone who they were or whence they came, and their identities remained a mystery for nearly a week. They were returned to their mother in Nice. Mormon died in the 1970s. Lolo is presently living in Paris.

Ralph Hollis continues to work as a WHOI Chief *Alvin* pilot.

J. Bruce Ismay, one of the *Titanic*'s owners, soon became the most infamous man to sail on salt water since Captain Bligh—for having entered a lfieboat while hundreds of women still remained aboard his ship. He testified that he had searched for women passengers but could find none. Few believed him, and in frustration and seclusion he died. Now, seventy-five years later, Edith Russell's diary vindicates him, to one degree or another. She wrote, in 1934: "I went out on the boat deck and stood in a direct line of light with Mr. Bruce Ismay. . . . He called out, 'What are you doing on this boat? I thought all women had already left!' And he cried out, 'If there are any women around come over to this staircase at once!' I walked over to Mr. Ismay, who pushed me swiftly down the narrow iron staircase. . . . Bruce Ismay certainly saved my life, and I don't doubt that he saved many more."

In making judgments, one must always keep in mind that the *Titanic* was like a dimly lit skyscraper turned on its side. One generally did not see what was happening beyond a radius of forty feet. Hundreds of women could be crawling around inside, and an observer would never know it.

Jason Jr, has been retired. Its successor, *Jason,* is now under construction. Bob Ballard is looking forward to a Friday the 13th launch.

Johnny the cook, who walked into the *Argo* control room and became one of the first people to see the *Titanic* in its grave, and then ran to tell Bob Ballard the ship had been found, was then on his first expedition. He fell in love with the sea that summer and decided to spend the rest of his life there.

The *Knorr*, the ship that found the wreck of the *Titanic,* remains in service.

The *Titanic*'s lifeboats, thirteen of which were recovered by the *Carpathia*, were returned to the White Star Line in New York. The word *Titanic* and the boats' numbers were removed, and they were shipped back to England, where the Board of Trade Regulations would soon be requiring lifeboat space for all. The lifeboats appear to have been transferred to other White Star liners. (Why not? They were in good condition. They'd only been used once.) They were placed there anonymously, presumably because passengers would have thought it a bad omen to be carrying the *Titanic*'s lifeboats—especially on her nearly identical sisters, *Olympic* and *Britannic*. A fourteenth lifeboat (Collapsible A, Rosa Abbott's boat) was recovered by White Star's *Oceanic* on May 13, 1912, about 230 miles from the site of the sinking. It still contained three bodies left aboard when it was abandoned near the *Carpathia*. The bodies were sewn up in canvas bags for burial at sea, and Collapsible A was sunk.

Charles Lightoller, the *Titanic*'s second officer, stood in White Star Chairman J. Bruce Ismay's defense at the British inquiry, and his reputation suffered by association with Ismay. He never did attain command of his own ship, unless one counts his private sixty-foot yacht, with which he rescued 130 men at Dunkirk. Unarmed, bombed, and machine-gunned practically to splinters, the boat landed safely in England only by virtue of Lightroller's superior skill and seamanship. Walter Lord wrote about him in *The Miracle of Dunkirk*. Charles Lightoller died on December 8, 1952, at the age of seventy-eight. A personal friend of his later gave the whistle he had used on the morning of April 15, 1912—the same whistle that attracted Samuel Hemming to the overturned boat—to Walter Lord, and never forgave Lord for not resisting the urge to blow it. The whistle remains one of Lord's most cherished possessions and, except for that one time, has not been blown since the morning the *Titanic* went down.

Walter Lord is best known as the author of *A Night to Remember* and is widely regarded as the man who knows everything about the *Titanic*. This is true; but he is not merely an expert on the *Titanic*. He is somewhat like Isaac Asimov: an expert on everything. For a start, just for a start, he is constantly receiving phone calls from Texas, because he's the man to go to if you want to know about the Alamo.

Guglielmo Marconi, the Italian electrical engineer whose perfection and marketing of Nicola Telsa's invention made possible the rescue of the few people who did manage to get away on lifeboats, became one of the *Titanic*'s most celebrated heroes. No one ever told him that his countrymen were shepherded into rooms on E Deck aft and locked in.

T. W. McCawley, the *Titanic*'s gymnasium instructor, died on April 15, 1912.

Kirk McGeorge, left the *Alvin* team in November of 1986 to help establish one of the world's first touring submersibles.

The *Melville* remains in service.

Will Murdock, the *Titanic*'s first officer, died on April 15, 1912, apparently from a self-inflicted gunshot wound as the bridge dipped under. Witnesses suggest that he also shot one or two passengers before putting the gun to his own head. His body was never found.

The *Olympic*, the *Titanic*'s sister ship, was called back to Hartland and Wollf's Belfast shipyard and rebuilt in the aftermath of the *Titanic* disaster. The walls separating her watertight compartments were extended above E Deck, so she could withstand flooding of the first six compartments. In 1918, she collided with and sank a German submarine. The captain was awarded a medal and the *Olympic* was promptly dubbed "Old Reliable." In 1934 she collided with and sank a floating lighthouse off the New England coast. The captain was sued and the *Olympic* was promptly scrapped. Her wooden fittings now decorate London pubs.

The *Ortolon*, the *Atlantis II*'s naval escort ship to the *Titanic* site, has been equipped with bathyspheres for submarine rescue, and remains in service.

Charles Pellegrino continues to infect people with his enthusiasm for antimatter rockets and the exploration of outer space. There is, however, at least one instance of infection from the other direction. Charles talks a lot more about inner space than he used to. He even glances, from time to time, toward the Mediterranean and the lost Minoan fleet.

Harriet Quimby, the journalist and aviator whose historic flight across the English Channel was eclipsed by the *Titanic,* was killed in a plane crash at the Boston Air Show in October 1913. She was twenty-six years old. Her flight across the channel was not her only breakthrough. On September 4, 1911, at the Staten Island Fair, Harriet Quimby made the first takeoff and landing on a runway at night, a flight for which she was awarded $1500. Her parents watched from an automobile as she circled the fair grounds four times, flying in the light of the full moon, above a crowd of twenty thousand. Her mother rushed up to her as she stepped down from the monoplane, and then kissed her repeatedly. "You were up fully seven minutes, Harriet," she said, "and I think that I would have come up after you if you had remained in the air any longer." The daughter replied, "Oh, mother! You'll get used to it. It was grand. I didn't feel like ever coming to Earth again."

Morgan Robertson, the science-fiction writer who described a ship like the *Titanic* and named her *Titan,* and later wrote a book about a world war that began when Japanese planes bombed American harbors in Manila and Hawaii on a December morning, died in poverty and obscurity about 1915. After the sinking of the *Titanic*, friends gathered his books together for publication under one cover and produced a special 1000-copy, autographed edition. *Beyond the Spectrum* was one in a series of books about a global war, fought with fleets of submarines, and with aircraft that did not exist when the book was written. Though written in a style typical of the period's "penny dreadfuls," Robertson described Japanese internment camps in America and the use of a weapon whose flash effects were so powerful that it blinded anyone unfortunate enough to be looking in its direction. Robertson's other novels were about pirates, and it might be worth searching where he said the treasure was hidden.

Quartermaster George Rowe, the last member of the crew to learn that the *Titanic* had struck an iceberg and was sinking, continued to sail in the British Mercantile Service through both world wars. By 1955 he was retired and living near London. The very last person to learn that the *Titanic* was sinking was an immigrant girl of about eighteen who climbed into a lifeboat, dozed off, slept through all the commotion, and boarded the *Carpathia* thinking nothing out of the ordinary had occurred. According to producer William MacQuitty, who came to know her during the filming of *A Night to Remember*, the *Titanic* adventure was her first ocean voyage, and she was under the impression that ships operated somewhat like trains: you went halfway to your destination and then changed to another ship.

Edith Russell tried throughout the 1960s to get someone to write her biography, but was unable to interest an author or a publisher. Sadly, her musical toy pig seems to have enjoyed more fame than she did. It actually made a cameo appearance in the film version of *A Night to Remember*. In 1958, during one of her Atlantic crossings, Edith's luggage was lost and most of her *Titanic* memorabilia along with it (including the clothes she'd worn in the lifeboat). She willed what was left—her slippers and the toy pig—to Walter Lord. The pig's legs and tail are still broken, and one of her slippers is missing its diamond buckle, which had come loose as she prepared to enter boat number eleven. Edith died in a London hospital on April 4, 1975, at the age of ninety-eight.

Edith Russell's pig, being one of the most unusual and legendary *Titanic* artifacts, now spends most of its time in a bank vault. As this book was going to press, Lord removed the pig for a private ceremony. Charles Pellegrino had just become engaged to Gloria Tam, whose mother had always told her that the pig was a symbol of good luck in China (Gloria had been born in the year of the pig). Edith Russell's mother, of course, had told her the same thing, and the pig certainly proved lucky for Edith Russell. So, on June 23, 1988, after a traditional Chinese pig feast, Walter Lord brought Edith's pig out of confinement. Charles and Gloria then petted it for good luck.

John Salzig continues to work as a WHOI *Alvin* pilot.

David Sanders continues to work as a WHOI *Alvin* mechanic.

Larry Schumaker, who took Bob Ballard on his first *Alvin* dives, has retired from Woods Hole.

Mary Sloan was ushered by Thomas Andrews onto the last boat down. What happened to her after the *Carpathia* arrived in New York is unknown.

Captain Edward J. Smith was among the most tragic figures aboard the *Titanic*. When Thomas Andrews told him that the ship was going to sink, he knew the numbers: he knew how many people were aboard, he knew how many lifeboats he had, and he knew, at that moment, that people were going to die. As horrible as that realization was, it must have been made even more horrible by a curious sense of *déjà vu*. Some months earlier, on September 20, 1911, the naval cruiser *Hawke* struck the *Titanic's nearly identical sister ship Olympic.* Smith was then in command of the *Olympic*. The *Hawke* had been equipped with a ram specifically designed to sink ships with watertight compartments. The prow of the cruiser punched a twenty-foot-wide hole in the starboard side, and when the *Hawke* pulled out, several tons of luggage and cabin furniture were lying on her deck. The *Hawke* was badly damaged, a total loss. Captain Smith commented that "the *Olympic's* frame stood the shock well. There was no panic. Many passengers did not know there had been a collision, so slight was the shock felt in the dining saloon. The watertight doors, which automatically closed, held the compartments sealed." It seemed to Smith a miracle that the ship had survived such a thing. It seemed to him that these new, giant liners really were unsinkable after all. The great tragedy of the *Olympic* collision is that it might have made Captain Smith even more confident in the *Titanic's* supposed invincibility, which might explain why, seven months later, he was so willing to steam full ahead into an ice field he knew was there. Isador Straus, founder of Macy's, and Mrs. Straus were also on the *Olympic,* and were also impressed with its miraculous survival, and one might ordinarily conclude that this explains why Mr. Straus refused a seat in one of the *Titanic*'s lifeboats when it was offered ("I will not take a seat while younger men remain aboard!") and why Mrs. Straus was so willing to stay with him ("Where you go, I go."). But jumping to this conclusion would be wrong. The Strauses knew all too well that the *Titanic was dying*. *At about 1:10* A.M., Mrs. Straus helped her maid into boat number eight, and then removed her fur coat and put it around the girl's shoulders, telling her, "Keep warm, I won't be needing it."

Jim Speers enjoyed a meteoric career at the *New York Times* following his interview with Harold Bride. He lived to see the *Times* become the world's most respected and most read newspaper—an achievement due in part to its reporting of the *Titanic* story.

Paul Tibbetts continues to work as a WHOI *Alvin* pilot.

The *Titanic* rests 2.5 miles under the Grand Banks, in the vicinity of 41°46′N, 50°14′W, give or take fifteen miles in any direction. The liner stood on end and broke in half as it slid under. The four hundred-foot-long forward half sits upright on the bottom. Her prow is set on a westerly course, toward a port she has never seen. Although more than a half dozen expeditions have probed her, she still holds many unsolved questions, not the least of which is the possibility of sealed-off regions in the bow, filled with stagnant water, anoxic mud and preserved organic furnishings, including horsehair sofas and, possibly, human bodies. Though Charles Pellegrino originally preferred to leave her as a memorial, he was tempted to consider ways of raising and displaying the *Titanic* once Ralph Hollis presented the possibility as an engineering challenge, and also as a challenge to raise and display her in a respectful manner. Pellegrino is quick to point out that one cannot simply pump the ship full of floatables and pop her up to the surface, as an American team did in Clive Cussler's novel, and the movie that followed. Even if the ship did not tear itself apart as it leaped into the air, the iron would surely turn to powder as soon as she began drying. Although details are not yet available to the public, Pellegrino and Powell's brainstorming sessions at Brookhaven National Laboratory took up the *Titanic* challenge in 1989. At an estimated cost of $40 million, the 450-foot-long bow section would have been raised 200 feet below the wind and waves of the North Atlantic, then driven (very gently) to port at four knots and displayed in a tank of icy fresh water. Note that the $40 million price tag covers salvage only. Building a proper display would cost almost ten times as much. Anoxic, antiseptic water cooled to the very edge of freezing will forestall all decay, just as cold water at the bottom of Lake Ontario preserves wooden ships and even fabric and food almost indefinitely. The tank permits display of the *Titanic* in its true historic context: resting in an environment closely resembling the bed of the Atlantic. An insulated ceiling blocks out all light. Visitors move through transparent passageways in trains similar to those seen at Epcot Center's Living Seas pavilion. The passageways wind over the forecastle and the boat deck, the only light being the light the trains bring with them. Passengers experience the *Titanic* very much as the first *Alvin* explorers experienced her. Meanwhile, exploration of the wreck can be conducted by divers equipped with rebreathers; and via 3-D virtual reality (of the kind experienced at Epcot's version of *Fantastic Voyage*), visitors could experience actual archaeological odysseys into the *Titanic*'s cargo holds, the Marconi shack, and the ruins of Edith Russell's stateroom.

A variation on the Powell/Pellegrino/Xerad Corporation design will first be used to raise large objects other than the *Titanic* (including, perhaps, the 400-year-old "galleon" *Cinque Chagas* and the sediment that surrounds it) from the bottom of the ocean. Charles Pellegrino and Roy Cullimore's comparative study of film footage from every *Titanic* expedition, and of the iron stalactites ("rusticles") growing from the ship's frame, reveal a bacterial assault that behaves like a constantly accelerating case of tooth decay on the *Titanic*'s metal. By 1994 the roof of the gymnasium had collapsed, a large steel door on the port side had fallen away, and submarine explorers began reporting disturbing creakings and quakings when they alighted on the decks. Paradoxically, 1912 newspapers recovered from the *Titanic*'s debris field are still readable—even olives, and what appear to be remnants of a chicken dinner have been preserved—while inch-thick steel is being eaten year by year before our eyes. The ship more closely resembles an increasingly dangerous house of cards than cliffs of riveted steel plates.

By 1996, the bacteria (entirely new to science, and as strange as anything we may hope to find on Mars) had metabolized as much as 20% of the *Titanic*'s iron. In a very real sense, something is alive on the *Titanic*—and it is the *Titanic* itself.

This discovery alone has made our world a little more mysterious and a little more beautiful, and barely suggests what future surprises await us. Archaeological evidence of looting by the ship's crew, and the discovery of readable paper (the first ever recovered from a shipwreck) hint that the *Titanic* still has secrets to tell. More and more of the tale will be (and is being) lost under a constantly shifting bacterial environment.

That the *Titanic* is becoming a house of cards renders the hull too fragile for the "Xerad plan" (raising the bow section in one piece) and calls instead for Pellegrino's "*T. rex* plan," in which the ship is raised "one card at a time" as the pieces collapse and fall off. The proposed underwater display would thus begin as a fiberglass reconstruction of the wreck site, with the actual foremast and other loose structures set into place. As the ship continues to collapse (from the upper decks down), the pieces are raised one by one until the fiberglass is slowly replaced by the actual *Titanic*. The name "*T. rex* plan" derives from the fact that almost every *Tyrannosaurus* seen in museums began as fiberglass and plaster models with a few real teeth, a claw, and perhaps a femur or two added. As new bones became available (usually over decades), more and more of the fiberglass was replaced until at last eighty percent of the skeleton was real *T. rex*.

If the *Titanic* is ever to be raised, the name of the game is likely to be "as above, so below."

Frank "Lucks" Towers, who survived the *Empress of Ireland* and the *Lucitania*, and claimed also to have survived the *Titanic*, is suspiciously absent from all known rosters of the *Titanic*'s crew, including the list of crew members who signed for their money after the *Carpathia* landed in New York. Although many people aboard the *Titanic*, including Edith Russell, are often misnamed on lists, Towers' absence on the payoff list (certainly he would have signed for whatever money was owed him) is cause for doubt that he was there at all. Unlike Edith Russell (who Anglicized her real name in order to advance her career), or the cardsharps, or Mr. Hoffman, Towers had no apparent reason for traveling under an assumed name. In his favor, Towers also claimed to have led Captain Smith and Thomas Andrews below deck and pointed the way to the damage. On this point survivors' accounts agree: a stoker *was* seen descending the bridge with the captain and the designer. Towers represents either one of history's most extraordinary tales of coincidence and survival, or one of its most remarkable liars.

Voyager 2 is presently racing out of the solar system at twenty-five miles per second. She will drift within 1.7 light-years of the star Ross 248, sometime in the spring of A.D. 42,165.

The White Star Line merged with the Cunard Line, owners of the rescue chip *Carpathia*, in 1934. Conrad eventually built the *Queen Elizabeth II*, a floating city some 100 feet longer than the *Titanic* that is widely regarded as "virtually unsinkable."

THE TITANIC'S CARGO MANIFEST

PORTS OF LOADING: Southampton/Cherbourg/Queenstown.

PORT OF DISCHARGE: New York

SAILING DATE: 10 April 1912.   ARRIVAL DATE: 17 April 1912.

cse = case, cs = cases, bls = bales, bgs = bags,
bndl = bundle, bbl = barrel, hhd = hogshead
Tulles = Silk/Nylon netting for veils or scarfs.

CONSIGNEE	DESCRIPTION OF GOODS
Wakem & McLaughlin.	1 cse Wine.
Thorer & Praetorius.	3 bls Skins.
Carter W. E.	1 cse Auto.
Fuchs & Lang Mfg. Co.	4 cs Printers Blankets.
Spaulding, A. G. & Bros.	34 cs Athletic Goods (golf clubs)
Park & Tilford.	1 cse toothpaste,
	5 cs Drug sundries,
	1 cse Brushware.
Maltus & Ware.	8 cs Orchids.
Spencerian Pen Co.	4 cs Pens.
Sherman Sons & Co.	7 cs Cottons.
Claflin & Co.	12 cs Cotton Laces.
Muser Bros.	3 cs Tissues.
Isler & Guye.	4 bls Straw.

CONSIGNEE	DESCRIPTION OF GOODS
Hydeman & Lassner.	1 cse Tulle.
Petry, P. H. & Co.	1 cse Tulle.
Metzger, A. S.	2 cse Tulle.
Mills & Gibbs.	29 cs Cotton, 1 cse Gloves.
Field, Marshall & Co.	1 cse Gloves.
N.Y. Motion Picture Co.	1 cse Films.
Thorburn, J. M., & Co.	8 cs Bulbs.
Rawstick & H. Trad. Co.	28 bgs Sticks.
Dujardin & Ladnuck.	10 bxs Melons.
Amer. Exp. Co.	25 cs Mdse.
Tiffany Co.	1 cask China,
	1 cse Silver Goods.
Lustig Bros.	4 cs Straw Hats.
Kuyper P. C. & Co.	1 cse Elastic Cords,
	1 cse Leather
Cohen, M. Bros.	5 Pkgs Skins.
Gross, Engel Co.	1 cse Skins.
Wilson, P. K. & Son.	61 cs Tulle.
Gallia Textile Co.	1 cse Lace Goods.
Calhoun Robbins & Co.	1 cse Cotton Laces,
	½ cse Brushware.
Victor & Achilles.	1 cse Brushware.
Baumgarten, Wm. & Co.	3 cs Furniture.
Speilman Co.	3 cs Silk Crape.
Nottingham Lace Works.	2 cs Cottons.
Naday & Fleischer.	1 cse Laces.
Rosenthal, Leo J., Co.	4 cs Cottons.
Waken & McLaughlin.	25 cs Biscuits,
	42 cs Wines.
Leeming T., & Co.	7 cse Biscuits.
Crown Perfume Co.	3 cs Soap Perfumes.
Meadows, T., & Co.	5 cs Books, 3 bxs Samples,
	1 cse Parchments.
Thomas & Pierson.	2 cs Hardware, 2 cs Books,
	2 cs Furniture.
Amer. Exp. Co.	1 cse Elastics,
	1 cse Gramaphone,
	4 cs Hosiery, 5 cs Books,
	1 cse Canvas, 3 cs Prints,
	1 cse Rubber Goods,

	5 cs Films, 1 cse Tweed,
	1 cse Sero Fittings (Syringes),
	A quantity of Oak Beams,
	1 cse Plants,
	1 cse Speedometer,
	1 pkg Effects, 2 cs Samples,
	8 cs Paste, 4 cs Books,
	2 cs Camera and Stand.
Sheldon, G. W. & Co.	1 cse Machinery.
Maltus & Ware.	15 cs Alarm Apparatus,
	4 cs Orchids.
Hempstead & Sons.	30 cs Plants.
Brasch & Rothenstein.	2 cs Lace Collars,
	2 cs Books.
Isler & Guye.	53 pkgs Straw.
Baring Brothers & Co.	68 cs Rubber,
	10 bags Galls(suspenders?)
Altman, B. & Co.	1 cse Cottons.
Stern S.	60 cs Salt Powder.
Arnold, F. R. & Co.	6 cs Soap.
Schieffelin & Co.	17 pkgs Wool Fat.
American Motor Co.	1 pkg Candles.
Strohmeyer & Arpe.	75 bls Fish.
National City Bank N.Y.	11 bls Rubber.
Kronfeld, Saunders & Co.	5 cs Shells.
Richard C. B.	1 cse Films.
Corbel, M. J. & Co.	2 cs Hat Leather, & c.
Snow's Express Co.	2 cs Books.
Van Ingen, E. H. & Co.	1 cse Woolens.
Lippincot, J. B. & Co.	10 cs Books.
Lazard Freres.	1 bale Skins.
Aero Club of America.	1 crate Machinery,
	1 cse Printed Matter.
Whitcombe, McGeachim & Co.	386 rolls Linoleum.
Wright & Graham.	437 casks Tea.
Ullmann, J.	4 bales Skins.
Arnold & Zeiss.	134 cs Rubber.
Brown Brothers & Co.	76 cs Dragons Blood, 2 cs Gum.
American Shipping Co.	3 cs Books.
Adams Express Co.	95 cs Books.

CONSIGNEE	DESCRIPTION OF GOODS
Lasker & Bernstein.	117 cs Sponges.
Oelrichs & Co.	2 cs Pictures & c.
Stachert, G. H. & Co.	12 pkgs Periodicals.
Milbank, Leamann & Co.	3 cs Woolens.
Vandergrift, F. B. & Co.	53 cs Champagne.
Downing, R. F. & Co.	1 cs Felt, 1 do Meal,
	8 do Tennis balls,
	1 do Engine Packing.
Dublin, Morris & Kornbluth.	2 pkgs Skins.
Hersog, Simon & Sons.	4 pkgs Skins.
International Trading Co.	1 cse Surgical Goods,
	1 cse Ironware.
Fitt & Scott.	4 cs Printed Matter,
	1 cse Cloth.
Davies Turner & Co.	4 cs Printed Matter,
	1 cse Machinery, 1 do Picture,
	1 cse Books, 1 do Mdse,
	1 do Notions, 1 do Photo.
Sheldon, G. W. & Co.	1 cse Elastics, 2 cs Books,
	1 box Golf Balls,
	5 cs Instruments.
American Express Co.	2 parcels Merchandise.
Vandergrift, F. B. & Co.	1 case Merchandise.
Budd S.	1 parcel Merchandise.
Lamke & Buechner.	1 parcel Merchandise.
Nicholas, G. S. & Co.	1 cse Merchandise.
Walker, G. A.	1 cse Merchandise.
Adams Express Co.	4 rolls Linoleum, 1 cse Hats,
	3 bales Leather, 5 cs Books,
	6 cs Confectionery,
	1 cse Tin Tubes, 2 cs Soap,
	2 cs Boots.
Wells Fargo & Co.	3 cs Books, 2 cs Furniture,
	1 cse Pamphlets, 1 do Paints,
	1 cse Eggs, 1 do Whiskey.
International News Co.	10 pkgs Periodicals.
Van Ingen, E. H. & Co.	1 Parcel.
Stearns, R. H. & Co.	1 cse Cretonne (fabric for curtains/ slipcovers) Silk.
Downing, R. F. & Co.	1 cse Iron Jacks, 1 do Bulbs.

CONSIGNEE	DESCRIPTION OF GOODS.
Jacobson, James.	1 cse Hosiery.
Carbon Machinery Equipment Co.	1 cse Clothing.
Sanger, R. & Co.	8 cse Hairnets.
Fleitmann & Co.	1 cse Silk Goods.
Rusch & Co. (Rauch?)	1 cse Tissues.
New York Merchandise Co.	1 cse Hairnets.
Blum, J. A.	2 cs Silk Goods.
Tiedeman, T. & Sons.	3 cs Silk Goods.
Costa, F.	1 cse Silk Goods.
Tolson, H. M. & Co.	1 cse Gloves.
Matthews, G. T. & Co.	30 pkgs Tea.
Richards, C. B. & Co.	2 cs Books and Lace.
Tice & Lynch.	5 cs Books, 1 bag Frames, 1 cse Cotton, 2 cs Stationery.
U.S. Express Co.	1 cse Scientific Instruments 1 cse Sundries, 3 cs Test Cords, 1 cse Briar Pipes, 1 cse Sundries, 2 cs Printed Matter.
Papa, Chas. & Co.	1196 bags Potatoes.
Bauer, J. P. & Co. (Sauer?)	318 bags Potatoes.
Rusch & Co.	1 cse Velvets.
Mallouk, H.	1 cse Laces.
Bardwill Bros.	8 cs Laces.
Heyliger, A. V.	1 cse Velvet.
Peabody, H. W. & Co.	18 bls Straw Goods.
Simon, A. L. & Co.	1 cse Raw Feathers.
Wilson, P. K. & Sons.	2 cs Linens.
Manhattan Shirt Co.	3 cs Tissue.
Broadway Trust Co.	3 cs Coney Skins. (rabbit)
Prost, G.	1 cse Auto Parts.
Young Bros.	1 cse Feathers.
Wimpfhelmer, A. Co.	3 cs Leather.
Brown Bros. & Co.	15 cs Rabbit Hair.
Goldrier, Morris.	11 cs Feathers.
Cobb, G. H.	1 cse Tissue.
Andaffren Ref. Mach. Co.	11 cs Refrigerating Machinery.
Sutar, Alfred. (Sufar?)	18 cs Machinery.
Amer. Express Co.	1 cse Packed Packages,

	3 cse Tissue, 2 bbls Mercury, 1 bbl Earth, 2 bbls Glassware, 3 cs Printed Matter, 1 cse Straw Braids, 1 cse Straw Hats, 1 cse Cheese.
Meadows, Thos. & Co.	3 cs Hosiery.
Urchs & Hegnoer.	3 cs Silk Goods.
Cauvigny Brush Co.	1 cse Brushware.
Johnson, J. G. & Co.	2 cs Ribbons.
Judkins & McCormick.	2 cs Flowers.
Spielman Co.	1 cse Gloves.
American Express Co.	18 cs Merchandise.
Wakem & McLaughlin.	6 bales Cork.
Acker, Merrell & Condit.	75 cs Anchovies, 1 cse Liquor, 225 cs Mustard.
Engs, P. W. & Sons	190 cs Liquor, 25 cs Syrups.
Schall & Co.	25 cs Preserves.
N.Y. & Cuba Mail S.S. Co.	12 cs Butter, 18 cs Oil, 2 hhds Vinegar, 6 cs Preserves, 19 cs Vinegar, 8 cs Dry Fruit, 10 bndls of 2 cs Wine.
DuBois, Geo. C.	16 hhds Wine.
Hollander, H.	185 cs Wine, 110 cs Brandy.
Van Renssaller, C. A.	10 hhds Wine, 15 cs Cognac.
Brown Bros. & Co.	100 cs Shelled Walnuts.
Bernard, Judas & Co.	70 bdls Cheese.
American Express Co.	20 bdls Cheese, 2 cs Cognac.
Mouquin Wine Co.	1 cse Liquor, 38 cs Oil.
Kanuth, Nachod & Kuhne.	107 cs Mushrooms, 1 cse Pamphlets.
Lazard Freres.	25 cs Sardines, 8 cs Preserves.
Acker, Merrell & Condit.	50 cs Wine.
DuBois, Geo. F.	6 casks Vermouth, 4 cs Wine.
Heidelbach, Ickelheimer & Co.	11 cs Shelled Walnuts.
Brown Bros. & Co.	100 bls Shelled Walnuts.
1st. Nat'l Bank of Chicago.	300 cs Shelled Walnuts.
Bischoff, H. & Co.	35 bags Rough Wood.
Baumert, F. X. & Co.	50 bdls Cheese.
Erie Despatch Co.	5 bdls Cheese.
Galle, B. & Co.	50 bdls Cheese.

CONSIGNEE	DESCRIPTION OF GOODS
Rathenberger & Co.	190 bdls Cheese.
Haupt & Burgi.	50 bdls Cheese.
Sheldon & Co.	10 bdls Cheese.
Percival, C.	50 bdls Cheese.
Stone, C. D. & Co.	30 bdls Cheese.
Phoenix Cheese Co.	30 bdls Cheese.
Petry, P. H. & Co.	10 bdls Cheese.
Reynolds & Dronig.	15 bdls Cheese.
Fougera, E.	41 cs Filter Paper.
Munroe, J. & Co.	22 cs Mushrooms, 15 cs Peas, 8 cs Beans, 13 cs Peas, 10 cs Mixed Vegetables, 25 cs Olives, 12 bdls Capers, 10 cs Fish, 20 cs Mdse.
Austin, Nichols & Co.	25 cs Olive Oil, 14 cs Mushrooms.

Order—14 cs Factice, 18 do Gum, 14 casks Gum, 225 casks Tea, 3 bls Skins, 4 cs Opium, 3 cs Window Frames, 8 bls Skins, 8 pkgs Skins, 1 cse Skins, 2 cs Horse Hair, 2 cs Silk Goods, 8 bls Raw Silk, 6 pkgs Hair Nets, 200 pkgs Tea, 246 cs Sardines, 30 rolls Jute Bagging, 1961 bags Potatoes, 7 cs Raw Feathers, 10 cs Hatters Fur, 3 cs Tissue, 1 cs Rabbit Hair, 31 pkgs Crude Rubber, 7 cs Vegetables, 5 cs Fish, 10 cs Syrups, 2 cs Liquors, 150 cs Shelled Walnuts, 15 bdls Cheese, 8 bls Buchu, 2 cs Grandfathers Clocks, 2 cs Leather.

Holders original Bill of Lading.
19 bls Goat Skins, 15 cs Calabashes, 5 bls Buchu, 4 cs Calabash Bowls, 3 bls Sheep Skins, 2 cs Embroidery, 8 octs(?) Wine, 22 cs Ostrich Feathers, 3 bls Skins, 33 bags Argols, 3 bls Sheep Skins.

A large fragment of ebony inlaid with gold, said to have been from the sarcophagus (or mummy case) of Queen Hatshepsut (who ruled Egypt around 1640 B.C.) was evidently shipped to New York in 1912. There is a persistent rumor among native Egyptologists that the casing fragment carried an evil curse and, on April 10, 1912, departed for America on the *Titanic*. Although many items were not logged at all or were logged under "disguise," a thorough reading of the *Titanic*'s cargo manifest fails to reveal Hatshepsut's presence, and it is noteworthy that Egypt's oral traditions state merely that the sarcophagus went down on *a* ship that sailed for New York in 1912, widely believed but not necessarily known to be the *Titanic*. According to historian Walter Lord, the story may have no more substance than the popular myth that the *Titanic*'s band played "Nearer My God to Thee" as the ship went down.

ACKNOWLEDGMENTS AND NOTES

I should start first by thanking some very special teachers who, when no one asked them to, took time out for a ten-year-old boy who loved insects and planets and fossils, but who read so poorly that he'd once been placed in a classroom with Down's syndrome children. The boy viewed himself as exceptionally stupid, and he viewed school as a place one merely survived in from Monday through Friday, daydreaming about rockets and hoping there would be no homework for the weekend. Mrs. Adelle Dobie took me out of the "special" class and taught me long division. Barbara and Dennis Harris assigned me special projects, sent me home to build electric generators and telegraphs, and gave me books that showed me how. I continued to read very slowly, but I loved what I was doing, so I struggled through the words, and the machines worked. My teachers also saw that I loved the sea, so I was encouraged to write book reports about the Beebe Barton bathysphere and the voyage of Captain Charles Wayville on the HMS *Challenger*. Soon I was reading H.G. Wells' *Time Machine,* Arthur C. Clarke's *Treasure of the Great Reef,* and Isaac Asimov's columns in *Science Digest*. In time, I came to love books. I even began looking forward to Mondays.

In most schools it is (and was then) considered counterproductive and even against the rules to assign individualized projects to a child who has fallen behind (especially one as hyperactive and outspoken as I was), to find out what that child loves most, and then to focus on those subjects as a means of catching him up with the rest of the school. Thank you, Mr. and Mrs. Harris; breaking the rules meant a lot to me.

Being blessed with teachers who make a difference is blessing enough for most children. I was doubly blessed with parents who made a difference. Mom, Dad: Thank you. I love you.

And add to these twin blessings the Nassau County 4-H club. There I found two more great teachers: Agnes Saunders and Ed McGunnigle. I also ran into a few strange little kids just like me: THE Don Peterson, Josh Stoff, and Jesse Stoff. In time, we grew up like brothers, and even developed a few "crazy" ideas, and wrote books together. We also lived through an odd coincidence: Jesse eventually walked away from evolutionary biology, the common ground on which we'd written many articles, a book, and discovered a few new oceans in space. He left fossils and meteorites behind, went into medicine, and developed treatments for a crippling and sometimes fatal disease that I was (unknown to any of us) showing symptoms of even when we were kids.

I am indebted to Robert Ballard of Woods Hole Oceanographic Institution (WHOI) for introducing me to hydrothermal vents, for bringing me along on *Argo*-Rise, and for (along with Walter Lord) making many encouraging sounds about my downblast theory. It was, however, the easiest paleontological puzzle I've ever had. Nothing needed to be dug out of rocks. The *Titanic* was all laid out for me in pictures.

Walter Lord provided a tremendous amount of information on Edith Russell, Thomas Andrews, and other personalities who found themselves thrown together on the *Titanic*'s slanting decks. I am especially indebted to him for Edith Russell's unpublished diaries. And I thank Edith Russell, though I never met her, for not bragging about her survival, as did many other survivors. Instead, she detailed the things she did that, in hindsight, appear strange and even stupid (*Rule*: always make sure the puppy is petted and kissed and lying comfortably under a blanket before you lock it in a bedroom on a sinking ship). The result is the most fascinating (and probably the most realistic account of how people behaved on the incredible night the *Titanic* went down.

I thank Eva Hart for her account of April 15, 1912, and especially for her opinions on the recent expeditions to the *Titanic*.

As in reconstructing a piece of pottery excavated from Mayan ruins, sometimes you have to fill in missing pieces as best you can. We know, for example, that Thomas Andrews brought his wife to the *Titanic* one night, while Halley's Comet was at its height of brightness and the ship still lay in its cradle. What they said to each other was never recorded, though the facts I present, as Mr. Andrews describes the ship to Helen, are accurate. The Andrews' impressions of each other, and Thomas Andrews affection for his ship, are derived from Helen Andrews' diaries, stewardess Mary Sloan's account of Thomas Andrews during the maiden voyage, and Shan F. Bullock's book *A Titanic Hero: Thomas Andrews, Shipbuilder*. Similarly, we know from the American and British inquiries into the loss of the *Titanic* that Harold Bride and Jack Phillips, in perhaps the strangest display of gallows humor the North Atlantic has ever seen, continued to say "many funny things" to each other almost until the water was up around their ankles. Always a wag, Bride was able to make Edward J. Smith laugh, even though the captain already knew that his ship was sinking with too few lifeboats. However, except for Bride's comments about sending the first SOS, the jokes themselves have not survived. For an insight into what might have been said in the Marconi shack that night, I relied largely on Thomas and Patrick McAvinue, who are famous (and infamous) for having kept the *Noa* (8 Ball Squadron) in laughter during the Korean War. (For this edition, the jokes themselves have surfaced, following the discovery of Harold Bride's descendants and a complete record of communications between the *Titanic* and the *Olympic*. The result is a truer reconstruction than was ever before possible of the mood in the Marconi Shack. As it turned out, the McAvinue reconstruciton was faithful to reality—spine-chillingly faithful.)

The timing of some events, as they have been traditionally reported, has been reset in this book. The times given by stressed passengers who only occasionally glanced at their watches are often conflicting, and tend to garble the order of such things as when the bridge dipped under, when water first rushed into the Marconi shack, and when the band must have stopped playing. Using a scale model of the *Titanic,* with watertight compartments and other features built in, I was able to reenact the sinking in a swimming pool, and have reset survivors' watches in accordance with the dictates of rising water.

I am deeply grateful to Jo-Jo, the wild dolphin that joined me in Turks and Cacos, coaxed me to stay in the water until I risked hypothermia, and gave me a glimpse of what life with Ho must have been like.

I thank William MacQuitty for his hospitality during my visit to London, and for fascinating conversations about his acquaintance with *Titanic* survivors, resulting from his filming of *A Night to Remember.*

George Skurla, Joel Taft, and Fred Haise (all of Grumman Aerospace) introduced me to the Space Shuttle *Challenger.* The loss of that beautiful ship was, to me, like the loss of an old friend.

For their participation in sessions about conditions inside ice worlds and the probing of our stellar neighborhood during the next hundred years, I am grateful to Jim Powell (Brookhaven National Laboratory), Hiroshi Takahashi (BNL), Robert L. Forward (Hughes Research Laboratory), Robert Jastrow (Dartmouth), William Newman (University of California, Jill Tarter (NASA/SETI), John Rather (Kamen Aerospace), Isaac Asimov (Boston Hospital and Columbia Memorial Hospital). I thank Dick Hoagland for first reporting on Stoff's and my theory about icebound, sulfide-metabolizing life near Jupiter and Saturn, and Arthur C. Clarke for a long, fascinating, and still on-going correspondence about the *Titanic,* Europa, and other things that go bump in the night.

I thank Tom Dettweiler, Cathy Scheer, Shelley Lauzon, Marge Stern, Terry Neilson, Ed Bland, Barrie Walden, Larry Schumaker and Kirk McGeorge for their hospitality during my stays at Woods Hole, and for the wealth of information they provided about probing the *Titanic,* and the machines that probed her.

I am grateful to everyone who sailed with me on the *Melville* and the *Atlantis II,* particularly Robert Ballard (who was among other things, kind enough to point out to me that I must never, never again say, "I can't wait to go down on *Alvin*" in a diner full of truckers who are unaware that *Alvin* is a submarine), Chet Ballard, Earl Young, "Skip," Martin Bowen, Emile Bergeron, Jean Franchteau, Roger Hekinian, Cindy van Dover, Chris von Alt, Jean Louis Cheninee, Haraldur Sigurdsson, Robert Aller, Per Hall, Peter Rude, Captain Reuben Baker, Ralph Hollis, David Sanders, John Salzig, Paul Tibbetts, Will Sellers, and of course *Angus, Argo,* and *Alvin.*

Thanks to Josh Stoff (Cradle of Aviation Museum), who brought up the fascinating case of Harriet Quimby.

Doug Colligan offered useful comments on some of the early chapters, and was kind enough to publish parts of them in the July 1986 issue of *Omni.*

Thanks to Russ Galen, my agent, who sold this thing—and to Tom Miller, who bought it.

Thanks are also due to Ann Craig (McGraw-Hill). *The* Don (Peterson), Ed Bishop (RPI), Steve Schoep (RIP) and Glen Marcus (Comicopia).

Finally, very special thanks go to Gloria Tam. Who knows why. Who knows all too well why.

And to Father Bob McGuire, who helped.

CHARLES PELLEGRINO, PH.D.
Rockville Centre, New York
12:40 A.M., April 15, 1987

SELECTED BIBLIOGRAPHY

BOOKS AND ARTICLES

Albion, Robert G. *Five Centuries of Famous Ships*. New York: McGraw-Hill, 1978.

Anderson, Roy. *White Star*. Prescot, Lancashire: T. Stephenson and Sons, 1964.

Baker, W. J. *A History of the Marconi Company*. London: Methuen and Company, 1970.

Ballard, Robert D. "How We Found *Titanic*," *National Geographic*, December 1985.

Ballard, Robert D. "A Long Last Look at *Titanic*," *National Geographic*, December 1986.

Ballard, Robert D. *The Discovery of the Titanic*. New York: Warner, 1987.

Brown, Alexander Crosby. *Women and Children Last: The Loss of the Steamship Arctic*. New York: G.P. Putnam, 1961.

Brownlee, Shannon. "Explorers of Dark Frontiers," *Discover*, February 1986.

Bullock, Shan F. *A Titanic Hero: Thomas Andrews, Shipbuilder*. Baltimore: Norman, Remington, 1913.

Clarke, Arthur C. *The Treasure of the Great Reef*. New York: Harper & Row, 1964.

Colligan, Doug and Charles R. Pellegrino. "*Titanic* Robots: Interview with Robert D. Ballard," *Omni*, July 1986.

Culliton, Barbara J. "Woods Hole Mulls *Titanic* Expedition," *Science*, vol. 197, 26 August 1977.

Collyer, Charlotte. "How I Was Saved from the *Titanic*," *Semi Monthly Magazine* (*Washington Post*), 26 May 1912.

Dodge, Washington. *The Last of the Titanic*. Riverside, Ct.: 7C's Press, 1912.

Dudley, Brian A. "The Construction of the *Titanic*," *Steamboat Bill*, Spring 1972.

Duff Gordon, Lady Cosmo. "I Was Saved from the *Titanic*," *Coronet*, June 1951.

Dunlap, Orrin. *Marconi: The Man and His Wireless*. New York: Macmillan, 1937.

The Engineer (Special), 4 March 1910, "The White Star Liners *Olympic* and *Titanic*."

Engineering (Special), 26 May 1911, "The White Star Liner *Titanic*."

Everett, Marshall, ed. *Wreck and Sinking of the Titanic*. L. H. Walter, 1912.

Francheteau, J., R. Hekinian, and R. D. Ballard. "Morphology and Evolution of Hydrothermal Deposits at the Axis of the East Pacific Rise," *Oceanologica Acta* vol. 8, no. 2, 1985.

Francheteau, Jean. "Basalt Pillars in Collapsed Lava Pools on the Deep Ocean Floor," *Nature,* vol. 281, pp. 209–211.

Francheteau, Jean, and Robert D. Ballard. "The East Pacific Rise near 21°N, 13°N and 20°S: Inferences for Along-Strike Variability of Axial Processes of the Mid-Ocean Ridge," *Earth and Planetary Science Letters,* vol. 64, pp. 93–113.

Griffin, Henry F. "Sixteen Boats and a Quiet Sea," *Outlook,* 27 April 1912.

Haas, Charles. *Titanie: Triumph and Tragedy.* New York: W. W. Norton, 1986.

Hekinian, Roger. "Undersea Volcanoes," *Scientific American,* July 1984.

Kennedy, C. and S. Prentice, eds. "A Night Still Remembered: Checking in with a Last Survivor," *MacCleans Magazine,* 23 January 1978.

Lightholler, Charles H. "Testimonies from the Field," *Christian Science Journal,* October 1912.

Lord, Barry. "*Hamilton and Scourge,* Two Remarkably Well-Preserved Schooners of Lake Ontario," *IATM Bulletin.* Winter 1986–1987.

Lord, Walter. "Maiden Voyage," *American Heritage,* December 1955.

Lord, Walter. *A Night to Remember.* New York: Holt, Rinehart and Winston, 1955; paperback by Bantam in current release.

Lord, Walter. *The Night Lives On.* New York: Morrow, 1986, Jove 1988.

Marconi, Degna. *My Father Marconi*. New York: McGraw-Hill, 1962.

Marcus, G. *The Maiden Voyage*. New York: Viking Press, 1969.

Nelson, D.A. and Emory Kristof. "Ghost Ships of the War of 1812," *National Geographic*, March 1983.

Oceanus (Special Issue). "Deep-Sea Hot Springs and Cold Seeps," Fall 1984.

Oceanus (Special Issue). *"Titanic,"* Winter 1985.

Oldham, Wilton J. *The Ismay Line. The Journal of Commerce* (Liverpool), 1961.

Pellegrino, Charles R. "Extraterrestrial Life: New Hope in Our Solar System," *Omni*, August 1984.

Pellegrino, Charles R. *Time Gate: Hurtling Backward through History*. Blue Ridge Summit, Pa.: TAB Books, 1985.

Pellegrino, Charles R. and Joshua Stoff. *Chariots for Apollo: The Untold Story Behind the Race to the Moon*. New York: Atheneum, 1985. Paperback by TAB Books, 1987.

Pellegrino, Charles R. and Jesse A. Stoff. *Darwin's Universe: Origins and Crises in the History of Life*. Blue Ridge Summit, Pa.: TAB Books, 1986.

Pellegrino, Charles R., James R. Powell and Isaac Asimov. *Making Star Trek Real: The Science Behind the Fiction*. Blue Ridge Summit, Pa.: TAB Books Inc., 1988.

Pellegrino, Powell, Asimov et al. *Interstellar Travel and Communication*. The American Association for the Advancement of Science (IN PRESS).

Powell, J.W. "Navaho, the 'Know-How' Missile," *Journal of the British Interplanetary Society*, February 1987.

Reichhardt, Tony. "ISO: Liberty Bell," *Space World,* January 1987.

Robertson, Morgan. *Futility.* (Also titled *The Wreck of the Titan.*) Facsimile copy available from the Titanic Historical Society. One of the few known copies of Robertson's *Beyond the Spectrum* is in the possession of Walter Lord.

Rostrom, Arthur H. "The Rescue of the *Titanic* Survivors," *Scribners Monthly,* March 1983.

Scientific American (Special), 17 June 1911, "The *Olympic* and the *Titanic*."

Stoff, J. A. and C. R. Pellegrino. *The Hidden Epidemic.* Random House, 1988. (Believe it or not, the *Titanic* rears its head in this book, particularly to the peculiar case of the ship's Chief Baker.)

The Shipbuilder (Special), Midsummer 1911, *"Olympic* and *Titanic,"* Reprinted by Patrick Stephens Ltd., 1983.

Thayer, John B. *The Sinking of the SS Titanic.* Riverside, Ct.: 7C's Press (1940). Reprinted 1974.

The Titanic Communicator, published by the Titanic Historical Society, provides excellent coverage of an unsinkable subject.

Tucker, Jonathan B. "Robot Subs," *High Technology,* February 1986.

Wade, Wyn Craig. *The Titanic: End of A Dream.* Middlesex, England: Penguin Books, 1979.

Walker, J Bernard. *An Unsinkable Titanic.* New York: Dodd, Mead, 1912.

Winocour, Jack, ed. *The Story of the Titanic as Told by Its Survivors: Lawrence Beesley, Archibald Gracie, Com-*

mander Lightoller, and Harold Bridge. New York: Dover Publications, 1960.

Wood, W. J. "Construction of the *Titanic,*" *Marine Review,* vol. 42, May, 1912.

Young, Filson. "God and Titan." *Saturday Review* (London), 20, April, 1912.

DOCUMENTS

Ballard, Robert D. "Geologic Processes of the Mid-Ocean Ridge," Winter 1986 *Argo*-Rise File: Voyages of the Research Vessel *Melville.*

Russell, Edith. Unpublished account of the sinking of the *Titanic.* Diary: April 11, 1934. (Copies in Lord and Pellegrino files).

Titanic Historical Society, Inc.; Indian Orchard, Mass. (Offices also in Philadelphia.): Letters and memoranda regarding Frederick Fleet, Mrs. Sylvia Lightoller, and Harold G. Lowe . . . Tape recordings and transcripts of the tenth anniversary of the THS, including interviews with survivors. *THS Archives.*

U.S. Congress, Senate. "Hearings of a Subcommittee of the Senate Commerce Committee Pursuant to S. Res. 283, to Investigate the Causes Leading to the Wreck of the White Star Liner *Titanic.*" *62nd Congress, 2nd Session, 1912, S. Document 726 (#6167).*

U.S. Congress, Senate. "Report of the Senate Committee on Commerce Pursuant to S. Res. 283, Directing the Committee to Investigate the Causes of the Sinking of the *Titanic,* with Speeches by William Alden Smith and

Isador Rayner," *62nd Congress, 2nd Session, 28 May, 1912, S. Report 806 (#6127).*

U.S. Congress, Senate. "Loss of the Steamship *Titanic*: Report of a Formal Investigation . . . As Conducted by the British Government, Presented by Mr. Alden Smith." *62nd Congress, 2nd Session, 20 August, 1912. S. Document 933 (#6179).*

Taped interviews with participants in the first *Titanic* expeditions (and also with survivor Eva Hart) remain in the author's files. Most of this material will eventually be copied and archived at Woods Hole Oceanographic Institution. Partial transcripts are presently in Walter Lord's files.

ABOUT THE AUTHOR

Dr. Charles Pellegrino wears many hats. He has been known to work simultaneously in crustaceology, paleontology, preliminary design of advanced rocket systems, and marine archaeology. He has been described by Stephen Jay Gould as a space scientist who occasionally looks down. Closely associated with the U.S. space program, he helped to frame the current U.S.-Soviet Space Cooperation Initiative as a means of reducing international tensions and the probability of nuclear war on Earth. At Brookhaven National Laboratory he and Dr. James Powell coordinate brainstorming sessions on the next 70 years in space; topics currently under discussion by Powell and Pellegrino range from the international industrialization of the moon and Mercury to matter-antimatter propulsion and plans for an interstellar voyage at 92 percent the speed of light.

In the late 1970s, Dr. Pellegrino and Dr. Jesse A. Stoff produced the original models that predicted the discovery of oceans inside certain moons of Jupiter and Saturn. While looking at the requirements for robot exploration of those new oceans, Pellegrino sailed with Dr. Robert Ballard during the first scientific mission of the deep-sea robot, *Argo*.

Dr. Pellegrino has produced seven books, writes a column in *Final Frontier,* and participates (as both scientist and laboratory rat) in medical experiments. He is an award-winning painter, a member of the AAAS and the New York Academy of Sciences, a fellow of the British Interplanetary Society, and a founding member of the Challenger Center. In his spare time he builds sand cities on the beach, lectures at Hofstra University, and smashes atoms.